Giles™

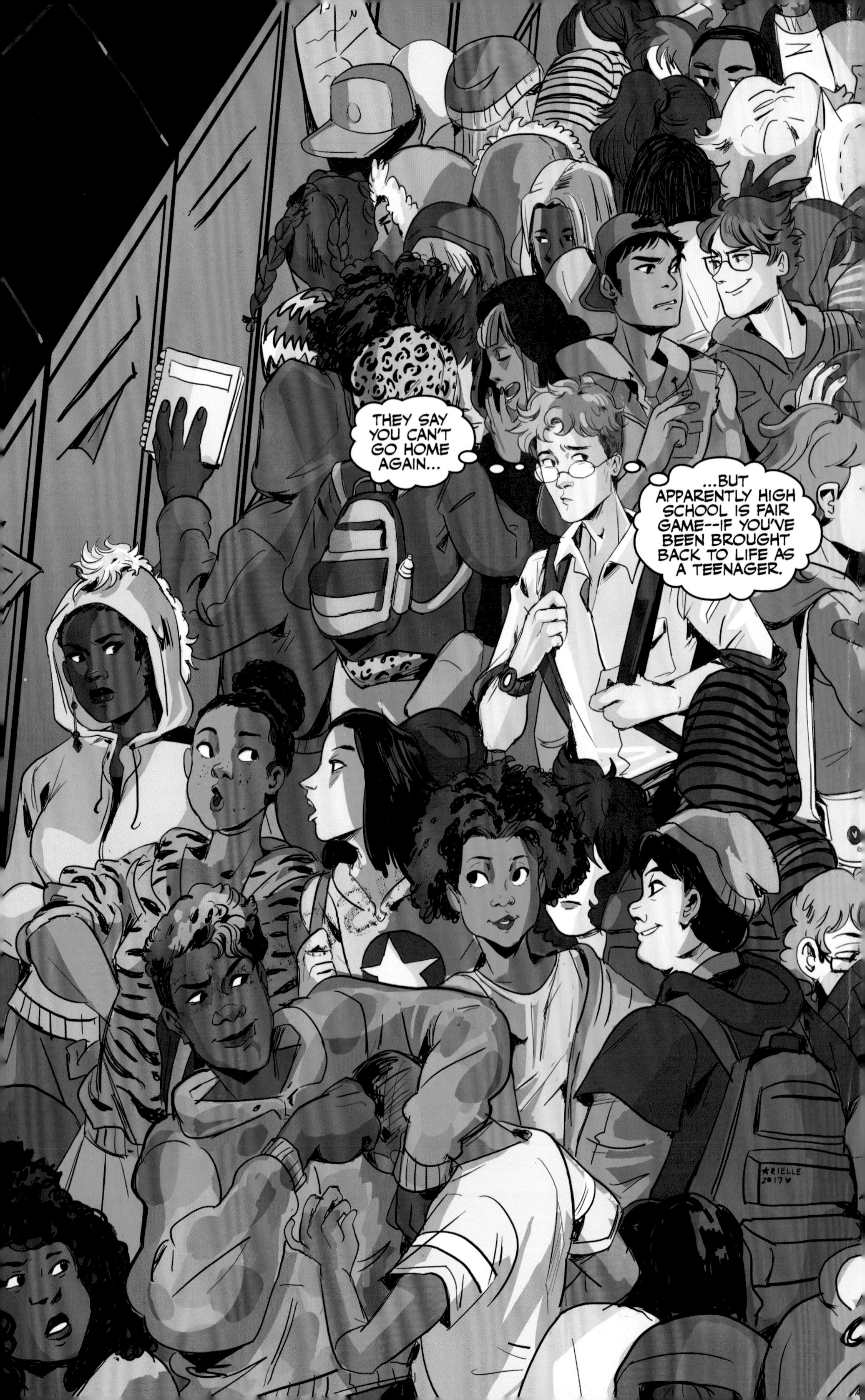
THEY SAY YOU CAN'T GO HOME AGAIN...
...BUT APPARENTLY HIGH SCHOOL IS FAIR GAME--IF YOU'VE BEEN BROUGHT BACK TO LIFE AS A TEENAGER.
★RIELLE 2017♥

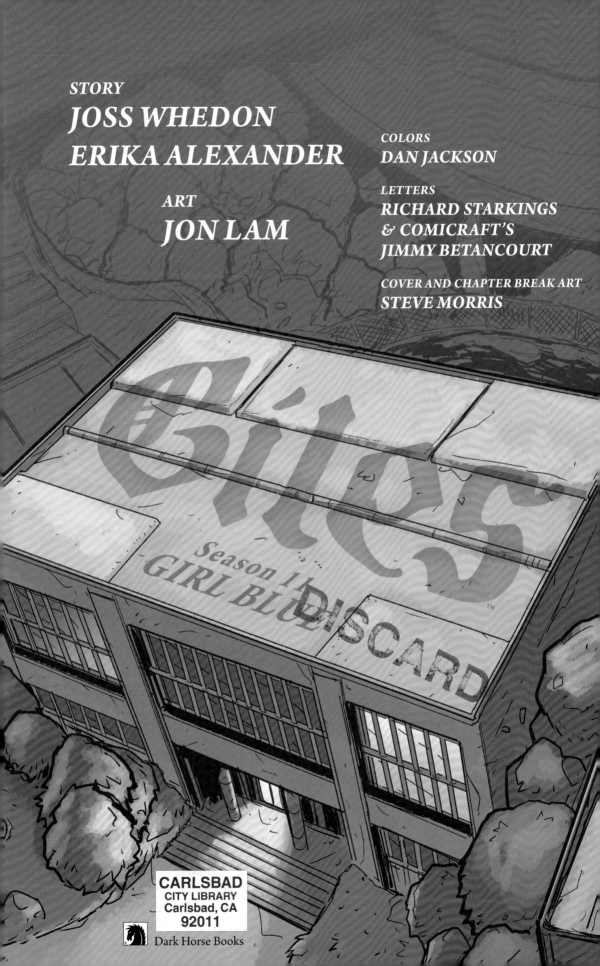

STORY
JOSS WHEDON
ERIKA ALEXANDER

ART
JON LAM

COLORS
DAN JACKSON

LETTERS
RICHARD STARKINGS
& COMICRAFT'S
JIMMY BETANCOURT

COVER AND CHAPTER BREAK ART
STEVE MORRIS

Dark Horse Books

president & publisher
Mike Richardson

editor
Freddye Miller

assistant editors
Jenny Blenk, Kevin Burkhalter, Judy Khuu

collection designer
Anita Magaña

digital art technician
Christianne Gillenardo-Goudreau

Special thanks to Nicole Spiegel at Twentieth Century Fox, Becca J. Sadowsky, and Randy Stradley.

The art on page 2 is the variant cover art from *Giles* Season 11 #1, by Arielle Jovellanos with Comicraft.

This story takes place during the events of *Buffy the Vampire Slayer* Season 11, created by Joss Whedon.

DarkHorse.com
First edition: September 2018
ISBN 978-1-50670-743-3

10 9 8 7 6 5 4 3 2 1
Printed in China

Published by Dark Horse Books
A division of Dark Horse Comics, Inc.
10956 SE Main Street
Milwaukie, OR 97222

To find a comics shop in your area, visit comicshoplocator.com

This volume reprints the comic book series *Giles* Season 11 #1–#4 from Dark Horse Comics, originally published February through May 2018.

Neil Hankerson, Executive Vice President · Tom Weddle, Chief Financial Officer · Randy Stradley, Vice President of Publishing · Nick McWhorter, Chief Business Development Officer · Matt Parkinson, Vice President of Marketing · Dale LaFountain, Vice President of Information Technology · Cara Niece, Vice President of Production and Scheduling · Mark Bernardi, Vice President of Book Trade and Digital Sales · Ken Lizzi, General Counsel · Dave Marshall, Editor in Chief · Davey Estrada, Editorial Director · Chris Warner, Senior Books Editor · Cary Grazzini, Director of Specialty Projects · Lia Ribacchi, Art Director · Vanessa Todd-Holmes, Director of Print Purchasing · Matt Dryer, Director of Digital Art and Prepress · Michael Gombos, Director of International Publishing and Licensing · Kari Yadro, Director of Custom Programs

OCTOBER 2018

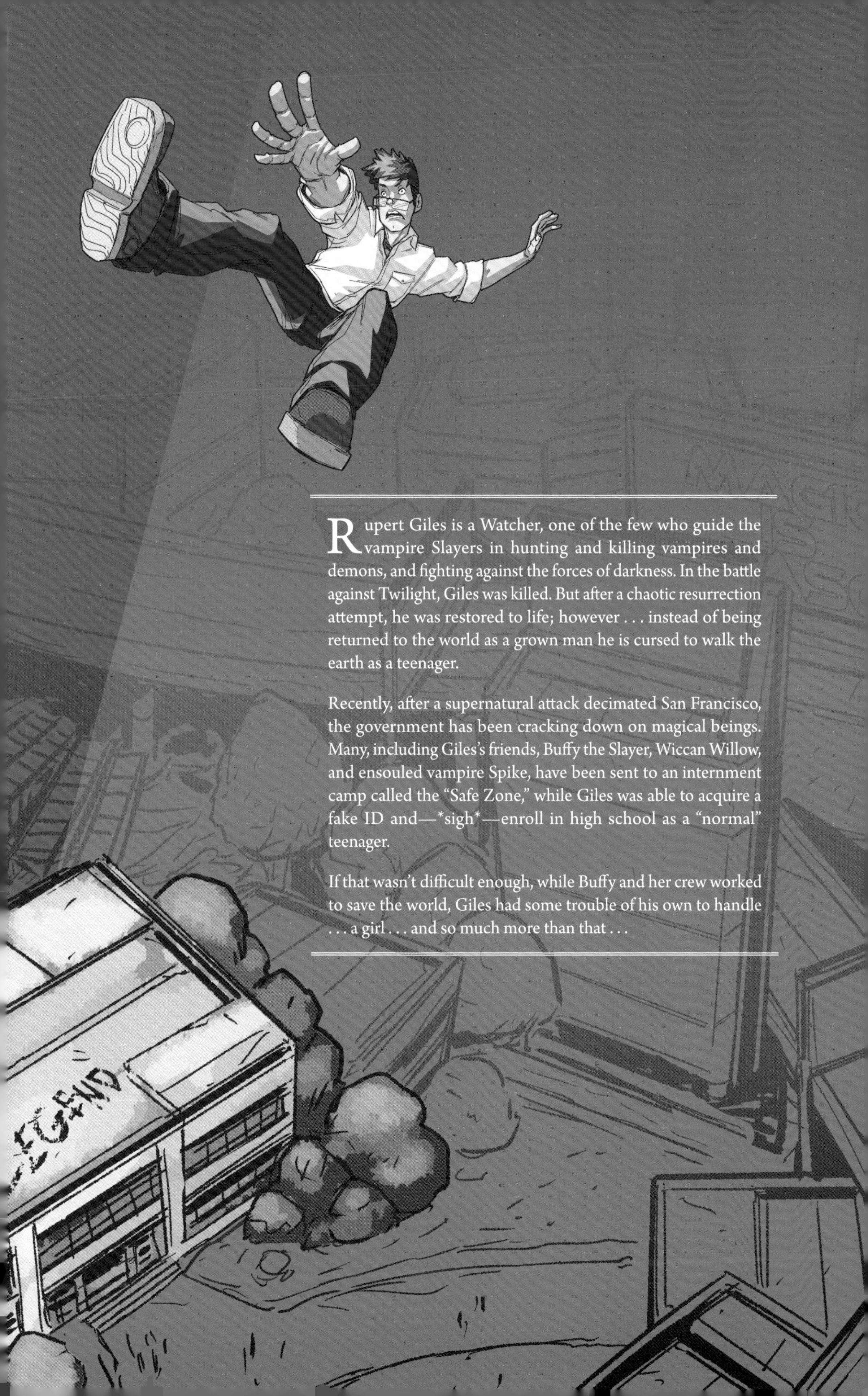

Rupert Giles is a Watcher, one of the few who guide the vampire Slayers in hunting and killing vampires and demons, and fighting against the forces of darkness. In the battle against Twilight, Giles was killed. But after a chaotic resurrection attempt, he was restored to life; however . . . instead of being returned to the world as a grown man he is cursed to walk the earth as a teenager.

Recently, after a supernatural attack decimated San Francisco, the government has been cracking down on magical beings. Many, including Giles's friends, Buffy the Slayer, Wiccan Willow, and ensouled vampire Spike, have been sent to an internment camp called the "Safe Zone," while Giles was able to acquire a fake ID and—*sigh*—enroll in high school as a "normal" teenager.

If that wasn't difficult enough, while Buffy and her crew worked to save the world, Giles had some trouble of his own to handle . . . a girl . . . and so much more than that . . .

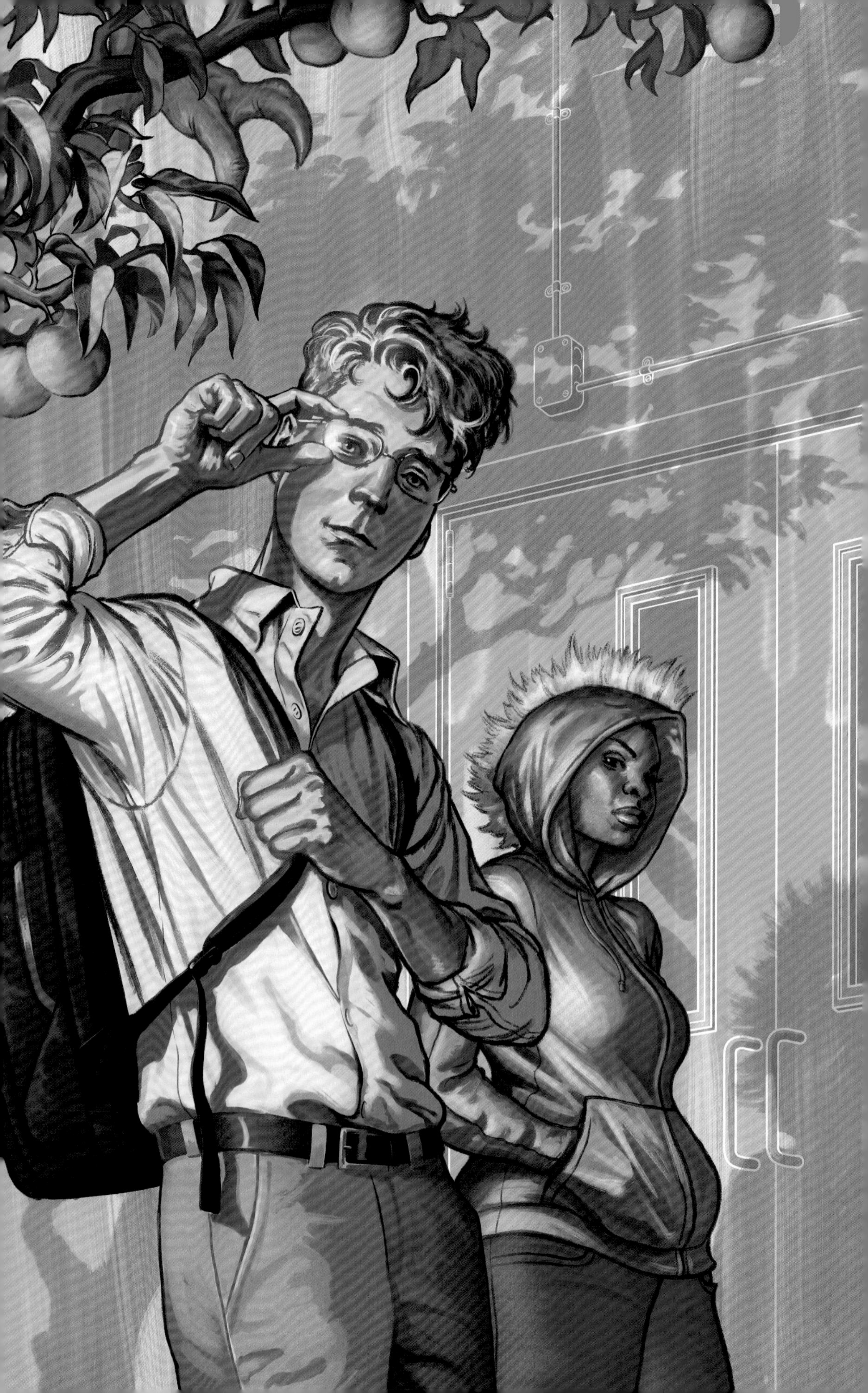

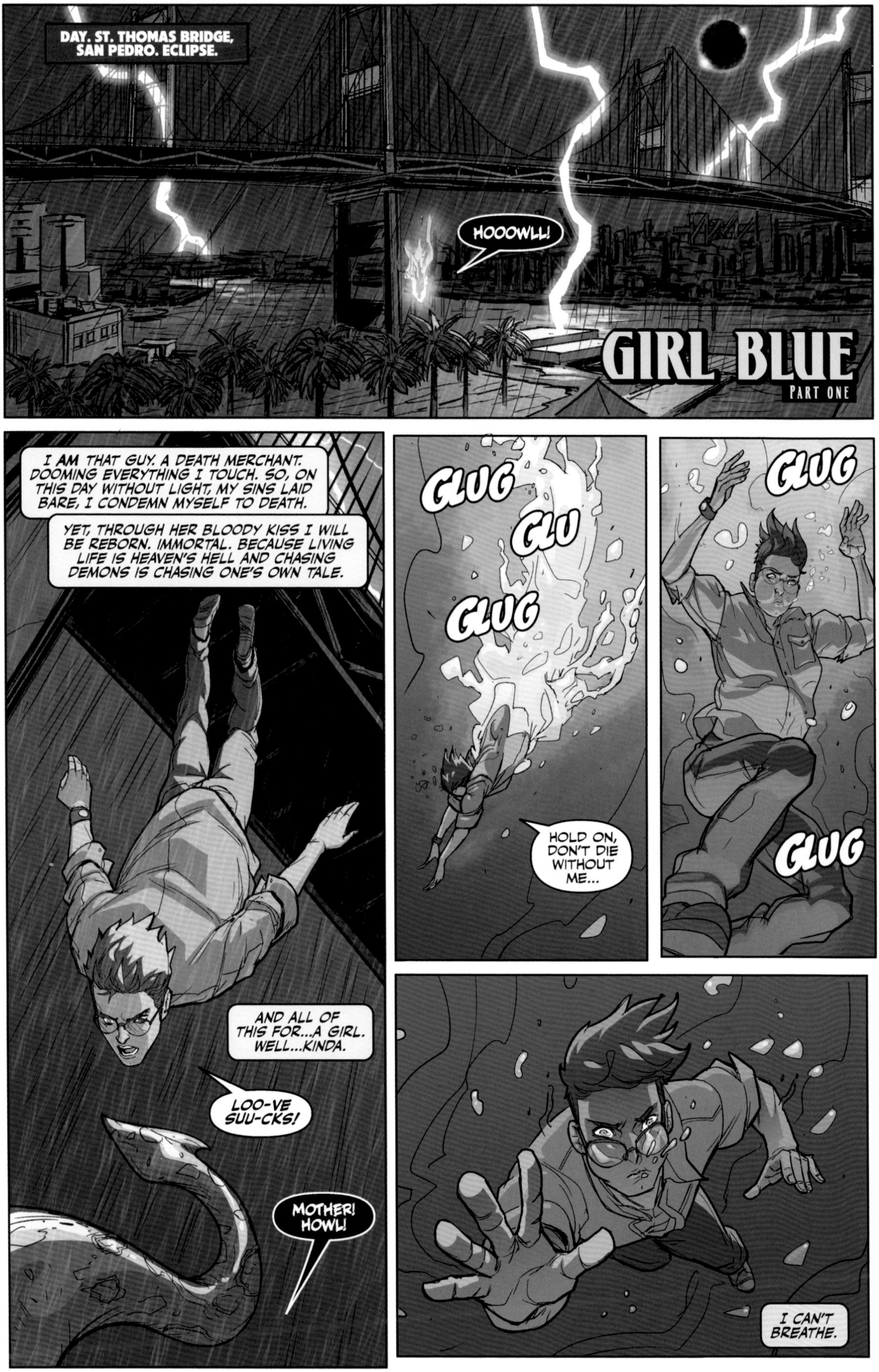
DAY. ST. THOMAS BRIDGE, SAN PEDRO. ECLIPSE.
HOOOWLL!
GIRL BLUE
PART ONE
I AM THAT GUY. A DEATH MERCHANT. DOOMING EVERYTHING I TOUCH. SO, ON THIS DAY WITHOUT LIGHT, MY SINS LAID BARE, I CONDEMN MYSELF TO DEATH.
YET, THROUGH HER BLOODY KISS I WILL BE REBORN. IMMORTAL. BECAUSE LIVING LIFE IS HEAVEN'S HELL AND CHASING DEMONS IS CHASING ONE'S OWN TALE.
AND ALL OF THIS FOR...A GIRL. WELL...KINDA.
LOO-VE SUU-CKS!
MOTHER! HOWL!
GLUG
GLU
GLUG
HOLD ON, DON'T DIE WITHOUT ME...
GLUG
GLUG
I CAN'T BREATHE.

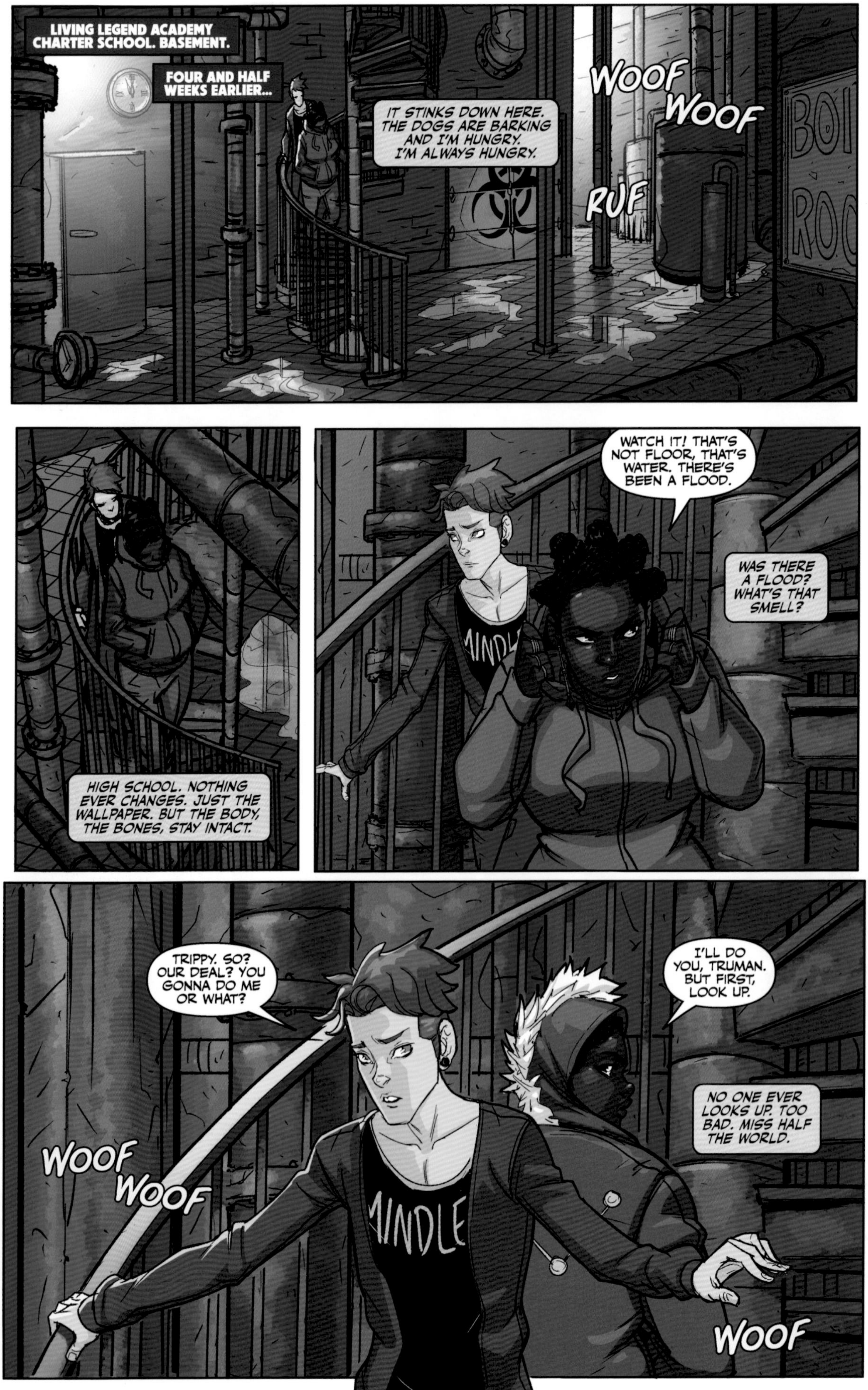
LIVING LEGEND ACADEMY CHARTER SCHOOL. BASEMENT.
FOUR AND HALF WEEKS EARLIER...
IT STINKS DOWN HERE. THE DOGS ARE BARKING AND I'M HUNGRY. I'M ALWAYS HUNGRY.
WOOF WOOF
RUF
HIGH SCHOOL. NOTHING EVER CHANGES. JUST THE WALLPAPER. BUT THE BODY, THE BONES, STAY INTACT.
WATCH IT! THAT'S NOT FLOOR, THAT'S WATER. THERE'S BEEN A FLOOD.
WAS THERE A FLOOD? WHAT'S THAT SMELL?
MINDLE
TRIPPY. SO? OUR DEAL? YOU GONNA DO ME OR WHAT?
I'LL DO YOU, TRUMAN. BUT FIRST, LOOK UP.
NO ONE EVER LOOKS UP. TOO BAD. MISS HALF THE WORLD.
MINDLE
WOOF WOOF
WOOF

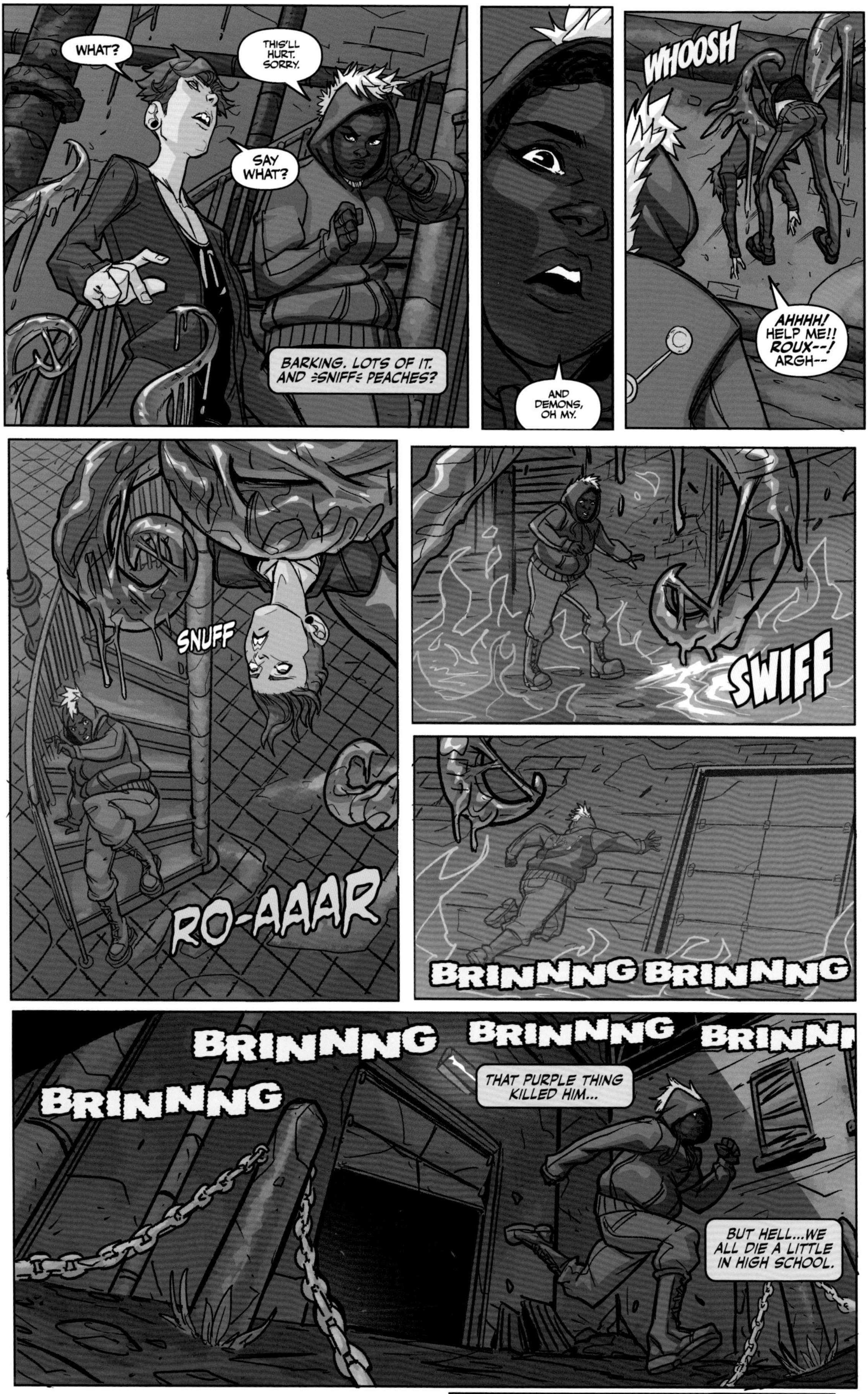
WHAT?
THIS'LL HURT. SORRY.
SAY WHAT?
BARKING. LOTS OF IT. AND =SNIFF= PEACHES?
AND DEMONS, OH MY.
WHOOSH
AHHHH! HELP ME!! ROUX--! ARGH--
SNUFF
RO-AAAR
SWIFF
BRINNNG BRINNNG
BRINNNG BRINNNG
BRINNNG
THAT PURPLE THING KILLED HIM...
BUT HELL...WE ALL DIE A LITTLE IN HIGH SCHOOL.
CUE MIXTAPE #1: "WE THE PEOPLE" BY A TRIBE CALLED QUEST

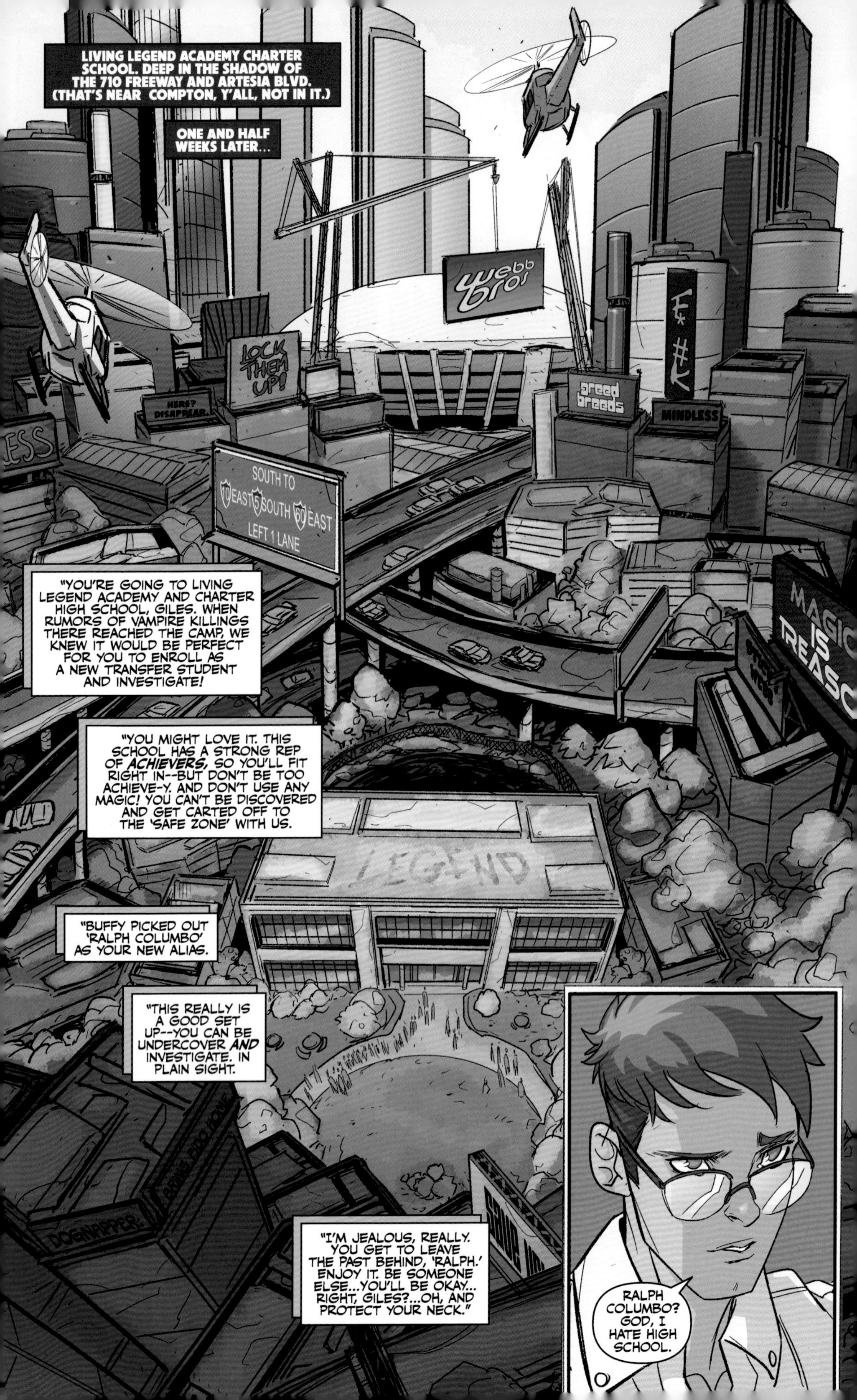
LIVING LEGEND ACADEMY CHARTER SCHOOL. DEEP IN THE SHADOW OF THE 710 FREEWAY AND ARTESIA BLVD. (THAT'S NEAR COMPTON, Y'ALL, NOT IN IT.)
ONE AND HALF WEEKS LATER...
webb bros
LOCK THEM UP!
greed breeds
MINDLESS
SOUTH TO 10 EAST 5 SOUTH 60 EAST LEFT 1 LANE
"YOU'RE GOING TO LIVING LEGEND ACADEMY AND CHARTER HIGH SCHOOL, GILES. WHEN RUMORS OF VAMPIRE KILLINGS THERE REACHED THE CAMP, WE KNEW IT WOULD BE PERFECT FOR YOU TO ENROLL AS A NEW TRANSFER STUDENT AND INVESTIGATE!
"YOU MIGHT LOVE IT. THIS SCHOOL HAS A STRONG REP OF *ACHIEVERS,* SO YOU'LL FIT RIGHT IN--BUT DON'T BE TOO ACHIEVE-Y. AND DON'T USE ANY MAGIC! YOU CAN'T BE DISCOVERED AND GET CARTED OFF TO THE 'SAFE ZONE' WITH US.
LEGEND
"BUFFY PICKED OUT 'RALPH COLUMBO' AS YOUR NEW ALIAS.
"THIS REALLY IS A GOOD SET UP--YOU CAN BE UNDERCOVER *AND* INVESTIGATE. IN PLAIN SIGHT.
DOGNAPPER
"I'M JEALOUS, REALLY. YOU GET TO LEAVE THE PAST BEHIND, 'RALPH.' ENJOY IT. BE SOMEONE ELSE...YOU'LL BE OKAY... RIGHT, GILES?...OH, AND PROTECT YOUR NECK."
RALPH COLUMBO? GOD, I HATE HIGH SCHOOL.

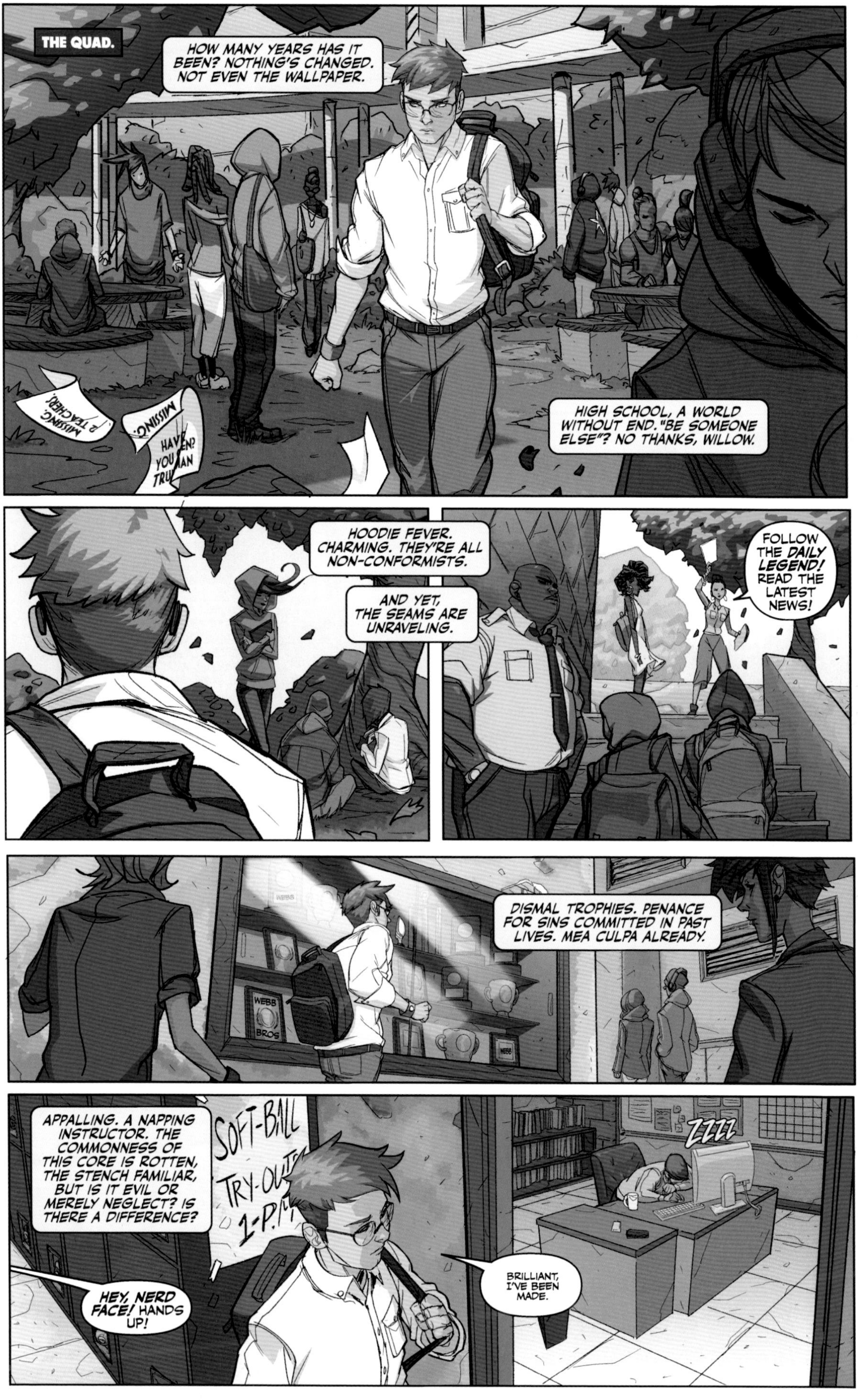
THE QUAD.
HOW MANY YEARS HAS IT BEEN? NOTHING'S CHANGED. NOT EVEN THE WALLPAPER.
MISSING: 2 TEACHERS.
MISSING:
HIGH SCHOOL, A WORLD WITHOUT END. "BE SOMEONE ELSE"? NO THANKS, WILLOW.
HOODIE FEVER. CHARMING. THEY'RE ALL NON-CONFORMISTS.
AND YET, THE SEAMS ARE UNRAVELING.
FOLLOW THE DAILY LEGEND! READ THE LATEST NEWS!
DISMAL TROPHIES. PENANCE FOR SINS COMMITTED IN PAST LIVES. MEA CULPA ALREADY.
WEBB BROS
WEBB
APPALLING. A NAPPING INSTRUCTOR. THE COMMONNESS OF THIS CORE IS ROTTEN, THE STENCH FAMILIAR, BUT IS IT EVIL OR MERELY NEGLECT? IS THERE A DIFFERENCE?
SOFT-BALL
ZZZZ
HEY, NERD FACE! HANDS UP!
BRILLIANT, I'VE BEEN MADE.

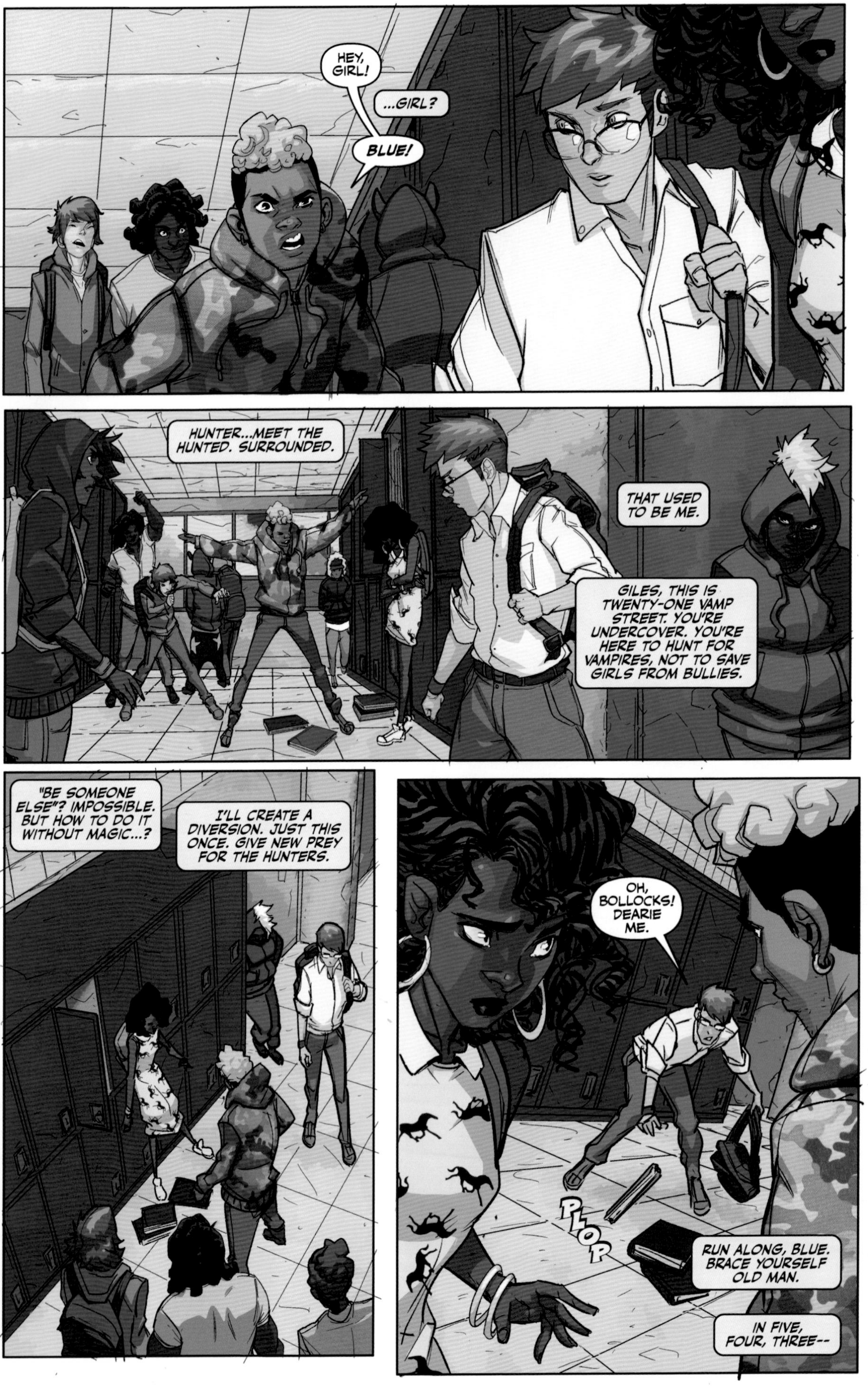
HEY, GIRL!
...GIRL?
BLUE!
HUNTER...MEET THE HUNTED. SURROUNDED.
THAT USED TO BE ME.
GILES, THIS IS TWENTY-ONE VAMP STREET. YOU'RE UNDERCOVER. YOU'RE HERE TO HUNT FOR VAMPIRES, NOT TO SAVE GIRLS FROM BULLIES.
"BE SOMEONE ELSE"? IMPOSSIBLE. BUT HOW TO DO IT WITHOUT MAGIC...?
I'LL CREATE A DIVERSION. JUST THIS ONCE. GIVE NEW PREY FOR THE HUNTERS.
OH, BOLLOCKS! DEARIE ME.
PLOP
RUN ALONG, BLUE. BRACE YOURSELF OLD MAN.
IN FIVE, FOUR, THREE--

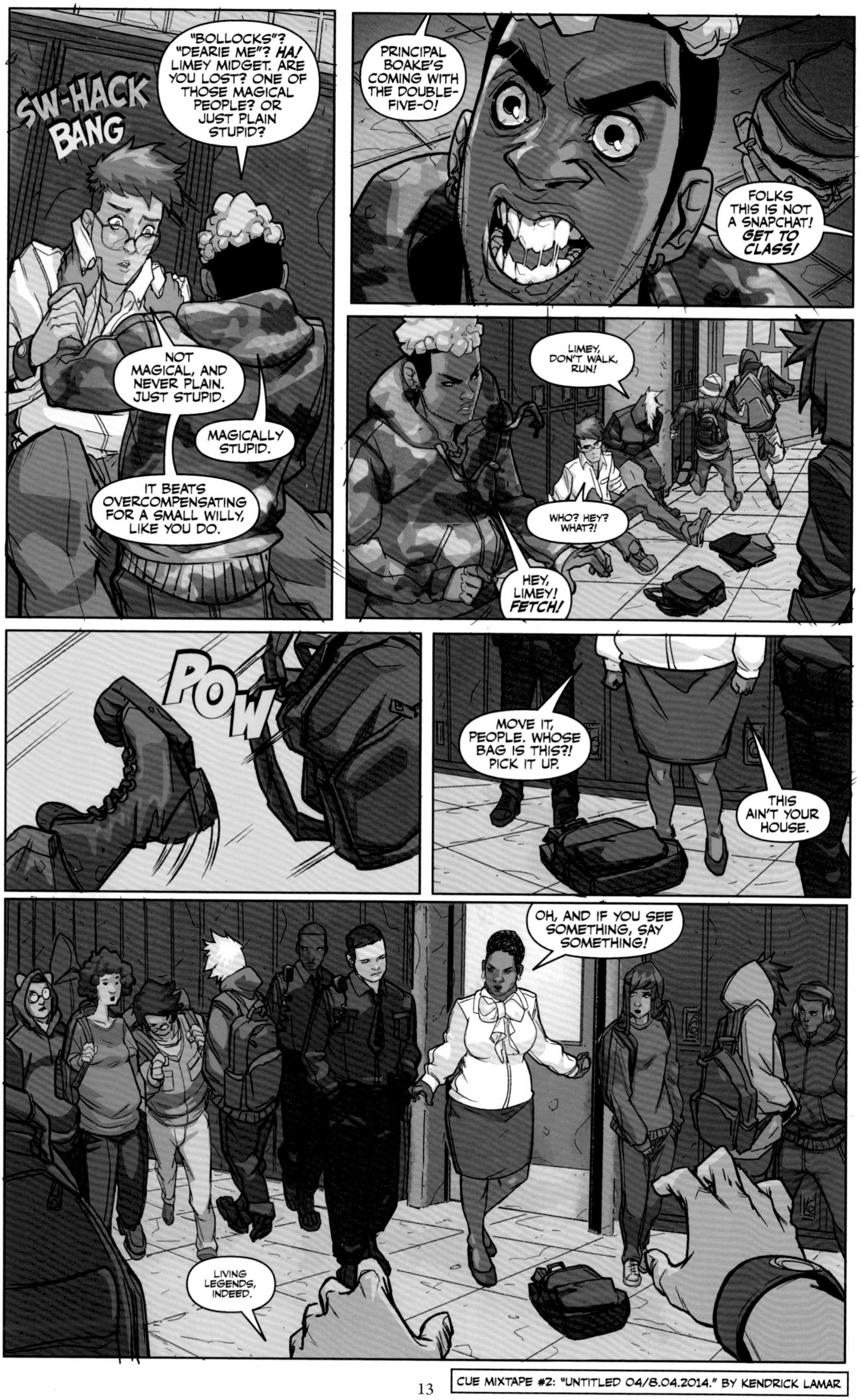
SW-HACK
BANG
"BOLLOCKS"? "DEARIE ME"? HA! LIMEY MIDGET. ARE YOU LOST? ONE OF THOSE MAGICAL PEOPLE? OR JUST PLAIN STUPID?
NOT MAGICAL, AND NEVER PLAIN. JUST STUPID.
MAGICALLY STUPID.
IT BEATS OVERCOMPENSATING FOR A SMALL WILLY, LIKE YOU DO.
PRINCIPAL BOAKE'S COMING WITH THE DOUBLE-FIVE-O!
FOLKS THIS IS NOT A SNAPCHAT! GET TO CLASS!
LIMEY, DON'T WALK, RUN!
WHO? HEY? WHAT?!
HEY, LIMEY! FETCH!
POW
MOVE IT, PEOPLE. WHOSE BAG IS THIS?! PICK IT UP.
THIS AIN'T YOUR HOUSE.
OH, AND IF YOU SEE SOMETHING, SAY SOMETHING!
LIVING LEGENDS, INDEED.

CUE MIXTAPE #2: "UNTITLED 04/8.04.2014." BY KENDRICK LAMAR

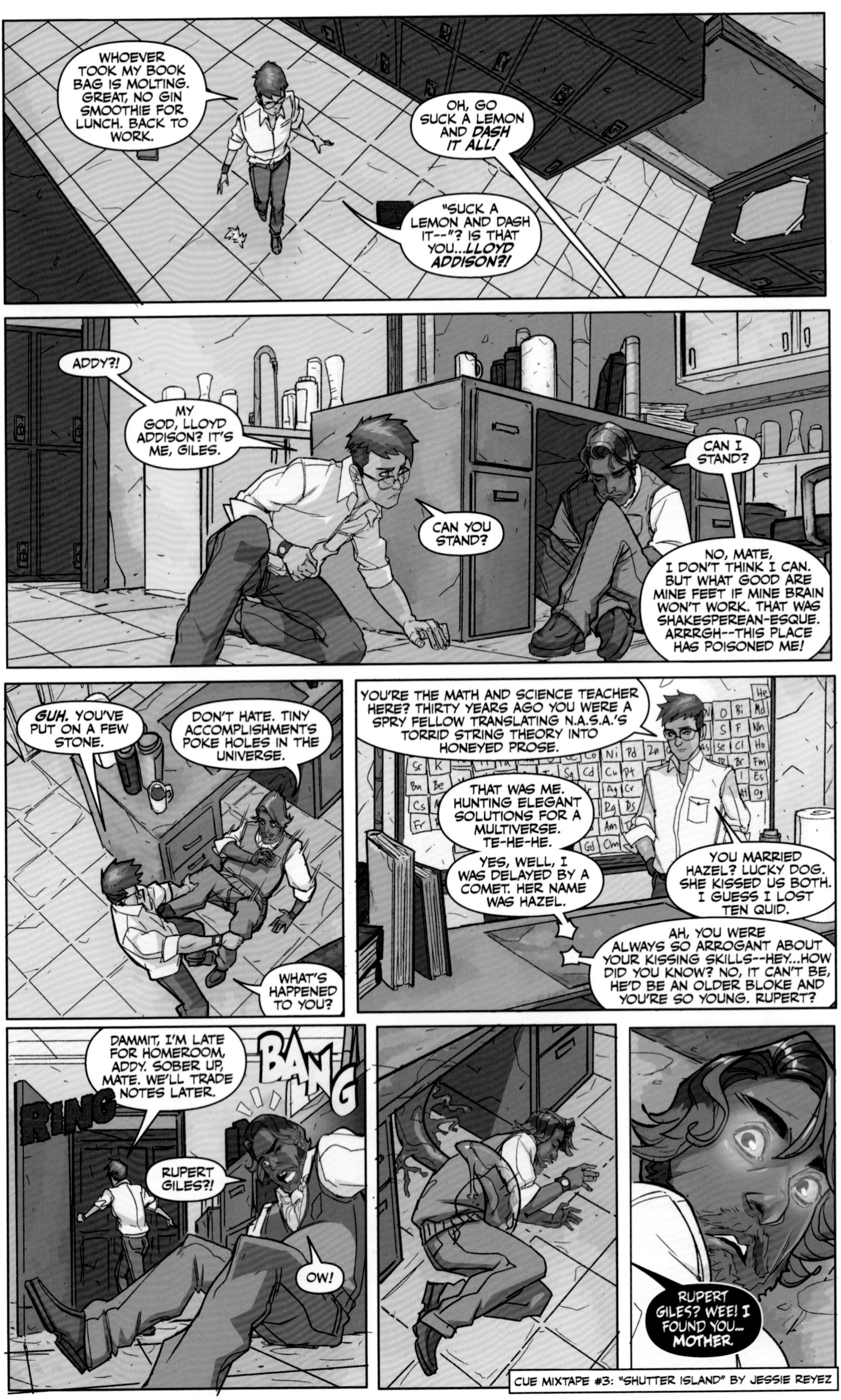
WHOEVER TOOK MY BOOK BAG IS MOLTING. GREAT, NO GIN SMOOTHIE FOR LUNCH. BACK TO WORK.
OH, GO SUCK A LEMON AND DASH IT ALL!
"SUCK A LEMON AND DASH IT--"? IS THAT YOU...LLOYD ADDISON?!
ADDY?!
MY GOD, LLOYD ADDISON? IT'S ME, GILES.
CAN I STAND?
CAN YOU STAND?
NO, MATE, I DON'T THINK I CAN. BUT WHAT GOOD ARE MINE FEET IF MINE BRAIN WON'T WORK. THAT WAS SHAKESPEREAN-ESQUE. ARRRGH--THIS PLACE HAS POISONED ME!
GUH. YOU'VE PUT ON A FEW STONE.
DON'T HATE. TINY ACCOMPLISHMENTS POKE HOLES IN THE UNIVERSE.
WHAT'S HAPPENED TO YOU?
YOU'RE THE MATH AND SCIENCE TEACHER HERE? THIRTY YEARS AGO YOU WERE A SPRY FELLOW TRANSLATING N.A.S.A.'S TORRID STRING THEORY INTO HONEYED PROSE.
THAT WAS ME. HUNTING ELEGANT SOLUTIONS FOR A MULTIVERSE. TE-HE-HE.
YES, WELL, I WAS DELAYED BY A COMET. HER NAME WAS HAZEL.
YOU MARRIED HAZEL? LUCKY DOG. SHE KISSED US BOTH. I GUESS I LOST TEN QUID.
AH, YOU WERE ALWAYS SO ARROGANT ABOUT YOUR KISSING SKILLS--HEY...HOW DID YOU KNOW? NO, IT CAN'T BE, HE'D BE AN OLDER BLOKE AND YOU'RE SO YOUNG. RUPERT?
DAMMIT, I'M LATE FOR HOMEROOM, ADDY. SOBER UP, MATE. WE'LL TRADE NOTES LATER.
BANG
RING
RUPERT GILES?!
OW!
RUPERT GILES? WEE! I FOUND YOU... MOTHER.
CUE MIXTAPE #3: "SHUTTER ISLAND" BY JESSIE REYEZ

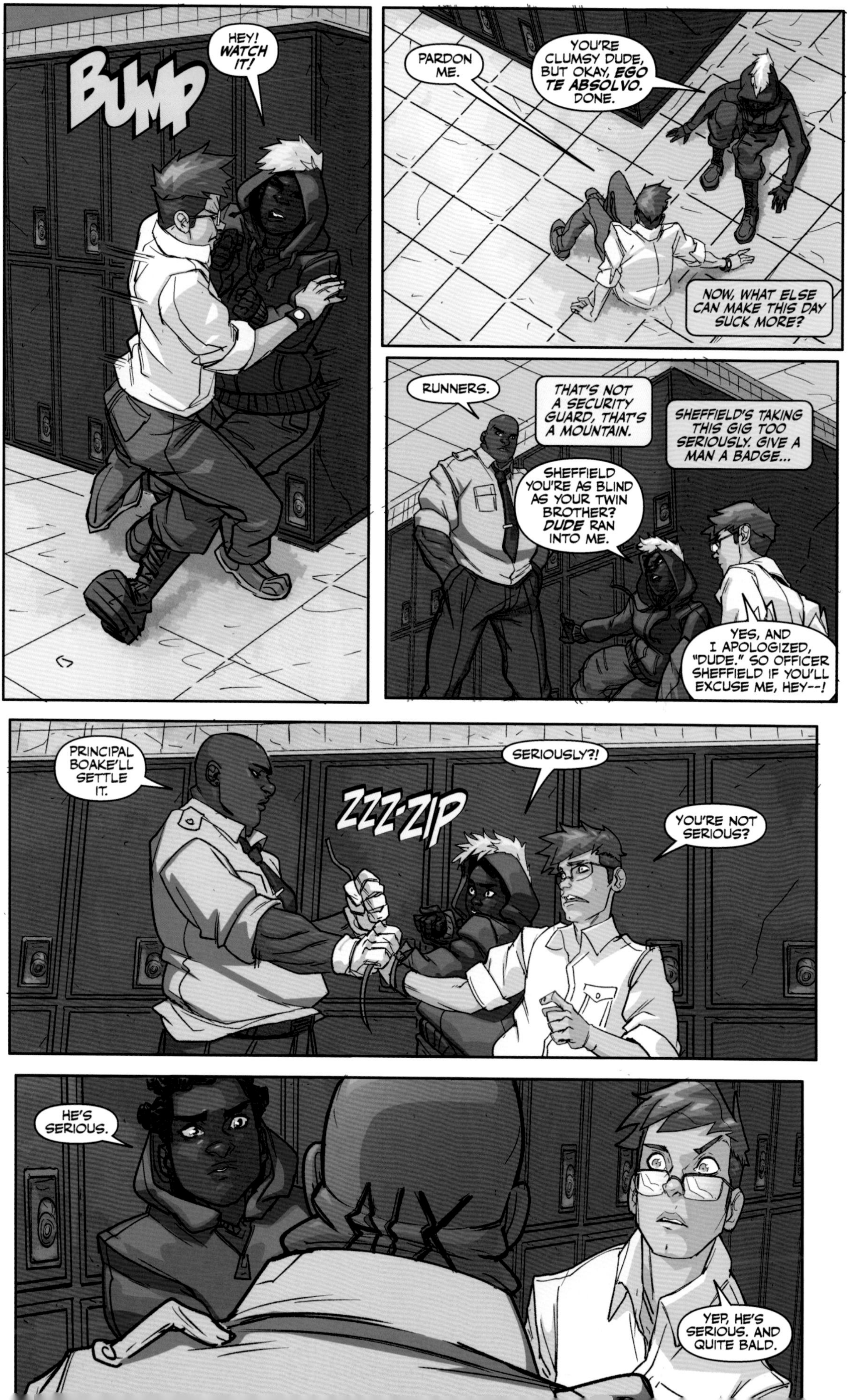
BUMP
HEY! WATCH IT!
PARDON ME.
YOU'RE CLUMSY DUDE, BUT OKAY, EGO TE ABSOLVO. DONE.
NOW, WHAT ELSE CAN MAKE THIS DAY SUCK MORE?
RUNNERS.
THAT'S NOT A SECURITY GUARD, THAT'S A MOUNTAIN.
SHEFFIELD'S TAKING THIS GIG TOO SERIOUSLY. GIVE A MAN A BADGE...
SHEFFIELD YOU'RE AS BLIND AS YOUR TWIN BROTHER? DUDE RAN INTO ME.
YES, AND I APOLOGIZED, "DUDE." SO OFFICER SHEFFIELD IF YOU'LL EXCUSE ME, HEY--!
PRINCIPAL BOAKE'LL SETTLE IT.
ZZZ-ZIP
SERIOUSLY?!
YOU'RE NOT SERIOUS?
HE'S SERIOUS.
YEP, HE'S SERIOUS. AND QUITE BALD.

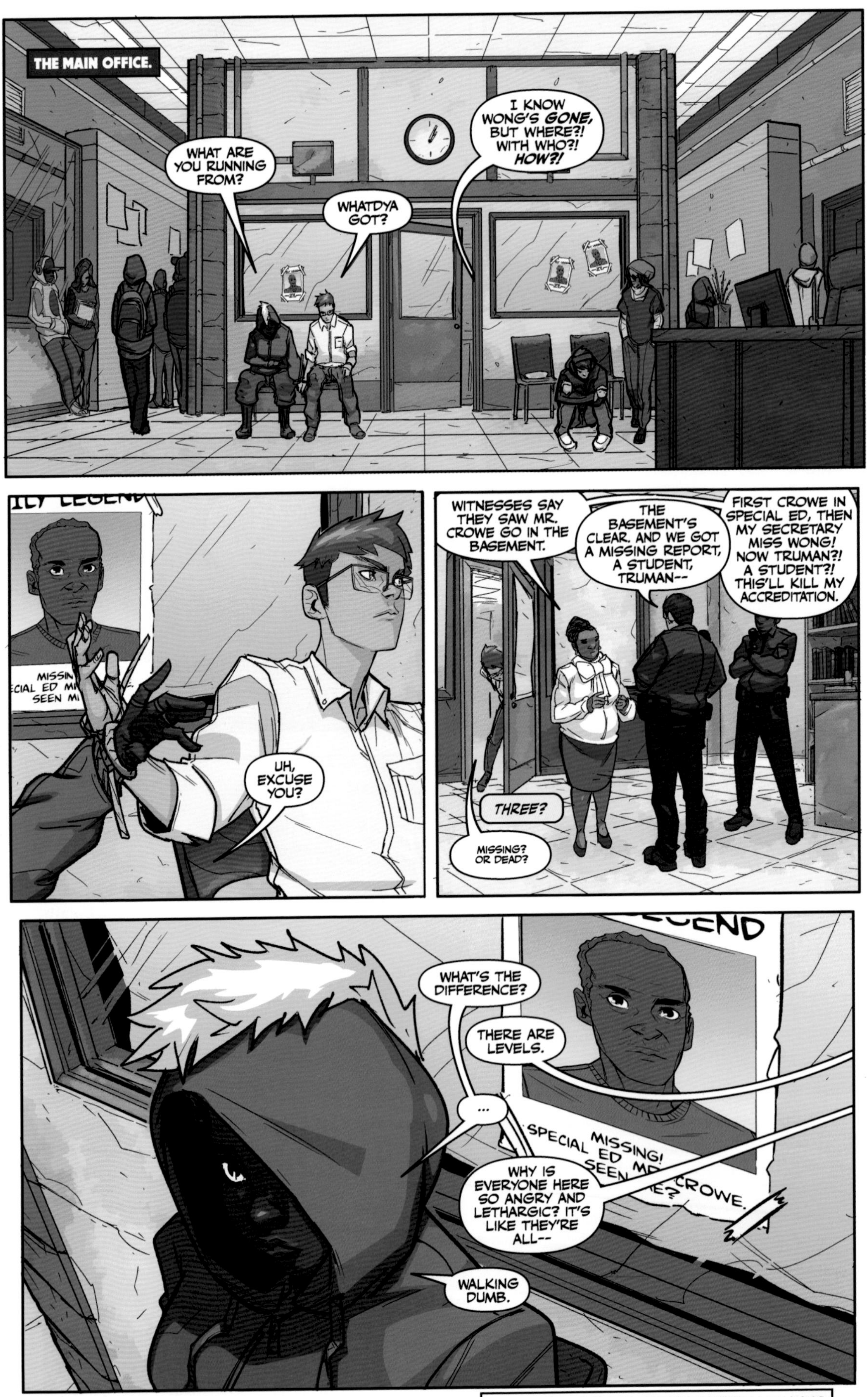
THE MAIN OFFICE.
WHAT ARE YOU RUNNING FROM?
WHATDYA GOT?
I KNOW WONG'S *GONE*, BUT WHERE?! WITH WHO?! *HOW?!*
UH, EXCUSE YOU?
WITNESSES SAY THEY SAW MR. CROWE GO IN THE BASEMENT.
THE BASEMENT'S CLEAR. AND WE GOT A MISSING REPORT, A STUDENT, TRUMAN--
FIRST CROWE IN SPECIAL ED, THEN MY SECRETARY MISS WONG! NOW TRUMAN?! A STUDENT?! THIS'LL KILL MY ACCREDITATION.
THREE?
MISSING? OR DEAD?
WHAT'S THE DIFFERENCE?
THERE ARE LEVELS.
...
WHY IS EVERYONE HERE SO ANGRY AND LETHARGIC? IT'S LIKE THEY'RE ALL--
WALKING DUMB.

CUE MIXTAPE #4: "LOST QUEEN" BY PHARRELL WILLIAMS

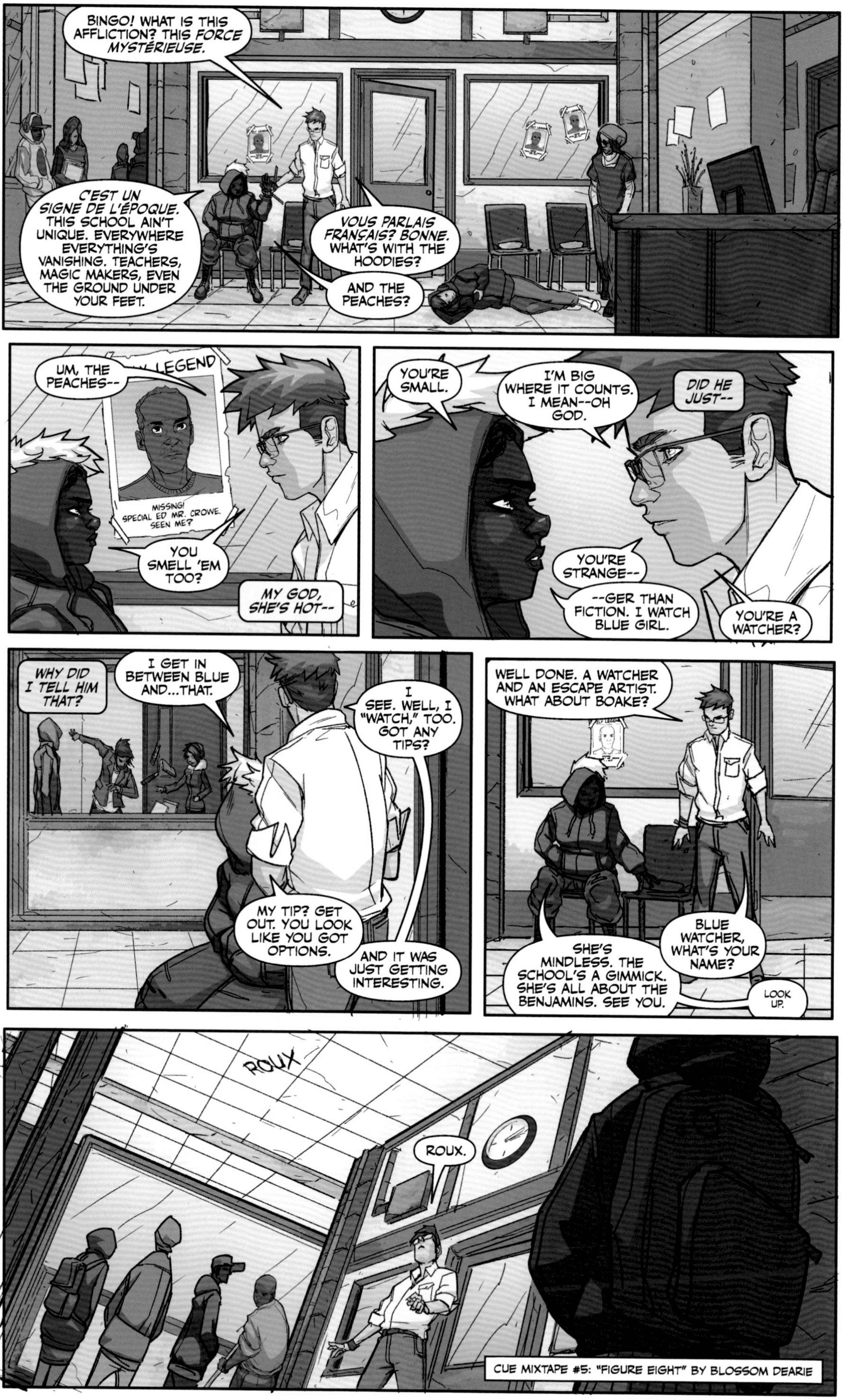
BINGO! WHAT IS THIS AFFLICTION? THIS *FORCE MYSTÉRIEUSE.*
C'EST UN SIGNE DE L'ÉPOQUE. THIS SCHOOL AIN'T UNIQUE. EVERYWHERE EVERYTHING'S VANISHING. TEACHERS, MAGIC MAKERS, EVEN THE GROUND UNDER YOUR FEET.
VOUS PARLAIS FRANÇAIS? BONNE. WHAT'S WITH THE HOODIES?
AND THE PEACHES?
UM, THE PEACHES--
LEGEND
MISSING! SPECIAL ED MR. CROWE. SEEN ME?
YOU SMELL 'EM TOO?
MY GOD, SHE'S HOT--
YOU'RE SMALL.
I'M BIG WHERE IT COUNTS. I MEAN--OH GOD.
DID HE JUST--
YOU'RE STRANGE--
--GER THAN FICTION. I WATCH BLUE GIRL.
YOU'RE A WATCHER?
WHY DID I TELL HIM THAT?
I GET IN BETWEEN BLUE AND...THAT.
I SEE. WELL, I "WATCH," TOO. GOT ANY TIPS?
MY TIP? GET OUT. YOU LOOK LIKE YOU GOT OPTIONS.
AND IT WAS JUST GETTING INTERESTING.
WELL DONE. A WATCHER AND AN ESCAPE ARTIST. WHAT ABOUT BOAKE?
SHE'S MINDLESS. THE SCHOOL'S A GIMMICK. SHE'S ALL ABOUT THE BENJAMINS. SEE YOU.
BLUE WATCHER, WHAT'S YOUR NAME?
LOOK UP.
ROUX
ROUX.
CUE MIXTAPE #5: "FIGURE EIGHT" BY BLOSSOM DEARIE

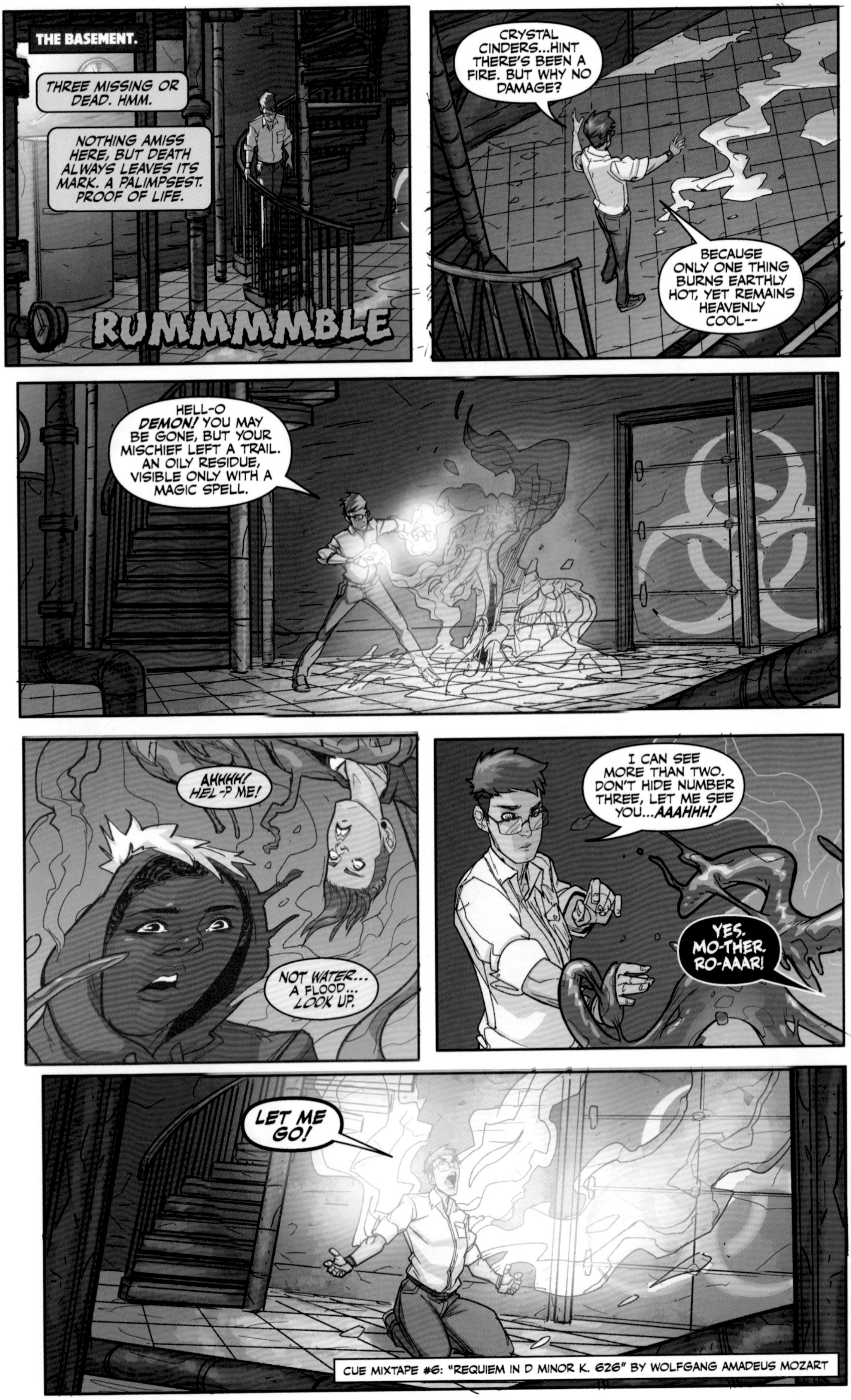
THE BASEMENT.
THREE MISSING OR DEAD. HMM.
NOTHING AMISS HERE, BUT DEATH ALWAYS LEAVES ITS MARK. A PALIMPSEST. PROOF OF LIFE.
RUMMMMMBLE
CRYSTAL CINDERS...HINT THERE'S BEEN A FIRE. BUT WHY NO DAMAGE?
BECAUSE ONLY ONE THING BURNS EARTHLY HOT, YET REMAINS HEAVENLY COOL--
HELL-O DEMON! YOU MAY BE GONE, BUT YOUR MISCHIEF LEFT A TRAIL. AN OILY RESIDUE, VISIBLE ONLY WITH A MAGIC SPELL.
AHHHH! HEL-P ME!
NOT WATER... A FLOOD... LOOK UP.
I CAN SEE MORE THAN TWO. DON'T HIDE NUMBER THREE, LET ME SEE YOU...AAAHHH!
YES. MO-THER. RO-AAAR!
LET ME GO!
CUE MIXTAPE #6: "REQUIEM IN D MINOR K. 626" BY WOLFGANG AMADEUS MOZART

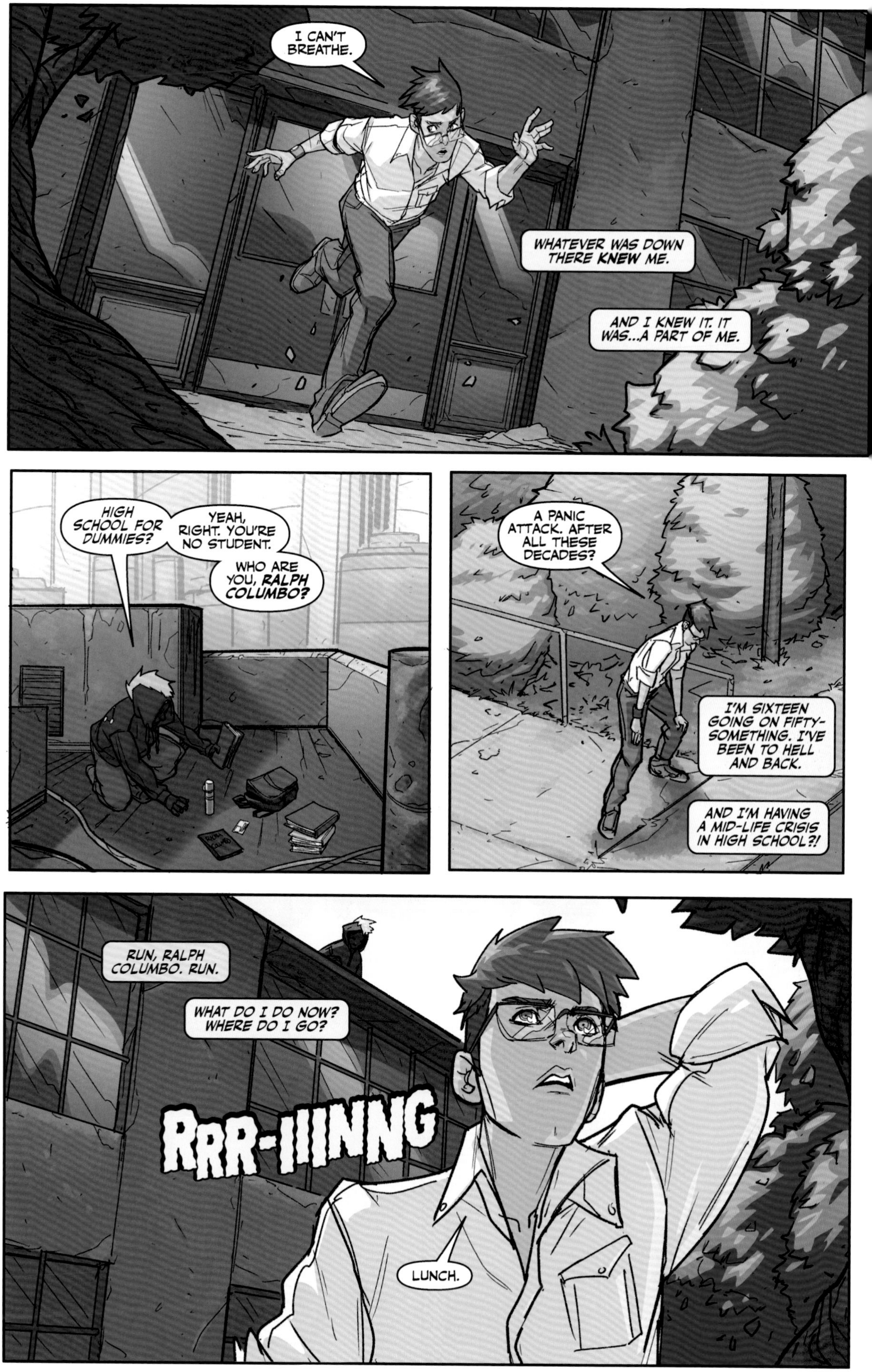
I CAN'T BREATHE.
WHATEVER WAS DOWN THERE KNEW ME.
AND I KNEW IT. IT WAS...A PART OF ME.
HIGH SCHOOL FOR DUMMIES?
YEAH, RIGHT. YOU'RE NO STUDENT.
WHO ARE YOU, RALPH COLUMBO?
A PANIC ATTACK. AFTER ALL THESE DECADES?
I'M SIXTEEN GOING ON FIFTY-SOMETHING. I'VE BEEN TO HELL AND BACK.
AND I'M HAVING A MID-LIFE CRISIS IN HIGH SCHOOL?!
RUN, RALPH COLUMBO. RUN.
WHAT DO I DO NOW? WHERE DO I GO?
RRR-IIINNG
LUNCH.

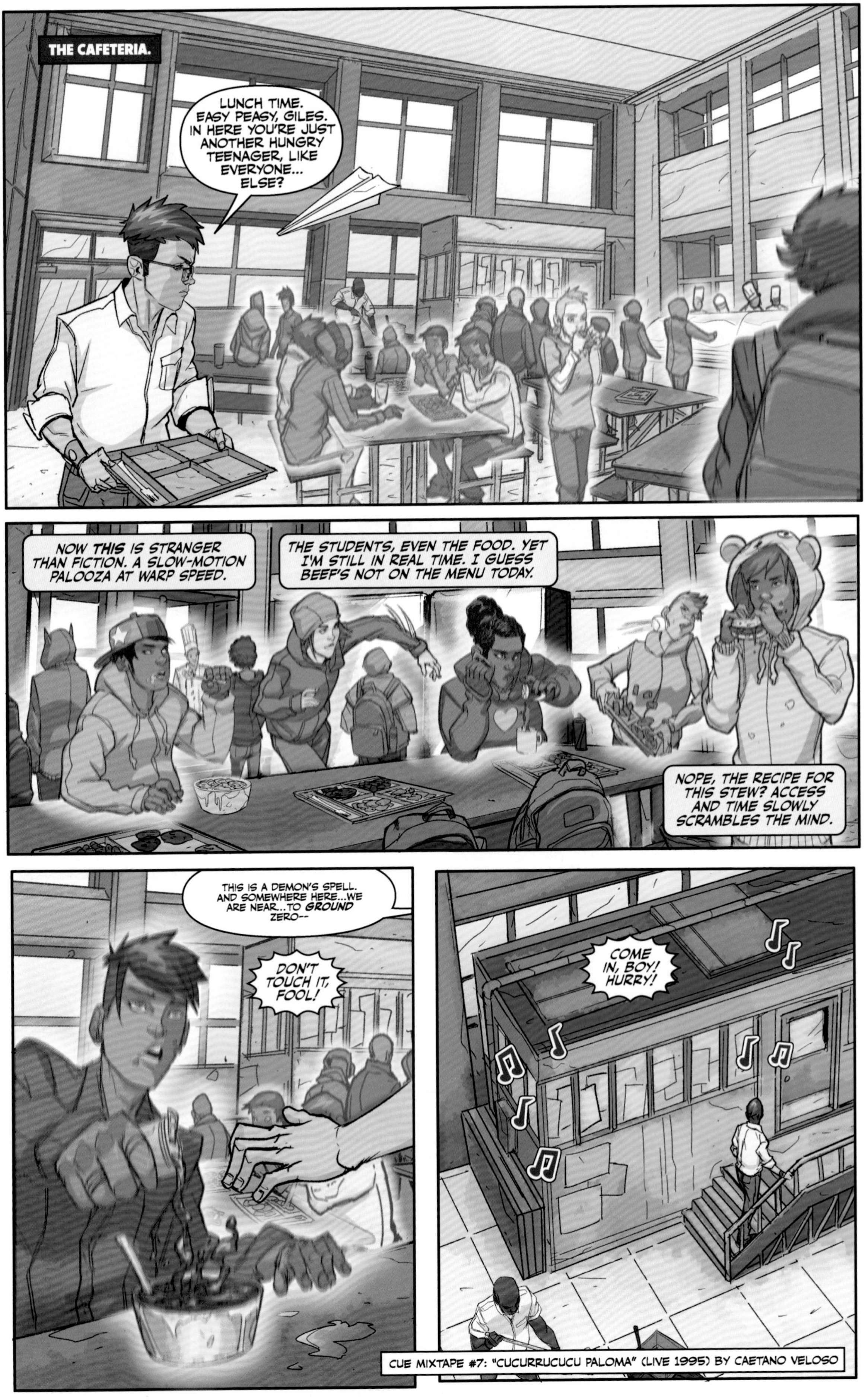
THE CAFETERIA.
LUNCH TIME. EASY PEASY, GILES. IN HERE YOU'RE JUST ANOTHER HUNGRY TEENAGER, LIKE EVERYONE... ELSE?
NOW THIS IS STRANGER THAN FICTION. A SLOW-MOTION PALOOZA AT WARP SPEED.
THE STUDENTS, EVEN THE FOOD. YET I'M STILL IN REAL TIME. I GUESS BEEF'S NOT ON THE MENU TODAY.
NOPE, THE RECIPE FOR THIS STEW? ACCESS AND TIME SLOWLY SCRAMBLES THE MIND.
THIS IS A DEMON'S SPELL. AND SOMEWHERE HERE...WE ARE NEAR...TO GROUND ZERO--
DON'T TOUCH IT, FOOL!
COME IN, BOY! HURRY!
CUE MIXTAPE #7: "CUCURRUCUCU PALOMA" (LIVE 1995) BY CAETANO VELOSO

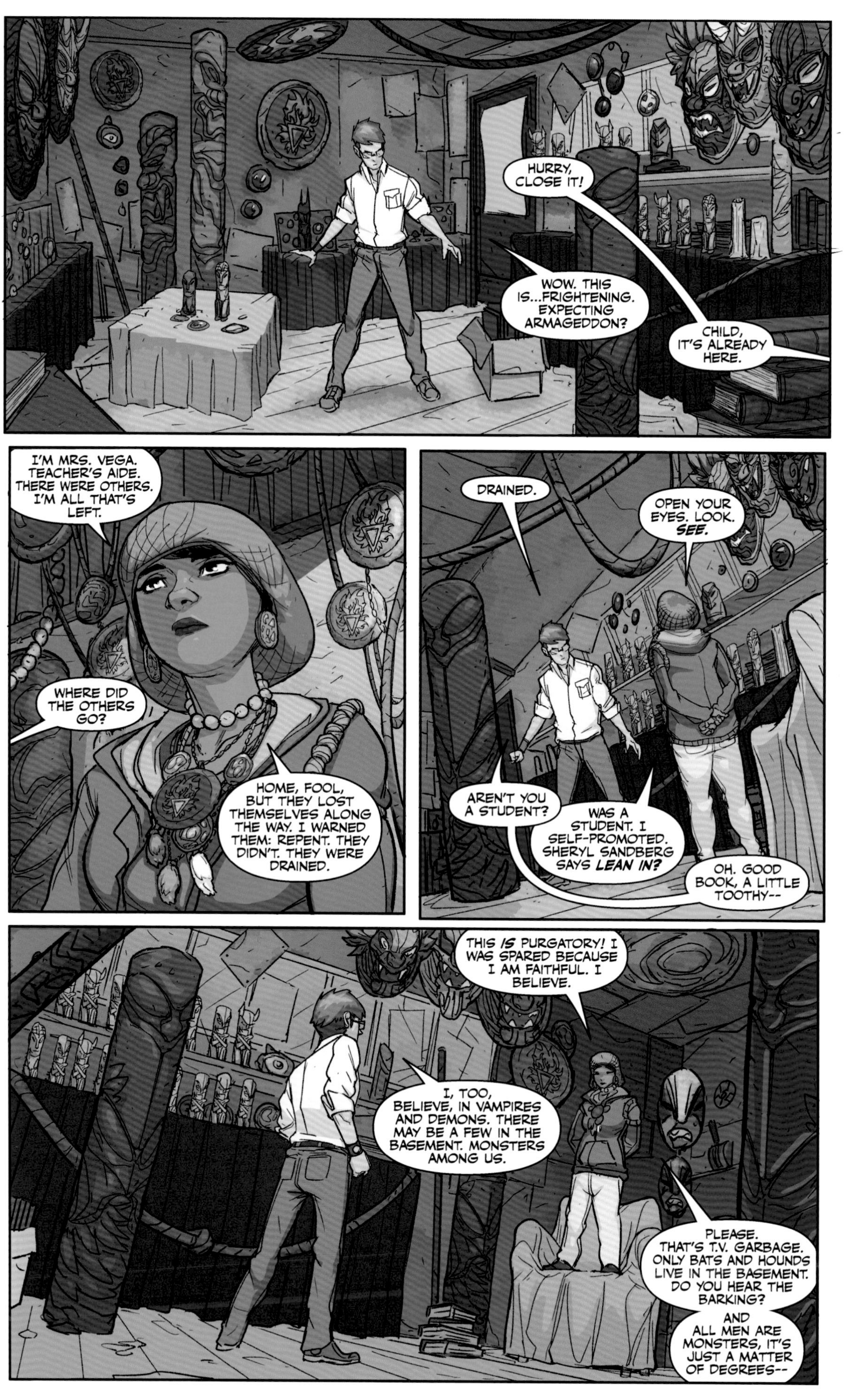
HURRY, CLOSE IT!
WOW. THIS IS...FRIGHTENING. EXPECTING ARMAGEDDON?
CHILD, IT'S ALREADY HERE.
I'M MRS. VEGA. TEACHER'S AIDE. THERE WERE OTHERS. I'M ALL THAT'S LEFT.
WHERE DID THE OTHERS GO?
HOME, FOOL, BUT THEY LOST THEMSELVES ALONG THE WAY. I WARNED THEM: REPENT. THEY DIDN'T. THEY WERE DRAINED.
DRAINED.
OPEN YOUR EYES. LOOK. SEE.
AREN'T YOU A STUDENT?
WAS A STUDENT. I SELF-PROMOTED. SHERYL SANDBERG SAYS LEAN IN?
OH. GOOD BOOK, A LITTLE TOOTHY--
THIS IS PURGATORY! I WAS SPARED BECAUSE I AM FAITHFUL. I BELIEVE.
I, TOO, BELIEVE, IN VAMPIRES AND DEMONS. THERE MAY BE A FEW IN THE BASEMENT. MONSTERS AMONG US.
PLEASE. THAT'S T.V. GARBAGE. ONLY BATS AND HOUNDS LIVE IN THE BASEMENT. DO YOU HEAR THE BARKING?
AND ALL MEN ARE MONSTERS, IT'S JUST A MATTER OF DEGREES--

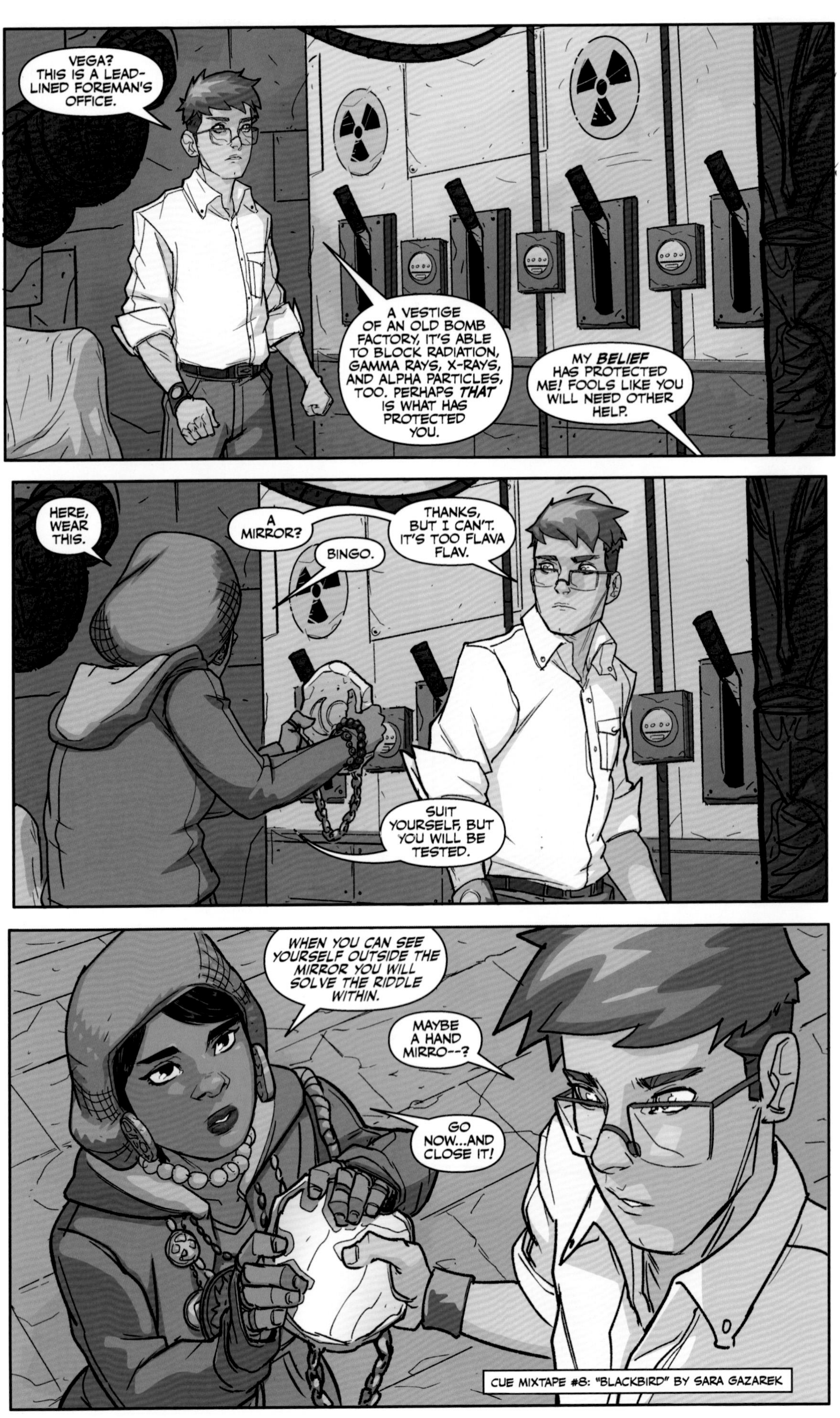
VEGA? THIS IS A LEAD-LINED FOREMAN'S OFFICE.
A VESTIGE OF AN OLD BOMB FACTORY, IT'S ABLE TO BLOCK RADIATION, GAMMA RAYS, X-RAYS, AND ALPHA PARTICLES, TOO. PERHAPS *THAT* IS WHAT HAS PROTECTED YOU.
MY ***BELIEF*** HAS PROTECTED ME! FOOLS LIKE YOU WILL NEED OTHER HELP.
HERE, WEAR THIS.
A MIRROR?
BINGO.
THANKS, BUT I CAN'T. IT'S TOO FLAVA FLAV.
SUIT YOURSELF, BUT YOU WILL BE TESTED.
WHEN YOU CAN SEE YOURSELF OUTSIDE THE MIRROR YOU WILL SOLVE THE RIDDLE WITHIN.
MAYBE A HAND MIRRO--?
GO NOW...AND CLOSE IT!
CUE MIXTAPE #8: "BLACKBIRD" BY SARA GAZAREK

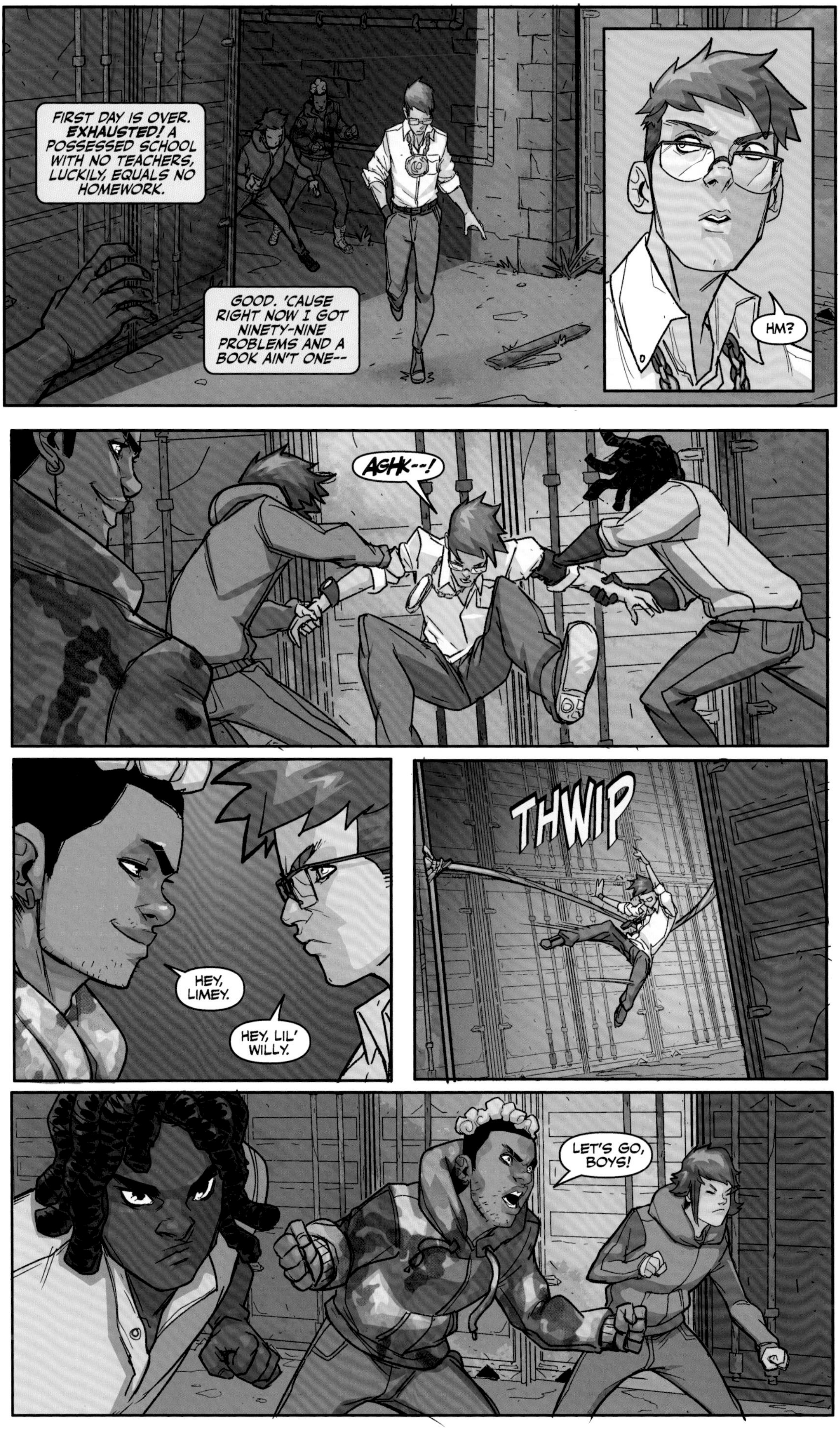
FIRST DAY IS OVER. **EXHAUSTED!** A POSSESSED SCHOOL WITH NO TEACHERS, LUCKILY, EQUALS NO HOMEWORK.
GOOD. 'CAUSE RIGHT NOW I GOT NINETY-NINE PROBLEMS AND A BOOK AIN'T ONE--
HM?
AGHK--!
HEY, LIMEY.
HEY, LIL' WILLY.
THWIP
LET'S GO, BOYS!

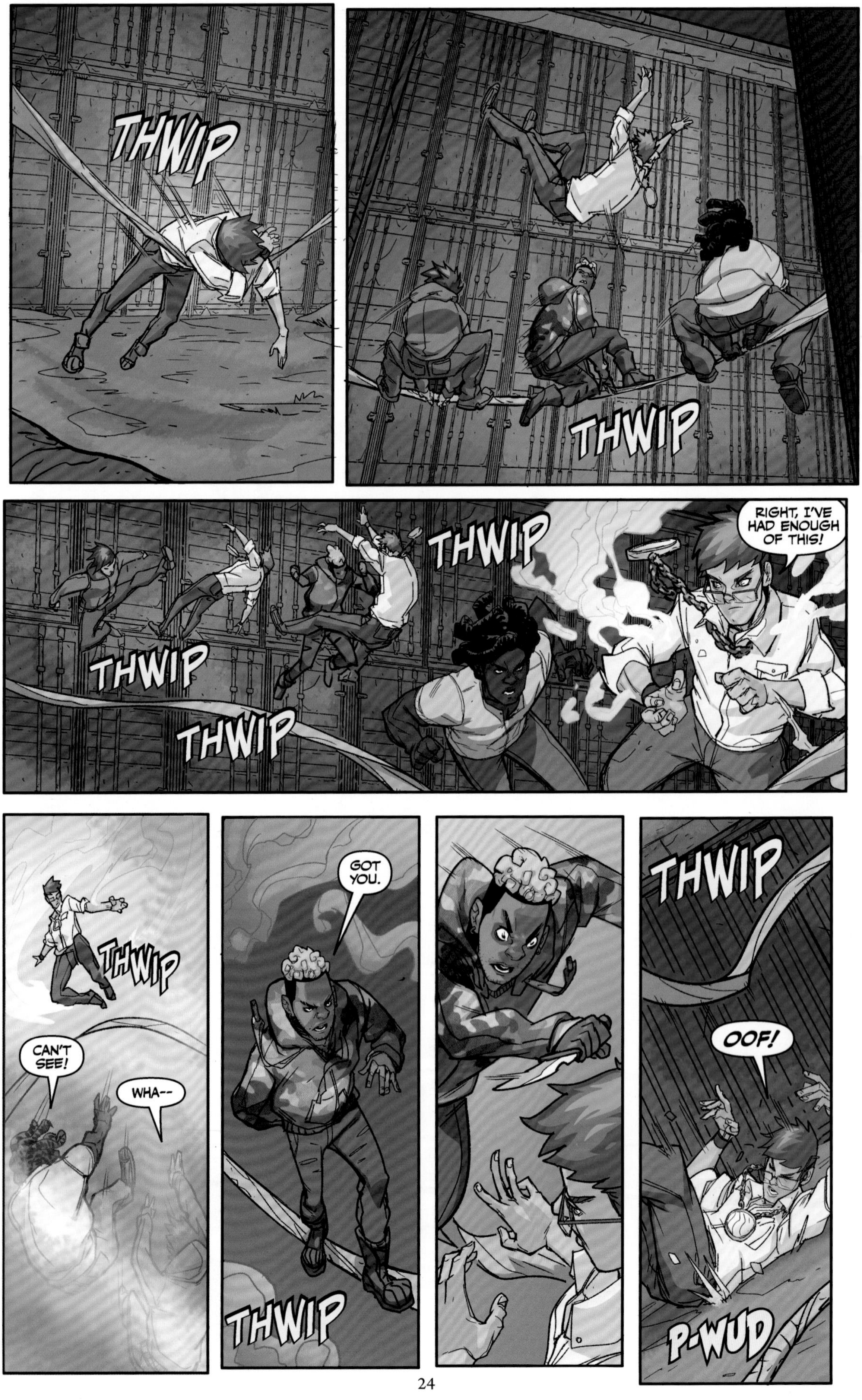
THWIP
THWIP
THWIP
RIGHT, I'VE HAD ENOUGH OF THIS!
THWIP
THWIP
THWIP
CAN'T SEE!
WHA--
GOT YOU.
THWIP
THWIP
OOF!
P-WUD

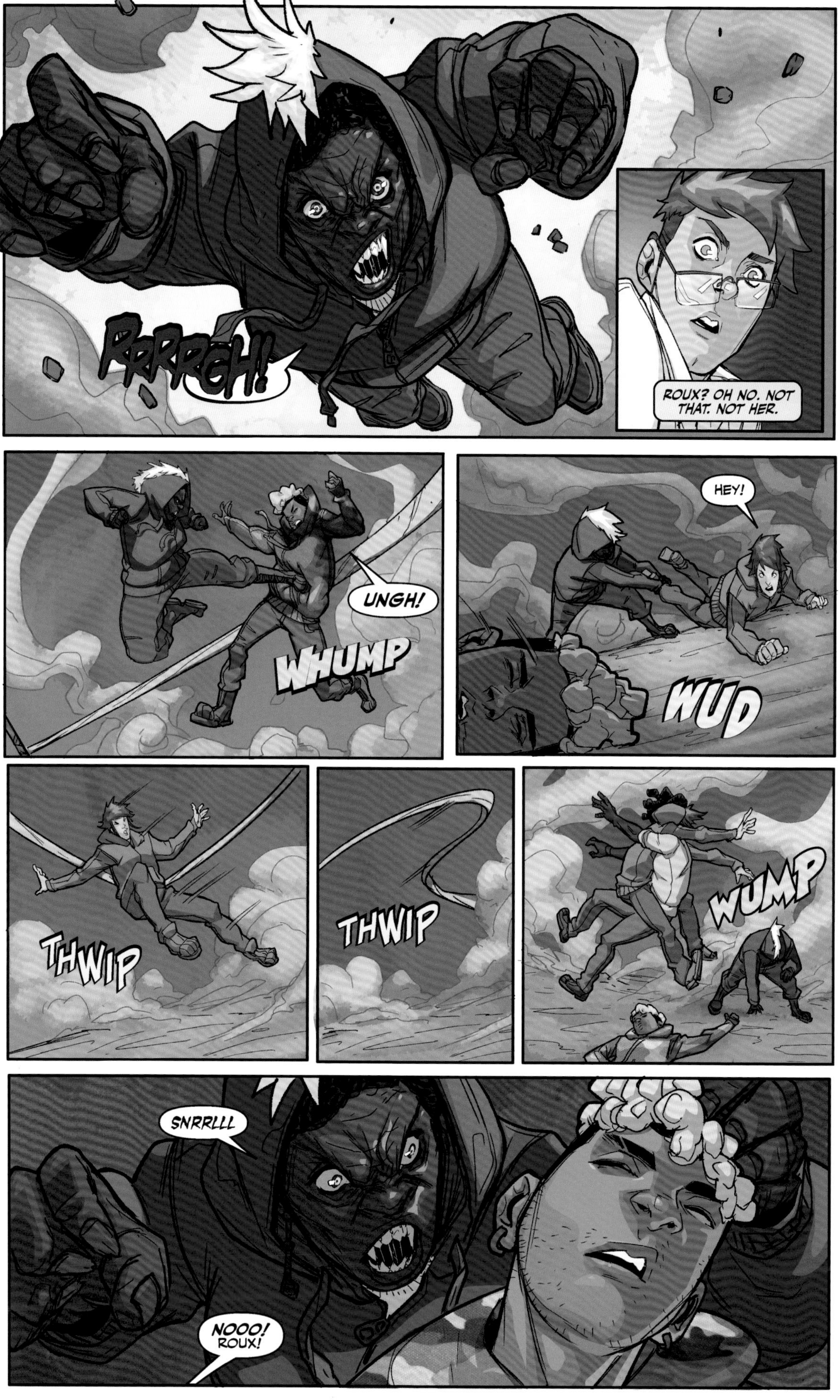
RRRRGH!
ROUX? OH NO. NOT THAT. NOT HER.
UNGH!
WHUMP
HEY!
WUD
THWIP
THWIP
WUMP
SNRRLLL
NOOO! ROUX!

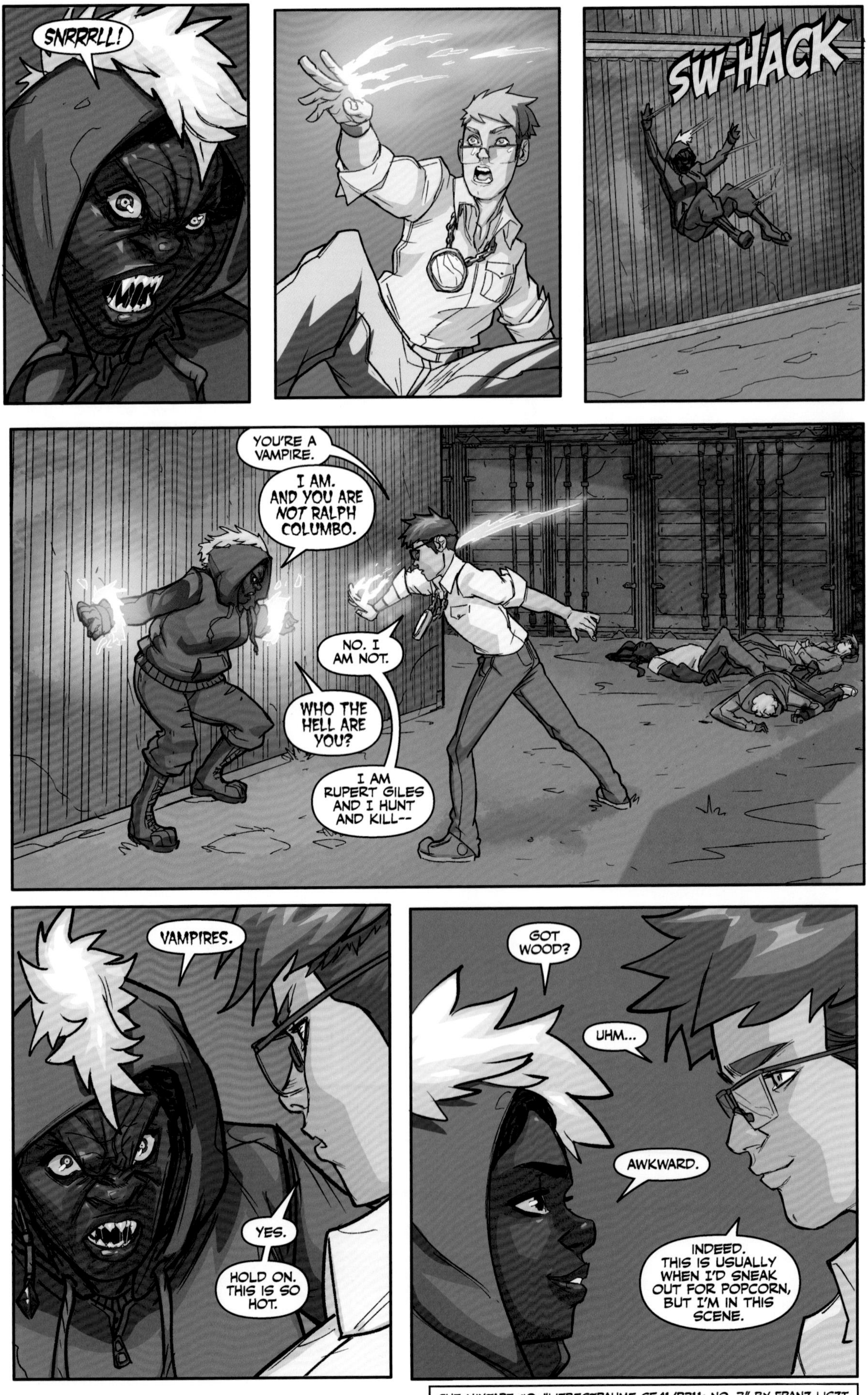
SNRRRLL!
SW-HACK
YOU'RE A VAMPIRE.
I AM. AND YOU ARE NOT RALPH COLUMBO.
NO. I AM NOT.
WHO THE HELL ARE YOU?
I AM RUPERT GILES AND I HUNT AND KILL--
VAMPIRES.
YES.
HOLD ON. THIS IS SO HOT.
GOT WOOD?
UHM...
AWKWARD.
INDEED. THIS IS USUALLY WHEN I'D SNEAK OUT FOR POPCORN, BUT I'M IN THIS SCENE.

CUE MIXTAPE #9: "LIEBESTRAUME S541/R211: NO. 3" BY FRANZ LISZT

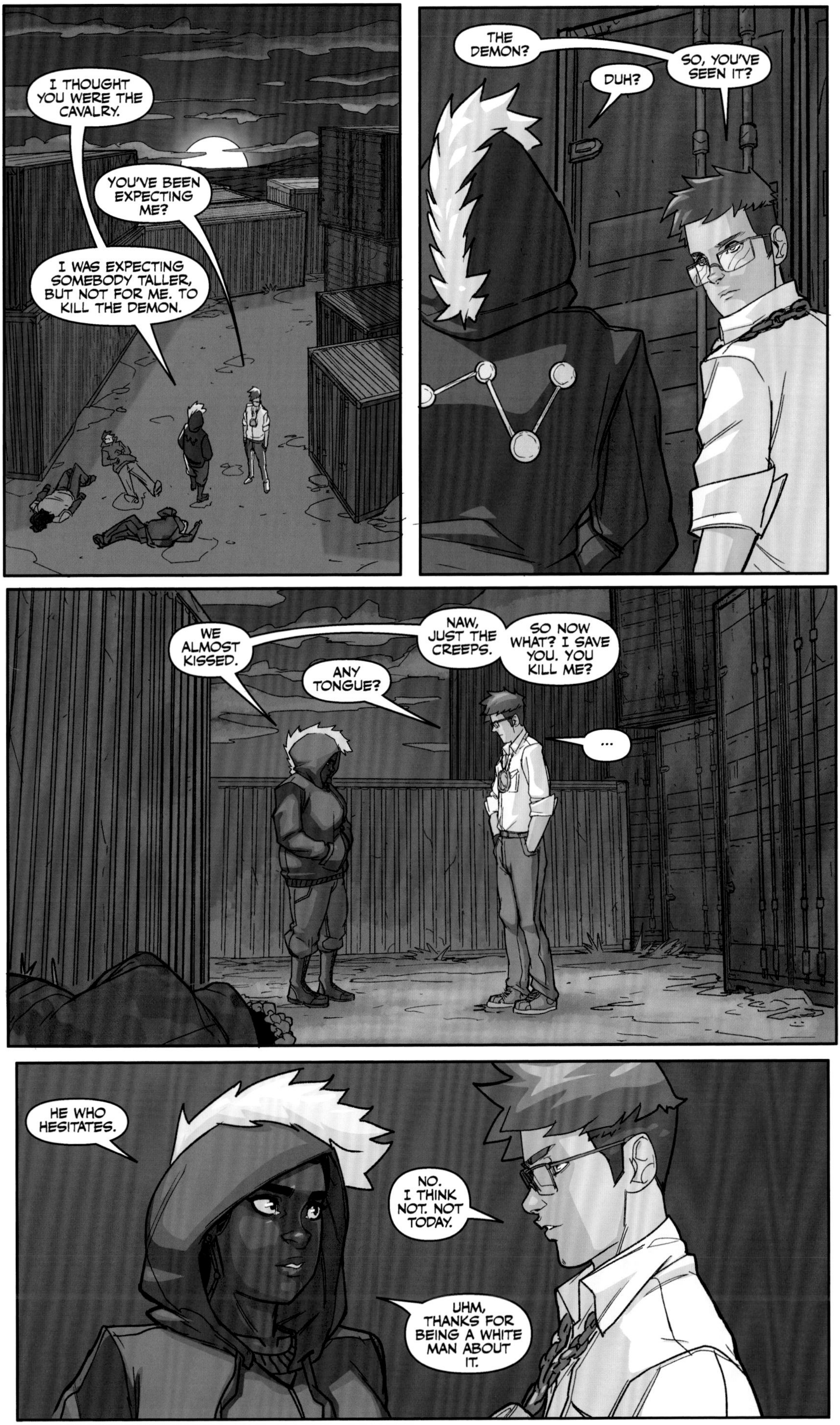
I THOUGHT YOU WERE THE CAVALRY.
YOU'VE BEEN EXPECTING ME?
I WAS EXPECTING SOMEBODY TALLER, BUT NOT FOR ME. TO KILL THE DEMON.
THE DEMON?
SO, YOU'VE SEEN IT?
DUH?
WE ALMOST KISSED.
ANY TONGUE?
NAW, JUST THE CREEPS.
SO NOW WHAT? I SAVE YOU. YOU KILL ME?
...
HE WHO HESITATES.
NO. I THINK NOT. NOT TODAY.
UHM, THANKS FOR BEING A WHITE MAN ABOUT IT.

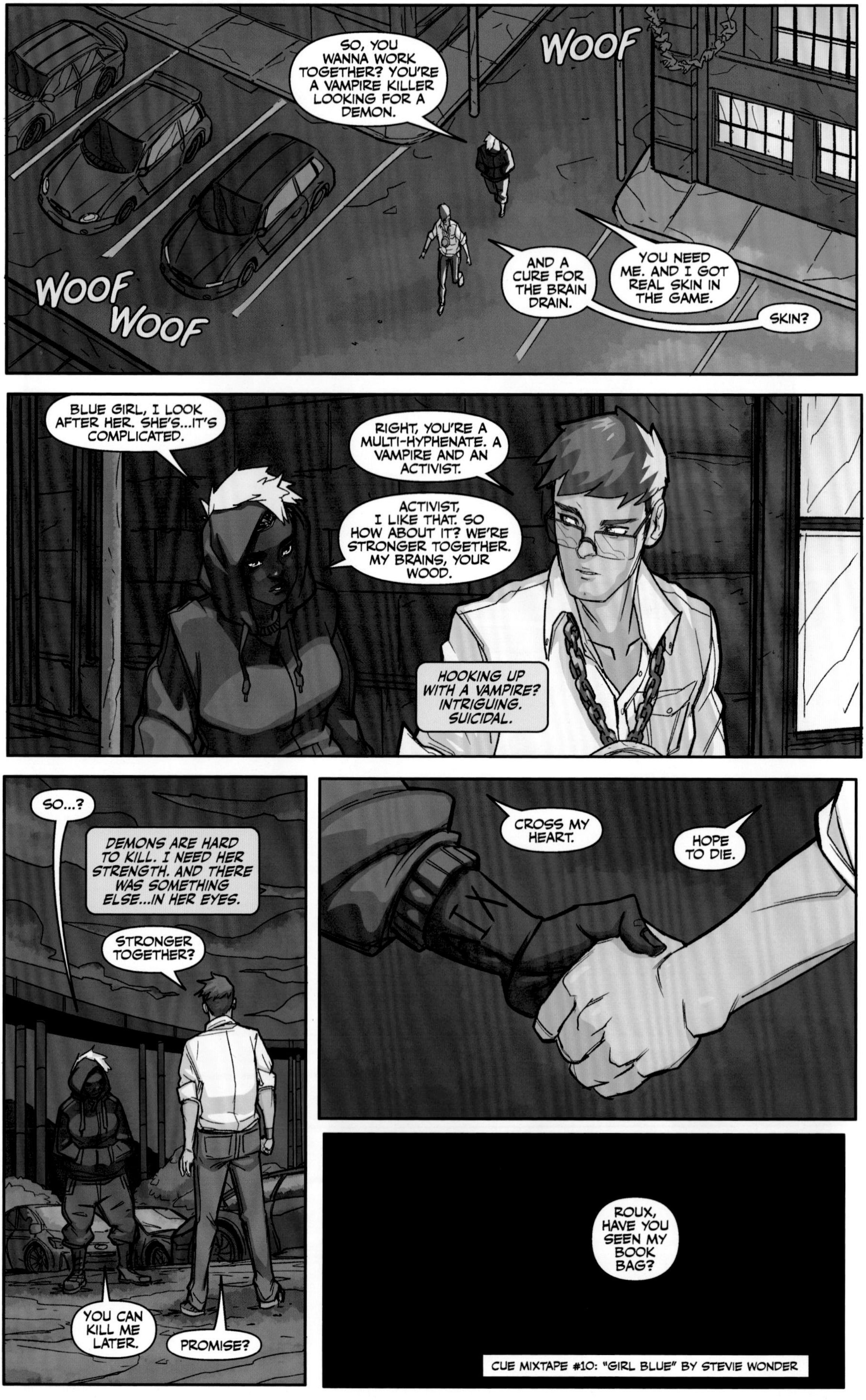

SO, YOU WANNA WORK TOGETHER? YOU'RE A VAMPIRE KILLER LOOKING FOR A DEMON.
WOOF
AND A CURE FOR THE BRAIN DRAIN.
YOU NEED ME. AND I GOT REAL SKIN IN THE GAME.
SKIN?
WOOF
WOOF
BLUE GIRL, I LOOK AFTER HER. SHE'S...IT'S COMPLICATED.
RIGHT, YOU'RE A MULTI-HYPHENATE. A VAMPIRE AND AN ACTIVIST.
ACTIVIST, I LIKE THAT. SO HOW ABOUT IT? WE'RE STRONGER TOGETHER. MY BRAINS, YOUR WOOD.
HOOKING UP WITH A VAMPIRE? INTRIGUING. SUICIDAL.
SO...?
DEMONS ARE HARD TO KILL. I NEED HER STRENGTH. AND THERE WAS SOMETHING ELSE...IN HER EYES.
STRONGER TOGETHER?
YOU CAN KILL ME LATER.
PROMISE?
CROSS MY HEART.
HOPE TO DIE.
ROUX, HAVE YOU SEEN MY BOOK BAG?
CUE MIXTAPE #10: "GIRL BLUE" BY STEVIE WONDER

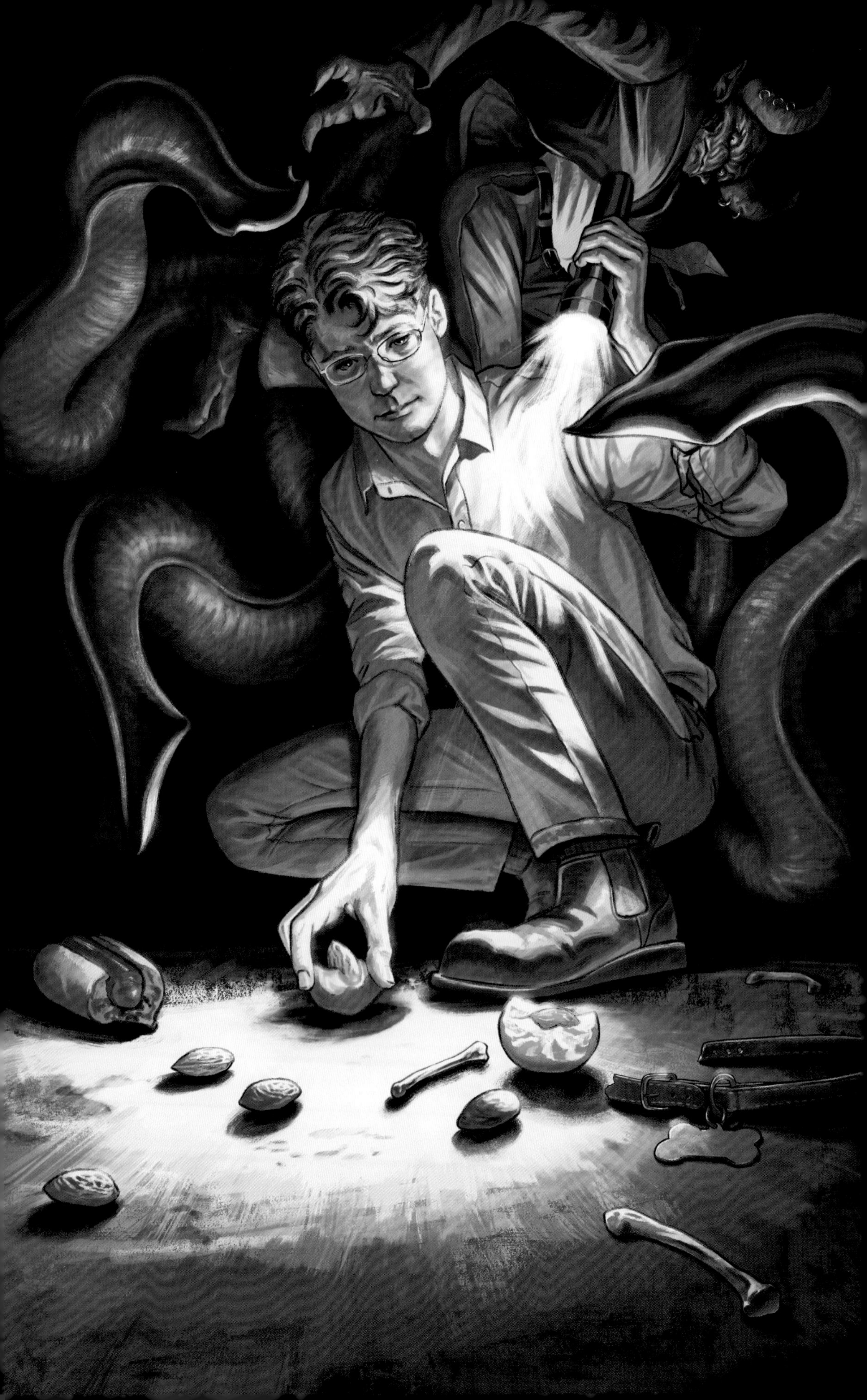

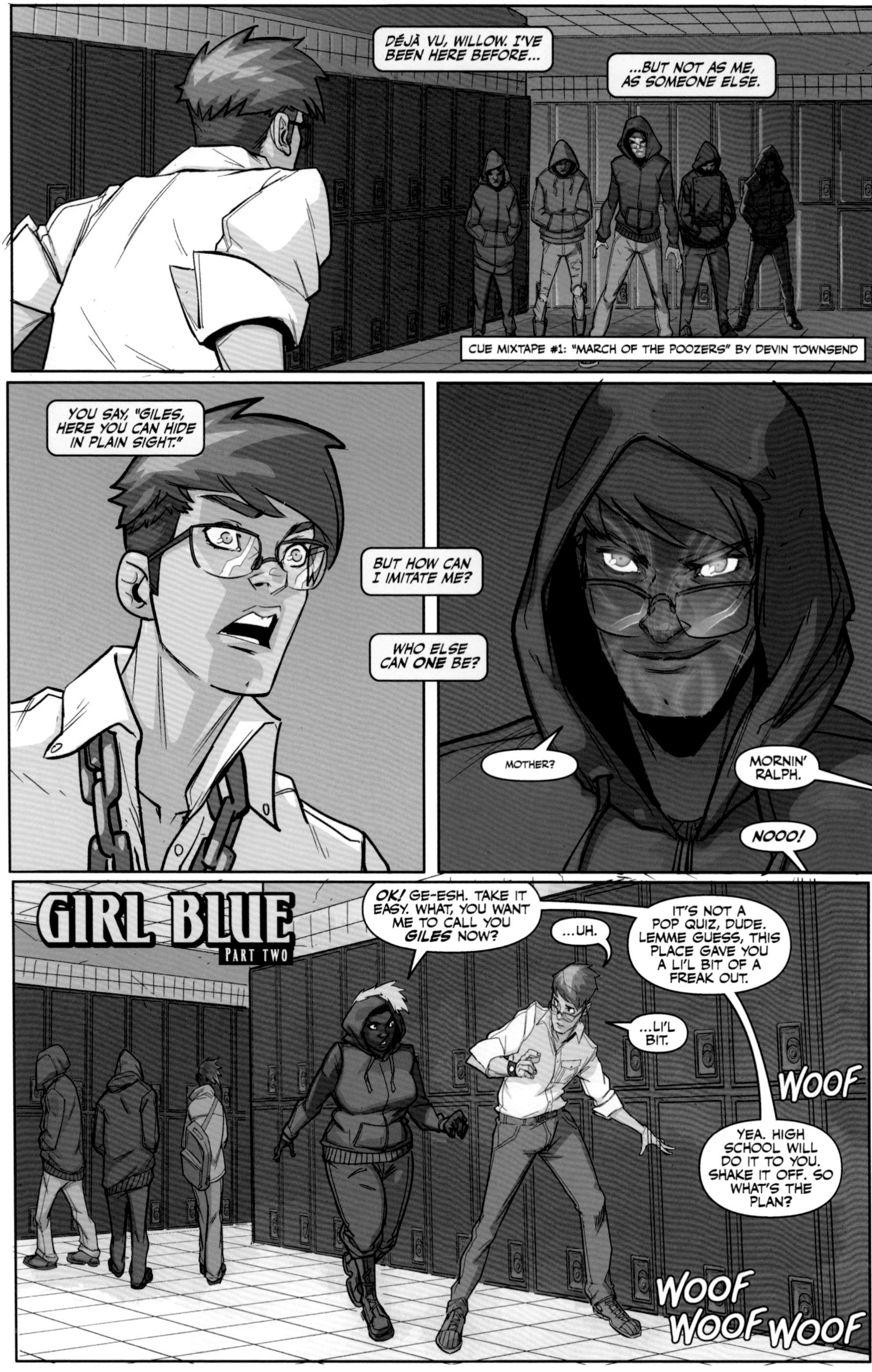
DÉJÀ VU, WILLOW. I'VE BEEN HERE BEFORE...
...BUT NOT AS ME, AS SOMEONE ELSE.
CUE MIXTAPE #1: "MARCH OF THE POOZERS" BY DEVIN TOWNSEND
YOU SAY, "GILES, HERE YOU CAN HIDE IN PLAIN SIGHT."
BUT HOW CAN I IMITATE ME?
WHO ELSE CAN ONE BE?
MOTHER?
MORNIN' RALPH.
NOOO!
GIRL BLUE
PART TWO
OK! GE-ESH. TAKE IT EASY. WHAT, YOU WANT ME TO CALL YOU GILES NOW?
...UH.
IT'S NOT A POP QUIZ, DUDE. LEMME GUESS, THIS PLACE GAVE YOU A LI'L BIT OF A FREAK OUT.
...LI'L BIT.
WOOF
YEA. HIGH SCHOOL WILL DO IT TO YOU. SHAKE IT OFF. SO WHAT'S THE PLAN?
WOOF WOOF WOOF WOOF

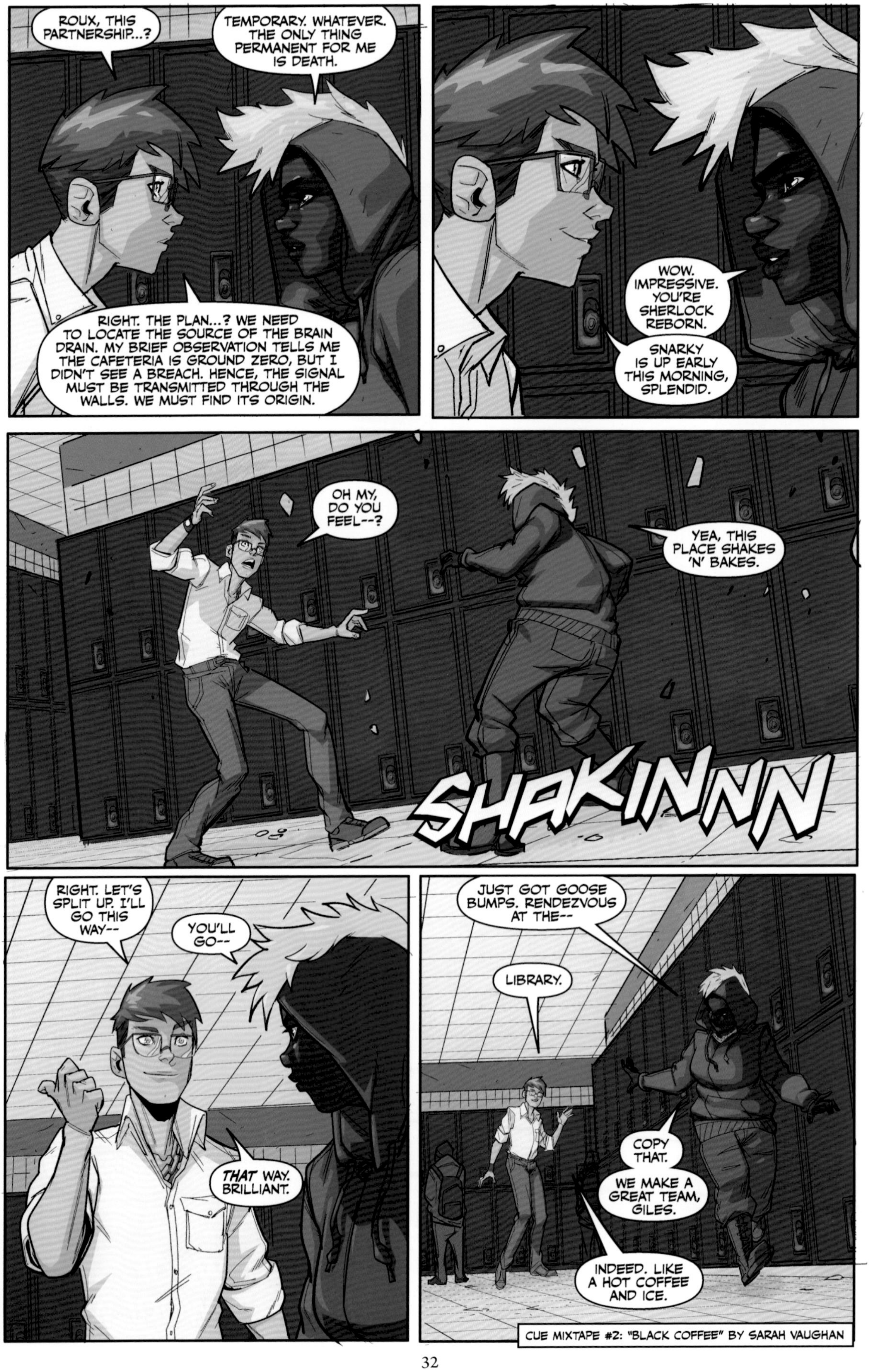

ROUX, THIS PARTNERSHIP...?
TEMPORARY. WHATEVER. THE ONLY THING PERMANENT FOR ME IS DEATH.
RIGHT. THE PLAN...? WE NEED TO LOCATE THE SOURCE OF THE BRAIN DRAIN. MY BRIEF OBSERVATION TELLS ME THE CAFETERIA IS GROUND ZERO, BUT I DIDN'T SEE A BREACH. HENCE, THE SIGNAL MUST BE TRANSMITTED THROUGH THE WALLS. WE MUST FIND ITS ORIGIN.
WOW. IMPRESSIVE. YOU'RE SHERLOCK REBORN.
SNARKY IS UP EARLY THIS MORNING, SPLENDID.
OH MY, DO YOU FEEL--?
YEA, THIS PLACE SHAKES 'N' BAKES.
SHAKINNN
RIGHT. LET'S SPLIT UP. I'LL GO THIS WAY--
YOU'LL GO--
THAT WAY. BRILLIANT.
JUST GOT GOOSE BUMPS. RENDEZVOUS AT THE--
LIBRARY.
COPY THAT.
WE MAKE A GREAT TEAM, GILES.
INDEED. LIKE A HOT COFFEE AND ICE.
CUE MIXTAPE #2: "BLACK COFFEE" BY SARAH VAUGHAN

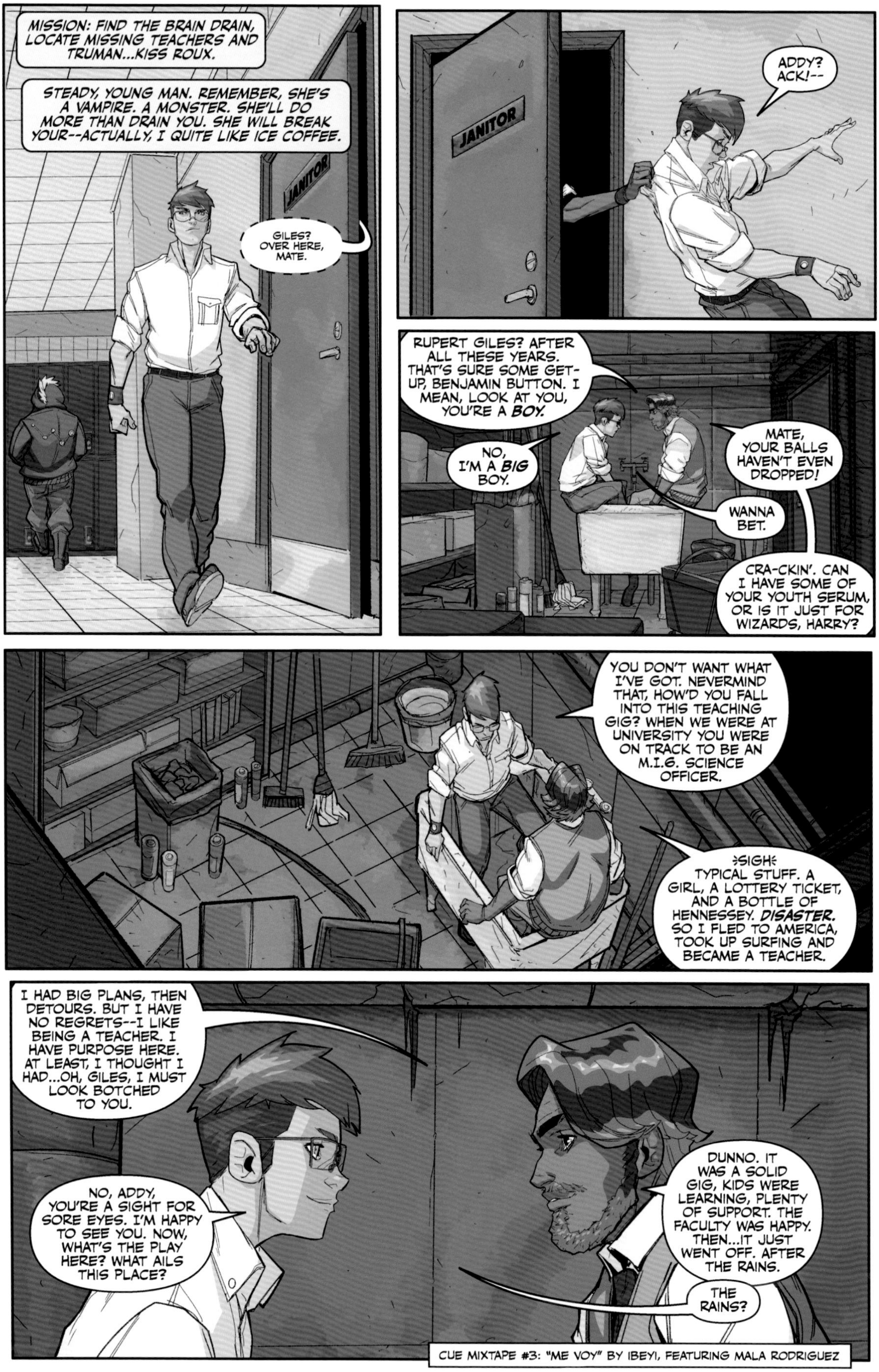
MISSION: FIND THE BRAIN DRAIN, LOCATE MISSING TEACHERS AND TRUMAN...KISS ROUX.
STEADY, YOUNG MAN. REMEMBER, SHE'S A VAMPIRE. A MONSTER. SHE'LL DO MORE THAN DRAIN YOU. SHE WILL BREAK YOUR--ACTUALLY, I QUITE LIKE ICE COFFEE.
JANITOR
GILES? OVER HERE, MATE.
JANITOR
ADDY? ACK!--
RUPERT GILES? AFTER ALL THESE YEARS. THAT'S SURE SOME GET-UP, BENJAMIN BUTTON. I MEAN, LOOK AT YOU, YOU'RE A BOY.
NO, I'M A BIG BOY.
MATE, YOUR BALLS HAVEN'T EVEN DROPPED!
WANNA BET.
CRA-CKIN'. CAN I HAVE SOME OF YOUR YOUTH SERUM, OR IS IT JUST FOR WIZARDS, HARRY?
YOU DON'T WANT WHAT I'VE GOT. NEVERMIND THAT, HOW'D YOU FALL INTO THIS TEACHING GIG? WHEN WE WERE AT UNIVERSITY YOU WERE ON TRACK TO BE AN M.I.6. SCIENCE OFFICER.
SIGH TYPICAL STUFF. A GIRL, A LOTTERY TICKET, AND A BOTTLE OF HENNESSEY. DISASTER. SO I FLED TO AMERICA, TOOK UP SURFING AND BECAME A TEACHER.
I HAD BIG PLANS, THEN DETOURS. BUT I HAVE NO REGRETS--I LIKE BEING A TEACHER. I HAVE PURPOSE HERE. AT LEAST, I THOUGHT I HAD...OH, GILES, I MUST LOOK BOTCHED TO YOU.
NO, ADDY, YOU'RE A SIGHT FOR SORE EYES. I'M HAPPY TO SEE YOU. NOW, WHAT'S THE PLAY HERE? WHAT AILS THIS PLACE?
DUNNO. IT WAS A SOLID GIG, KIDS WERE LEARNING, PLENTY OF SUPPORT. THE FACULTY WAS HAPPY. THEN...IT JUST WENT OFF. AFTER THE RAINS.
THE RAINS?
CUE MIXTAPE #3: "ME VOY" BY IBEYI, FEATURING MALA RODRIGUEZ

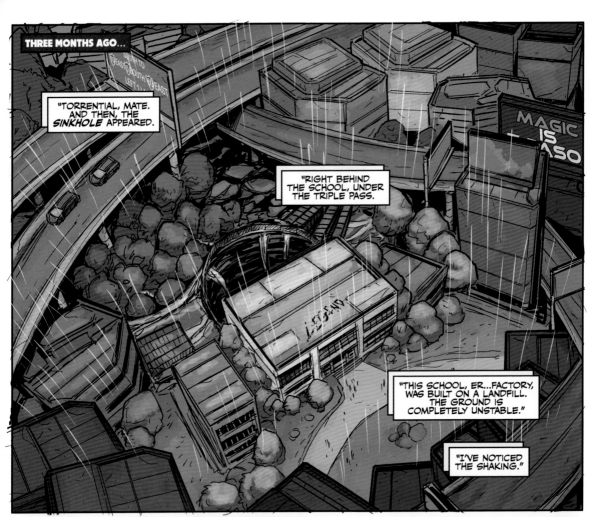

"TORRENTIAL, MATE. AND THEN, THE *SINKHOLE* APPEARED.

"RIGHT BEHIND THE SCHOOL, UNDER THE TRIPLE PASS."

MAGIC IS ASO

"THIS SCHOOL, ER...FACTORY, WAS BUILT ON A LANDFILL. THE GROUND IS COMPLETELY UNSTABLE."

"I'VE NOTICED THE SHAKING."

"RATTLE 'N' ROLL. IT'S BACKGROUND NOISE NOW, BUT THAT SINKHOLE... AFTER IT SHOWED UP, THE VIBE HAS NEVER BEEN THE SAME.

LEGEND

"SOMETHING UNHOLY WAS RELEASED. AND, GILES, IT SMELLED LIKE *PEACHES.*"

PEACHES?

ALL DAY, MATE, AND I *HATE* PEACHES. MY NANNY FORCED LEFTOVER FRUIT COBBLERS ON US EVERY BOXING DAY. ALTHOUGH I DON'T MIND BLACK PUDDING--

FOCUS, MAN. *"UNHOLY...?"*

YES, INHUMAN. JUST LURKING. THEN A FOG DESCENDED. NOT ALL AT ONCE. IT'S LIKE MY BRAIN WAS BEING DRAINED.

WHO ELSE IS AFFECTED?

EVERYONE. TEACHERS HAVE DISAPPEARED, MOST JUST LEFT. SOME, WHO KNOWS? AND THE KIDS, THEY ACT LIKE ZOMBIES OR WORSE...

WORSE?

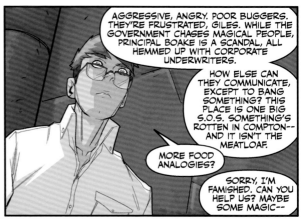

AGGRESSIVE, ANGRY. POOR BUGGERS. THEY'RE FRUSTRATED, GILES. WHILE THE GOVERNMENT CHASES MAGICAL PEOPLE, PRINCIPAL BOAKE IS A SCANDAL, ALL HEMMED UP WITH CORPORATE UNDERWRITERS.

HOW ELSE CAN THEY COMMUNICATE, EXCEPT TO BANG SOMETHING? THIS PLACE IS ONE BIG S.O.S. SOMETHING'S ROTTEN IN COMPTON-- AND IT ISN'T THE MEATLOAF.

MORE FOOD ANALOGIES?

SORRY, I'M FAMISHED. CAN YOU HELP US? MAYBE SOME MAGIC--

I'M NOT A WIZARD, NOR MAGICAL. I'M HUMAN. I JUST HAVE A FEW TRICKS UP MY--

WAIT, SELFIE TIME.

CLICK

FLASH

POOF

THANKS, MATE. WANNA PEACH?

WHERE WERE YOU HIDING THAT?

YOU DON'T WANT TO KNOW.

BUT YOU HATE PEACHES?

DETEST THEM.

SLURP

CUE MIXTAPE #4: "MIDNIGHT COWBOY" BY JOHN BARRY

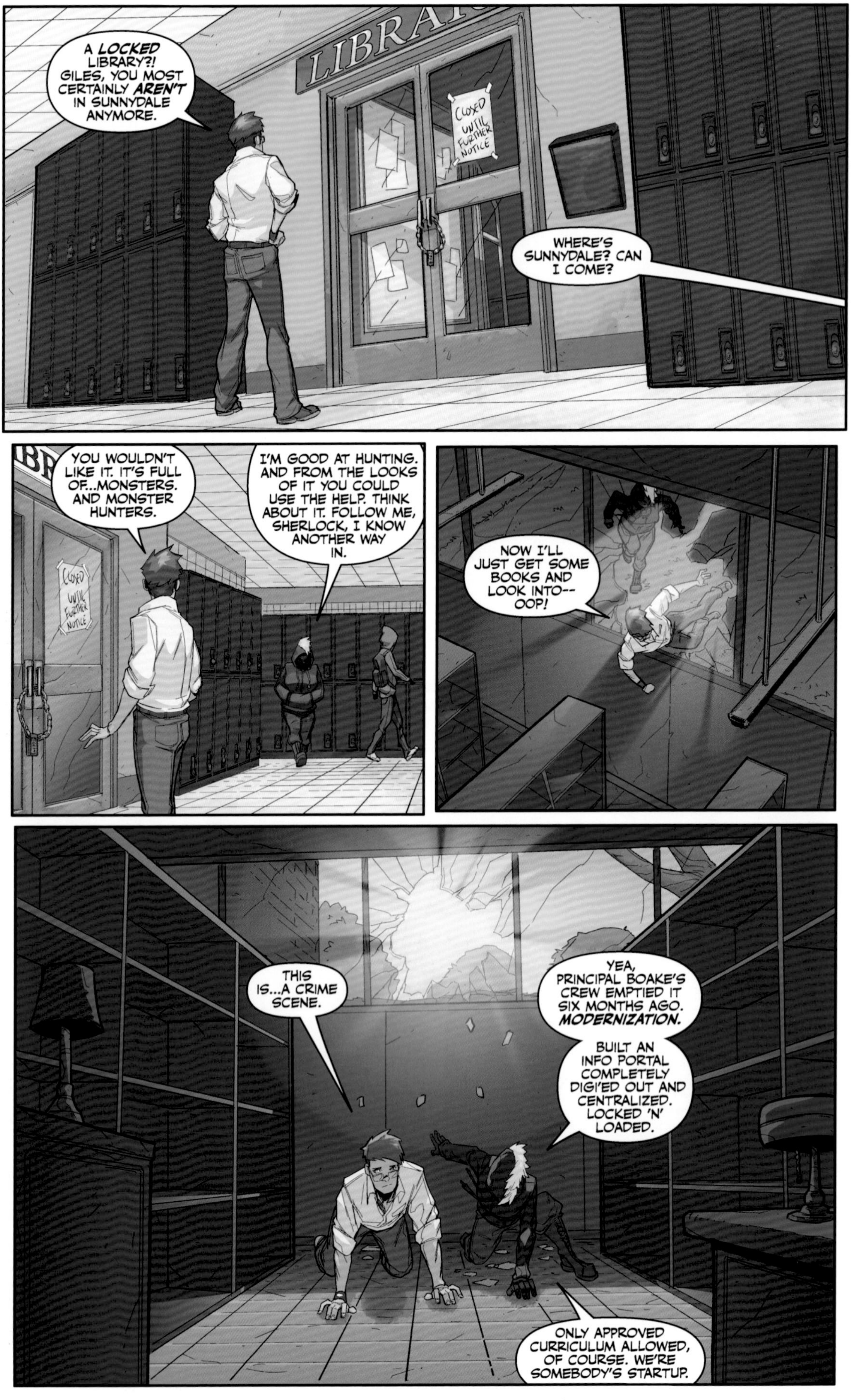

LIBRA
A LOCKED LIBRARY?! GILES, YOU MOST CERTAINLY AREN'T IN SUNNYDALE ANYMORE.
CLOSED UNTIL FURTHER NOTICE
WHERE'S SUNNYDALE? CAN I COME?
YOU WOULDN'T LIKE IT. IT'S FULL OF...MONSTERS. AND MONSTER HUNTERS.
I'M GOOD AT HUNTING. AND FROM THE LOOKS OF IT YOU COULD USE THE HELP. THINK ABOUT IT. FOLLOW ME, SHERLOCK, I KNOW ANOTHER WAY IN.
CLOSED UNTIL FURTHER NOTICE
NOW I'LL JUST GET SOME BOOKS AND LOOK INTO-- OOP!
THIS IS...A CRIME SCENE.
YEA, PRINCIPAL BOAKE'S CREW EMPTIED IT SIX MONTHS AGO. MODERNIZATION.
BUILT AN INFO PORTAL COMPLETELY DIGI'ED OUT AND CENTRALIZED. LOCKED 'N' LOADED.
ONLY APPROVED CURRICULUM ALLOWED, OF COURSE. WE'RE SOMEBODY'S STARTUP.

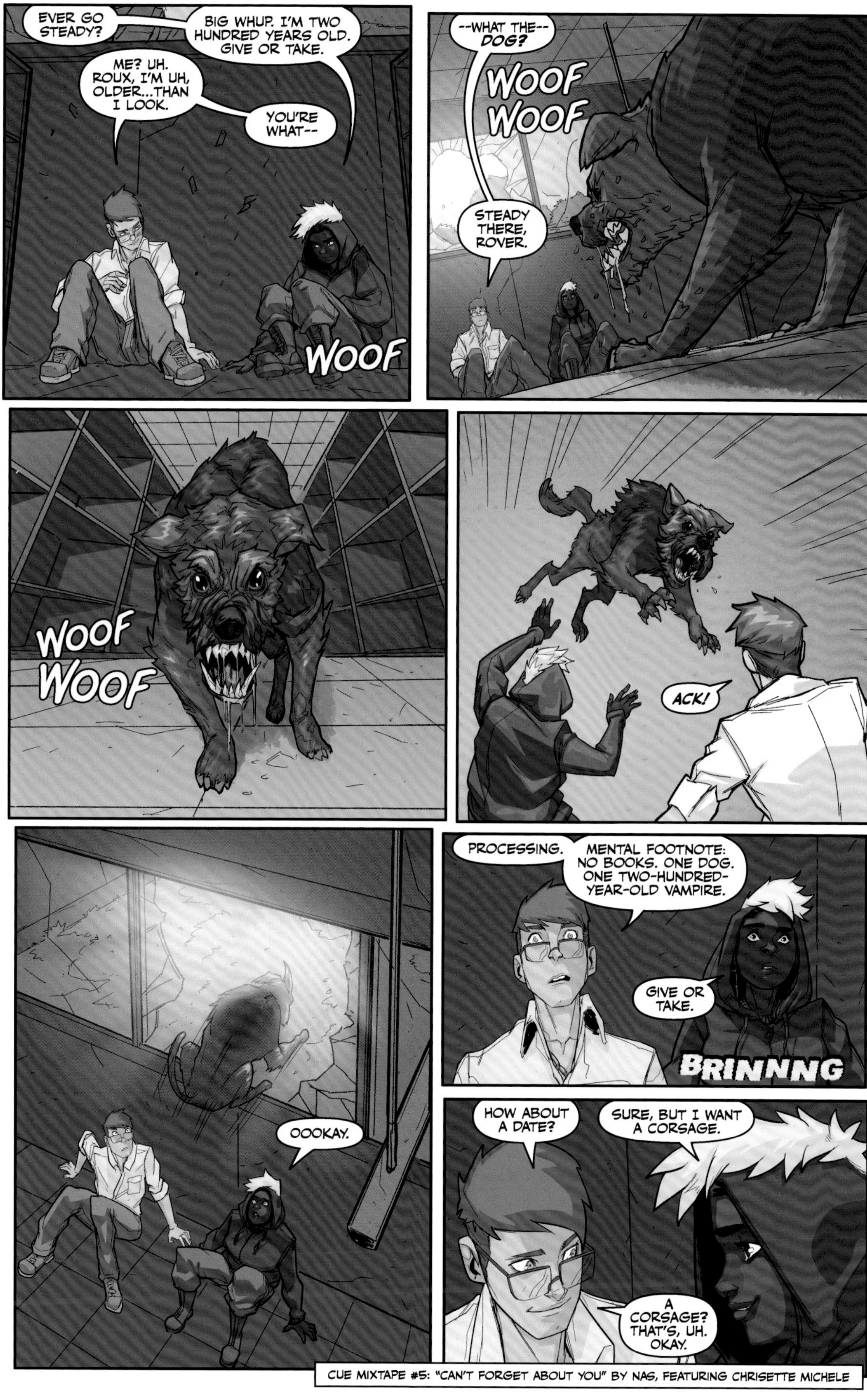

EVER GO STEADY?
BIG WHUP. I'M TWO HUNDRED YEARS OLD. GIVE OR TAKE.
ME? UH. ROUX, I'M UH, OLDER...THAN I LOOK.
YOU'RE WHAT--
WOOF
--WHAT THE-- DOG?
WOOF WOOF
STEADY THERE, ROVER.
WOOF WOOF
ACK!
OOOKAY.
PROCESSING.
MENTAL FOOTNOTE: NO BOOKS. ONE DOG. ONE TWO-HUNDRED-YEAR-OLD VAMPIRE.
GIVE OR TAKE.
BRINNNG
HOW ABOUT A DATE?
SURE, BUT I WANT A CORSAGE.
A CORSAGE? THAT'S, UH. OKAY.
CUE MIXTAPE #5: "CAN'T FORGET ABOUT YOU" BY NAS, FEATURING CHRISETTE MICHELE

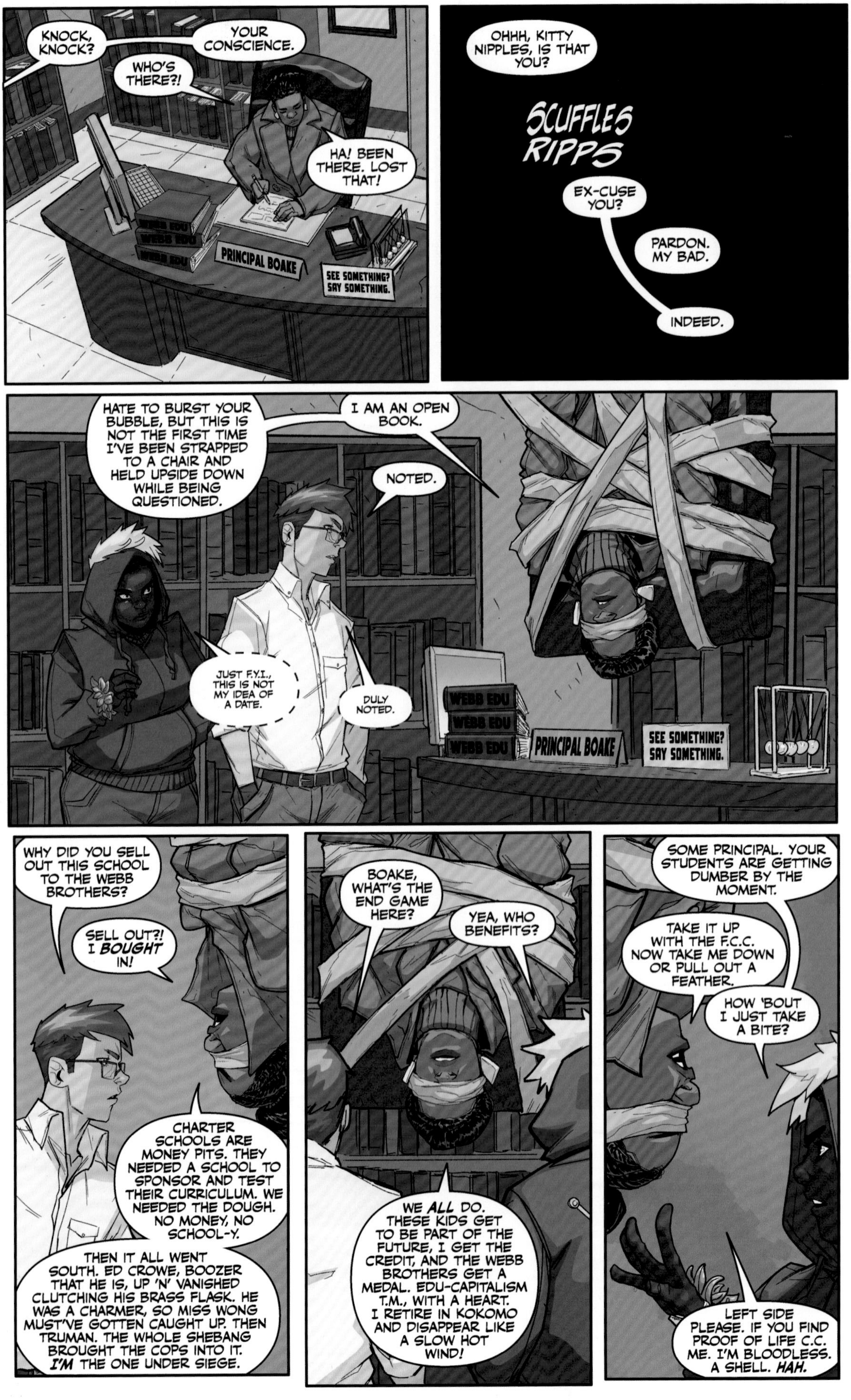
KNOCK, KNOCK?
YOUR CONSCIENCE.
WHO'S THERE?!
HA! BEEN THERE. LOST THAT!
WEBB EDU
WEBB EDU
WEBB EDU
PRINCIPAL BOAKE
SEE SOMETHING? SAY SOMETHING.
OHHH, KITTY NIPPLES, IS THAT YOU?
SCUFFLES RIPPS
EX-CUSE YOU?
PARDON. MY BAD.
INDEED.
HATE TO BURST YOUR BUBBLE, BUT THIS IS NOT THE FIRST TIME I'VE BEEN STRAPPED TO A CHAIR AND HELD UPSIDE DOWN WHILE BEING QUESTIONED.
I AM AN OPEN BOOK.
NOTED.
JUST F.Y.I., THIS IS NOT MY IDEA OF A DATE.
DULY NOTED.
WEBB EDU
WEBB EDU
WEBB EDU
PRINCIPAL BOAKE
SEE SOMETHING? SAY SOMETHING.
WHY DID YOU SELL OUT THIS SCHOOL TO THE WEBB BROTHERS?
SELL OUT?! I BOUGHT IN!
CHARTER SCHOOLS ARE MONEY PITS. THEY NEEDED A SCHOOL TO SPONSOR AND TEST THEIR CURRICULUM. WE NEEDED THE DOUGH. NO MONEY, NO SCHOOL-Y.
THEN IT ALL WENT SOUTH. ED CROWE, BOOZER THAT HE IS, UP 'N' VANISHED CLUTCHING HIS BRASS FLASK. HE WAS A CHARMER, SO MISS WONG MUST'VE GOTTEN CAUGHT UP. THEN TRUMAN. THE WHOLE SHEBANG BROUGHT THE COPS INTO IT. I'M THE ONE UNDER SIEGE.
BOAKE, WHAT'S THE END GAME HERE?
YEA, WHO BENEFITS?
WE ALL DO. THESE KIDS GET TO BE PART OF THE FUTURE, I GET THE CREDIT, AND THE WEBB BROTHERS GET A MEDAL. EDU-CAPITALISM T.M., WITH A HEART. I RETIRE IN KOKOMO AND DISAPPEAR LIKE A SLOW HOT WIND!
SOME PRINCIPAL. YOUR STUDENTS ARE GETTING DUMBER BY THE MOMENT.
TAKE IT UP WITH THE F.C.C. NOW TAKE ME DOWN OR PULL OUT A FEATHER.
HOW 'BOUT I JUST TAKE A BITE?
LEFT SIDE PLEASE. IF YOU FIND PROOF OF LIFE C.C. ME. I'M BLOODLESS. A SHELL. HAH.

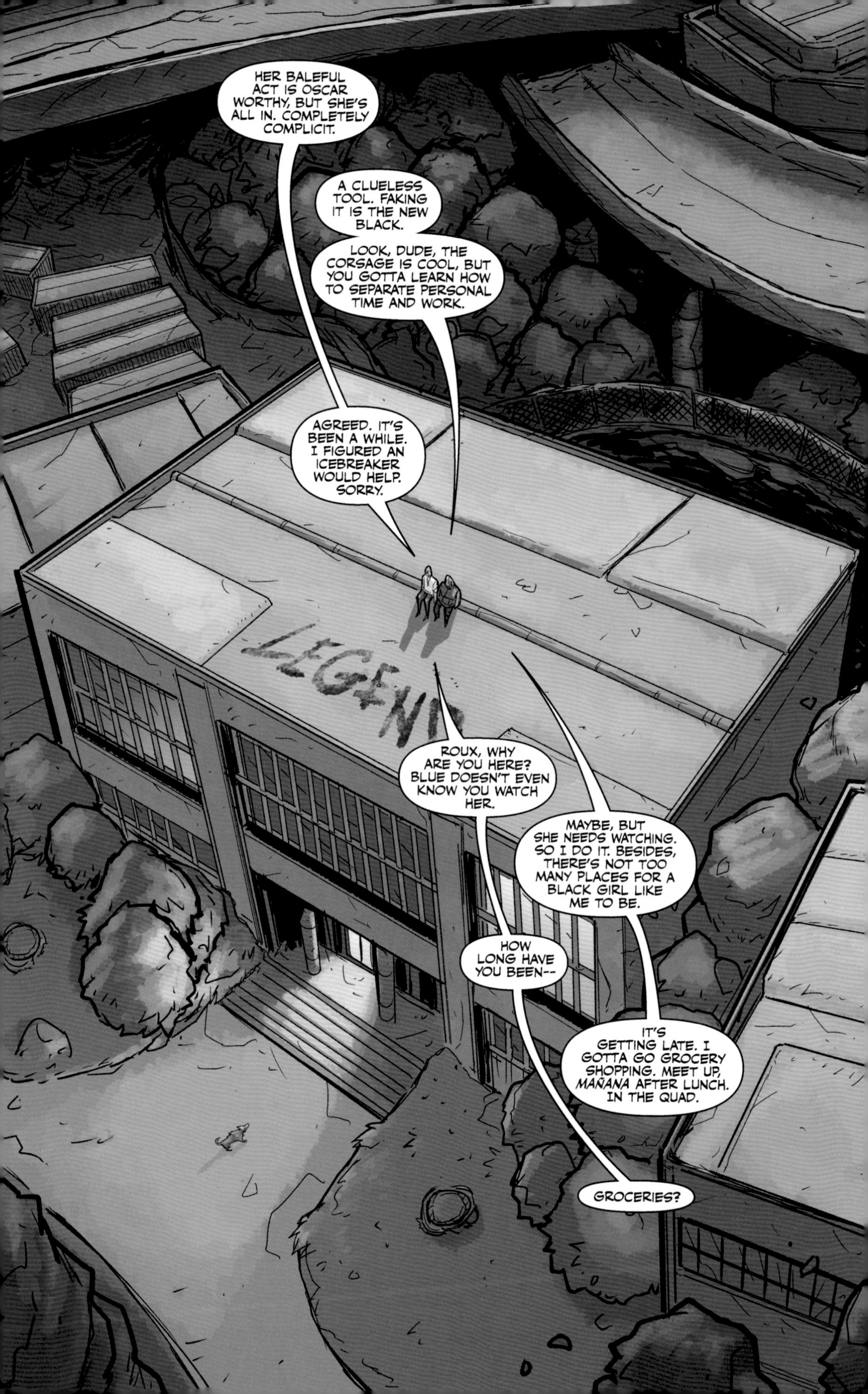
HER BALEFUL ACT IS OSCAR WORTHY, BUT SHE'S ALL IN. COMPLETELY COMPLICIT.
A CLUELESS TOOL. FAKING IT IS THE NEW BLACK.
LOOK, DUDE, THE CORSAGE IS COOL, BUT YOU GOTTA LEARN HOW TO SEPARATE PERSONAL TIME AND WORK.
AGREED. IT'S BEEN A WHILE. I FIGURED AN ICEBREAKER WOULD HELP. SORRY.
LEGEND
ROUX, WHY ARE YOU HERE? BLUE DOESN'T EVEN KNOW YOU WATCH HER.
MAYBE, BUT SHE NEEDS WATCHING. SO I DO IT. BESIDES, THERE'S NOT TOO MANY PLACES FOR A BLACK GIRL LIKE ME TO BE.
HOW LONG HAVE YOU BEEN--
IT'S GETTING LATE. I GOTTA GO GROCERY SHOPPING. MEET UP, *MAÑANA* AFTER LUNCH. IN THE QUAD.
GROCERIES?

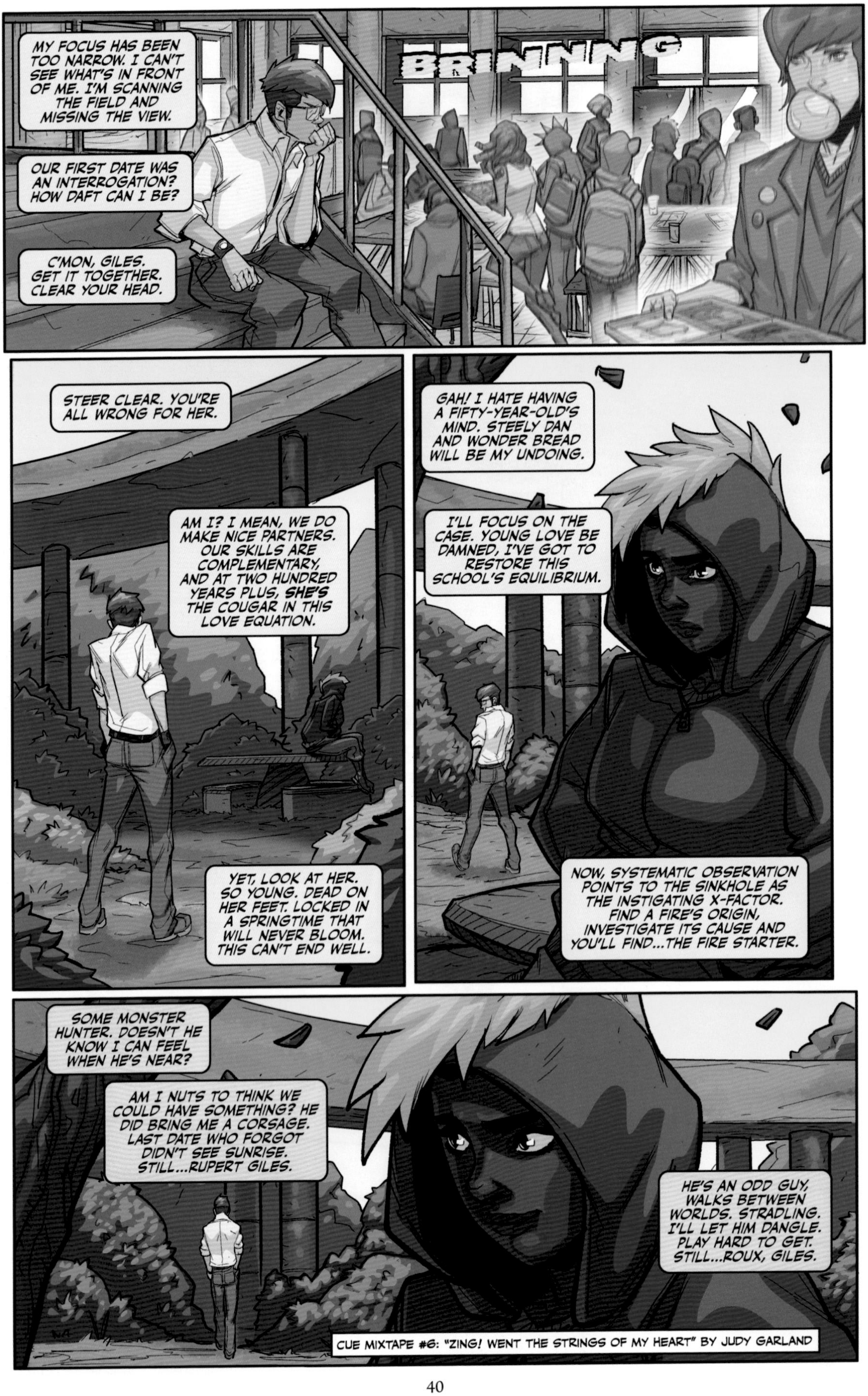
MY FOCUS HAS BEEN TOO NARROW. I CAN'T SEE WHAT'S IN FRONT OF ME. I'M SCANNING THE FIELD AND MISSING THE VIEW.
BRINNNG
OUR FIRST DATE WAS AN INTERROGATION? HOW DAFT CAN I BE?
C'MON, GILES. GET IT TOGETHER. CLEAR YOUR HEAD.
STEER CLEAR. YOU'RE ALL WRONG FOR HER.
AM I? I MEAN, WE DO MAKE NICE PARTNERS. OUR SKILLS ARE COMPLEMENTARY, AND AT TWO HUNDRED YEARS PLUS, **SHE'S** THE COUGAR IN THIS LOVE EQUATION.
YET, LOOK AT HER. SO YOUNG. DEAD ON HER FEET. LOCKED IN A SPRINGTIME THAT WILL NEVER BLOOM. THIS CAN'T END WELL.
GAH! I HATE HAVING A FIFTY-YEAR-OLD'S MIND. STEELY DAN AND WONDER BREAD WILL BE MY UNDOING.
I'LL FOCUS ON THE CASE. YOUNG LOVE BE DAMNED, I'VE GOT TO RESTORE THIS SCHOOL'S EQUILIBRIUM.
NOW, SYSTEMATIC OBSERVATION POINTS TO THE SINKHOLE AS THE INSTIGATING X-FACTOR. FIND A FIRE'S ORIGIN, INVESTIGATE ITS CAUSE AND YOU'LL FIND...THE FIRE STARTER.
SOME MONSTER HUNTER. DOESN'T HE KNOW I CAN FEEL WHEN HE'S NEAR?
AM I NUTS TO THINK WE COULD HAVE SOMETHING? HE DID BRING ME A CORSAGE. LAST DATE WHO FORGOT DIDN'T SEE SUNRISE. STILL...RUPERT GILES.
HE'S AN ODD GUY, WALKS BETWEEN WORLDS. STRADLING. I'LL LET HIM DANGLE. PLAY HARD TO GET. STILL...ROUX, GILES.
CUE MIXTAPE #6: "ZING! WENT THE STRINGS OF MY HEART" BY JUDY GARLAND

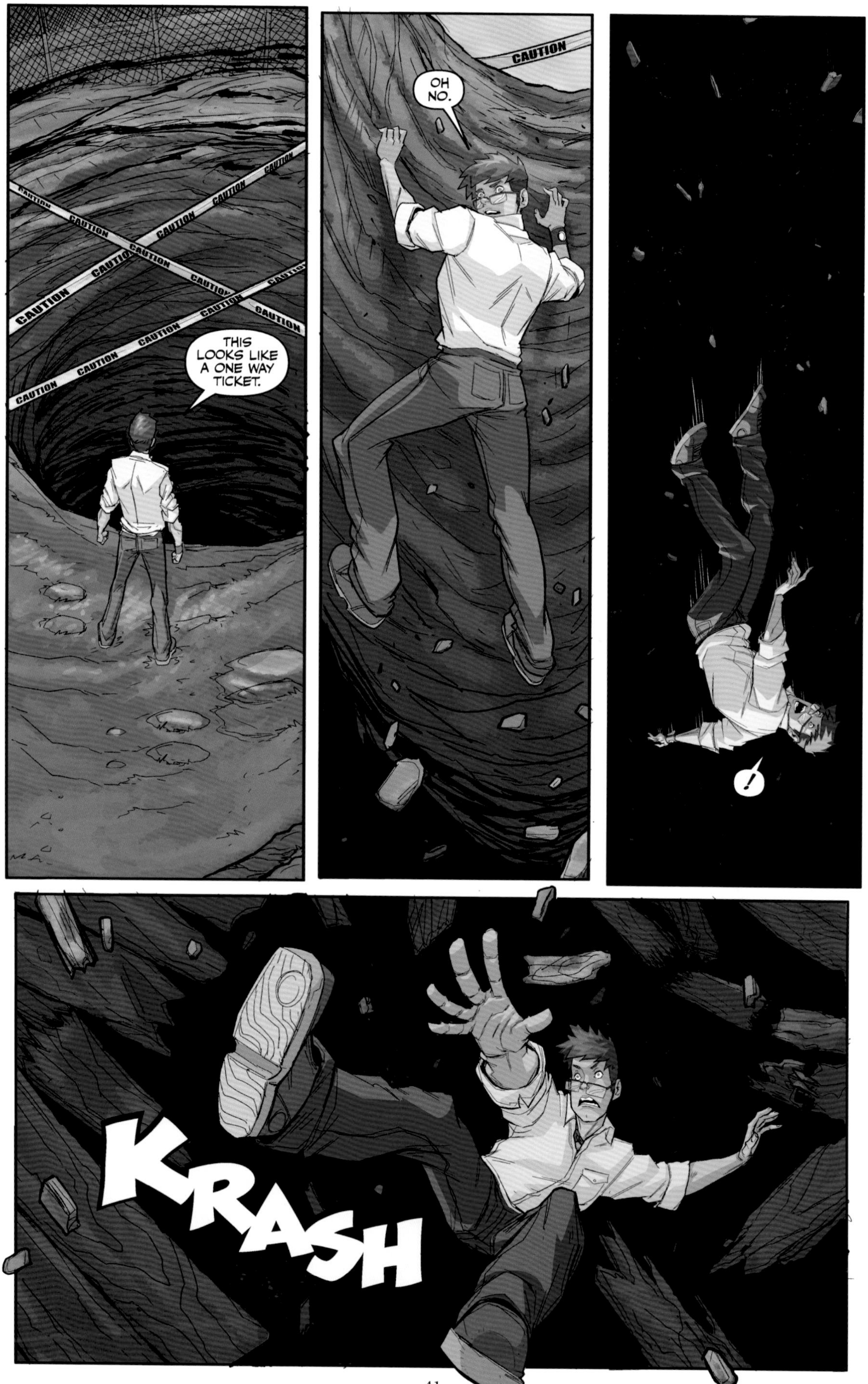
CAUTION
THIS LOOKS LIKE A ONE WAY TICKET.
OH NO.
!
KRASH

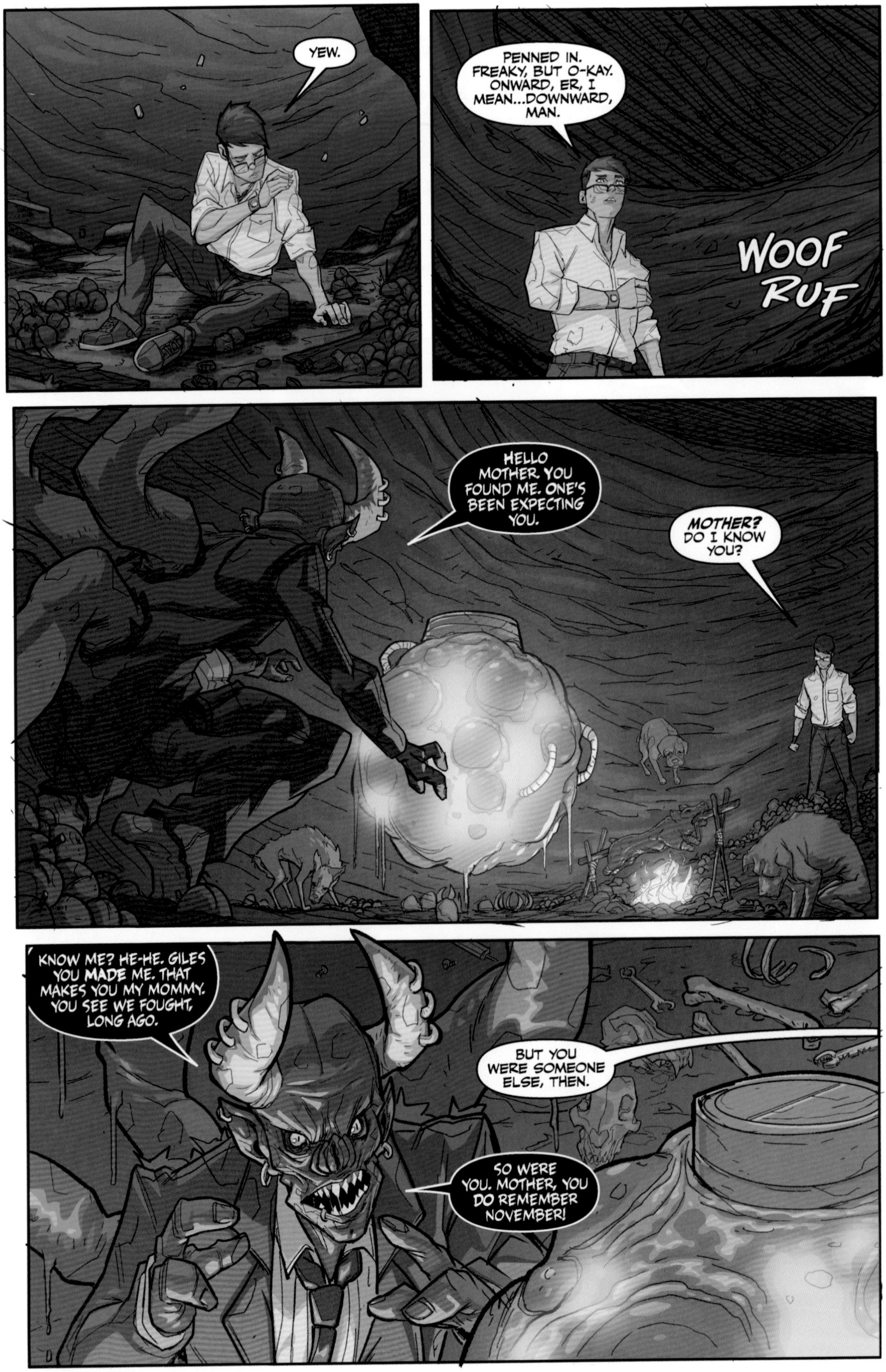
YEW.
PENNED IN. FREAKY, BUT O-KAY. ONWARD, ER, I MEAN...DOWNWARD, MAN.
WOOF
RUF
HELLO MOTHER. YOU FOUND ME. ONE'S BEEN EXPECTING YOU.
MOTHER? DO I KNOW YOU?
KNOW ME? HE-HE. GILES YOU MADE ME. THAT MAKES YOU MY MOMMY. YOU SEE WE FOUGHT, LONG AGO.
BUT YOU WERE SOMEONE ELSE, THEN.
SO WERE YOU. MOTHER, YOU DO REMEMBER NOVEMBER!

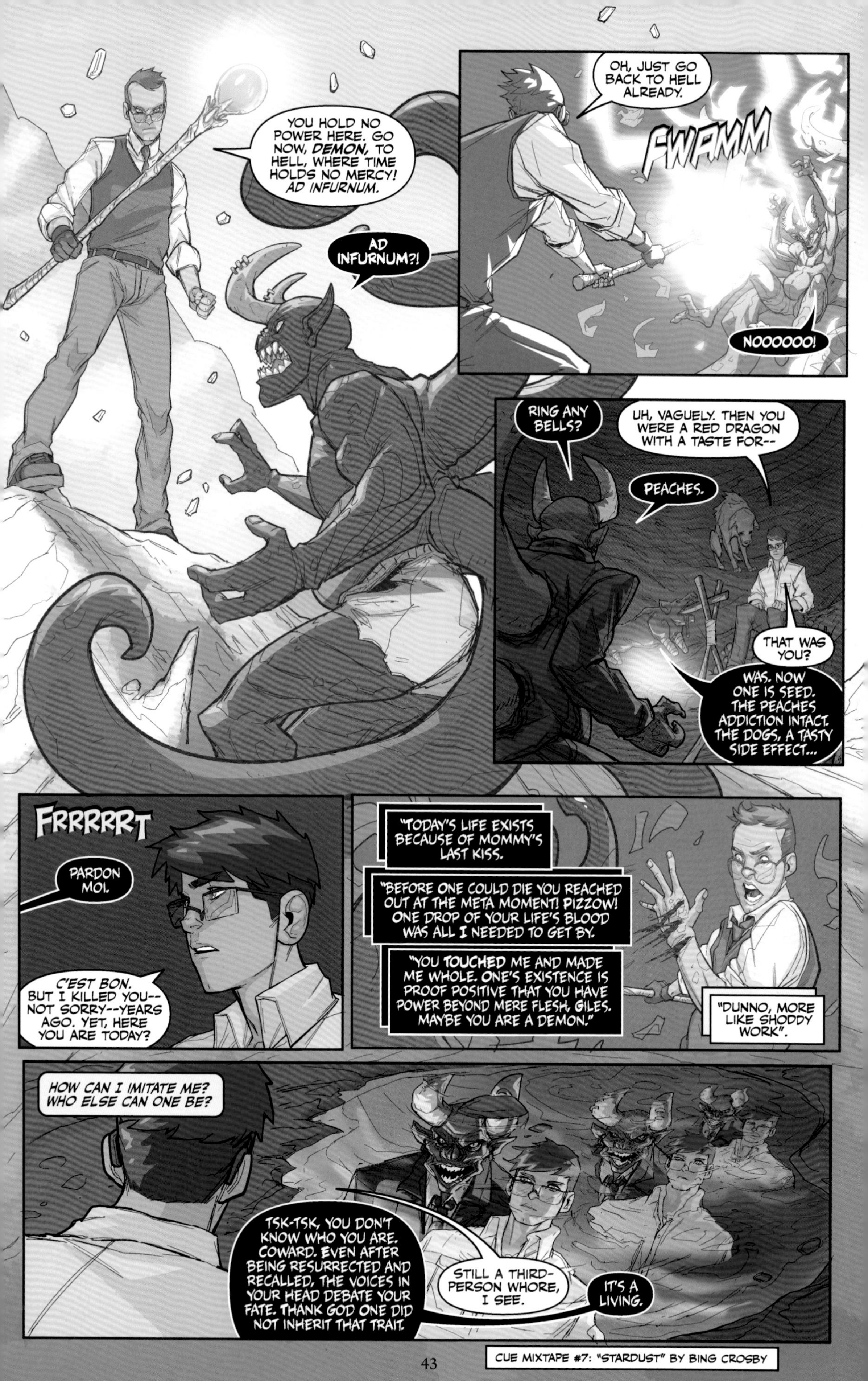
YOU HOLD NO POWER HERE. GO NOW, DEMON, TO HELL, WHERE TIME HOLDS NO MERCY! AD INFURNUM.
AD INFURNUM?!
OH, JUST GO BACK TO HELL ALREADY.
FWAMM
NOOOOOO!
RING ANY BELLS?
UH, VAGUELY. THEN YOU WERE A RED DRAGON WITH A TASTE FOR--
PEACHES.
THAT WAS YOU?
WAS. NOW ONE IS SEED. THE PEACHES ADDICTION INTACT. THE DOGS, A TASTY SIDE EFFECT...
FRRRRRT
PARDON MOI.
C'EST BON. BUT I KILLED YOU--NOT SORRY--YEARS AGO. YET, HERE YOU ARE TODAY?
"TODAY'S LIFE EXISTS BECAUSE OF MOMMY'S LAST KISS.
"BEFORE ONE COULD DIE YOU REACHED OUT AT THE META MOMENT! PIZZOW! ONE DROP OF YOUR LIFE'S BLOOD WAS ALL I NEEDED TO GET BY.
"YOU TOUCHED ME AND MADE ME WHOLE. ONE'S EXISTENCE IS PROOF POSITIVE THAT YOU HAVE POWER BEYOND MERE FLESH, GILES. MAYBE YOU ARE A DEMON."
"DUNNO, MORE LIKE SHODDY WORK".
HOW CAN I IMITATE ME? WHO ELSE CAN ONE BE?
TSK-TSK, YOU DON'T KNOW WHO YOU ARE. COWARD. EVEN AFTER BEING RESURRECTED AND RECALLED, THE VOICES IN YOUR HEAD DEBATE YOUR FATE. THANK GOD ONE DID NOT INHERIT THAT TRAIT.
STILL A THIRD-PERSON WHORE, I SEE.
IT'S A LIVING.
CUE MIXTAPE #7: "STARDUST" BY BING CROSBY

SO, WHY THIS SCHOOL? AS I RECALL, YOU LIKED BANKS.

A MIND IS A TERRIBLE THING TO WASTE, EXCEPT IF IT PAYS DIVIDENDS.

YOU'RE SELLING INTELLIGENCE?

BAH! WHY SELL INTELLIGENCE, WHEN ONE CAN MAKE A FORTUNE PEDDLING IGNORANCE. BESIDES, IT'S TRENDING. GOT FINANCIERS, PR., A PRESIDENT, EVERYTHING. ZAP A MIND, PLEASE DON'T REWIND.

AND THIS SCHOOL, I-DEAL. LOW HANGING FRUIT. BESIDES, WHO'S WATCHING? OH, FORGIVE ME, I KNOW WHO...

SHE WATCHES.

UMM. THE BLACK VAMP'S CUTE. OLD SCHOOL. VERY OLD INDEED. GOTTA REAL HUNGER FOR BLOOD. ASK TRUMAN.

CARE-FUL NOW HERO, SHE'S A SAVER. A REAL PACK RAT AND WHAT ONE CAN'T SEE WILL HURT YOU--

SHAKKN

SEED, THIS FOUNDATION IS QUITE, UH, TIPPY. WHY NOT REBUILD--?

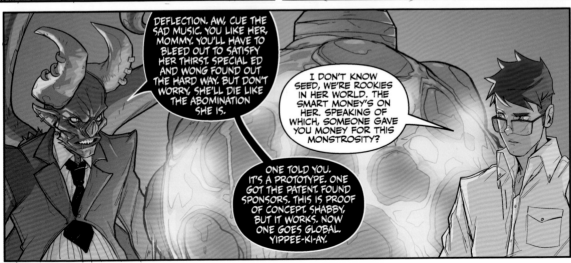

DEFLECTION. AW, CUE THE SAD MUSIC. YOU LIKE HER, MOMMY. YOU'LL HAVE TO BLEED OUT TO SATISFY HER THIRST. SPECIAL ED AND WONG FOUND OUT THE HARD WAY. BUT DON'T WORRY, SHE'LL DIE LIKE THE ABOMINATION SHE IS.

I DON'T KNOW SEED, WE'RE ROOKIES IN HER WORLD. THE SMART MONEY'S ON HER. SPEAKING OF WHICH, SOMEONE GAVE YOU MONEY FOR THIS MONSTROSITY?

ONE TOLD YOU. IT'S A PROTOTYPE. ONE GOT THE PATENT. FOUND SPONSORS. THIS IS PROOF OF CONCEPT. SHABBY, BUT IT WORKS. NOW ONE GOES GLOBAL. YIPPEE-KI-AY.

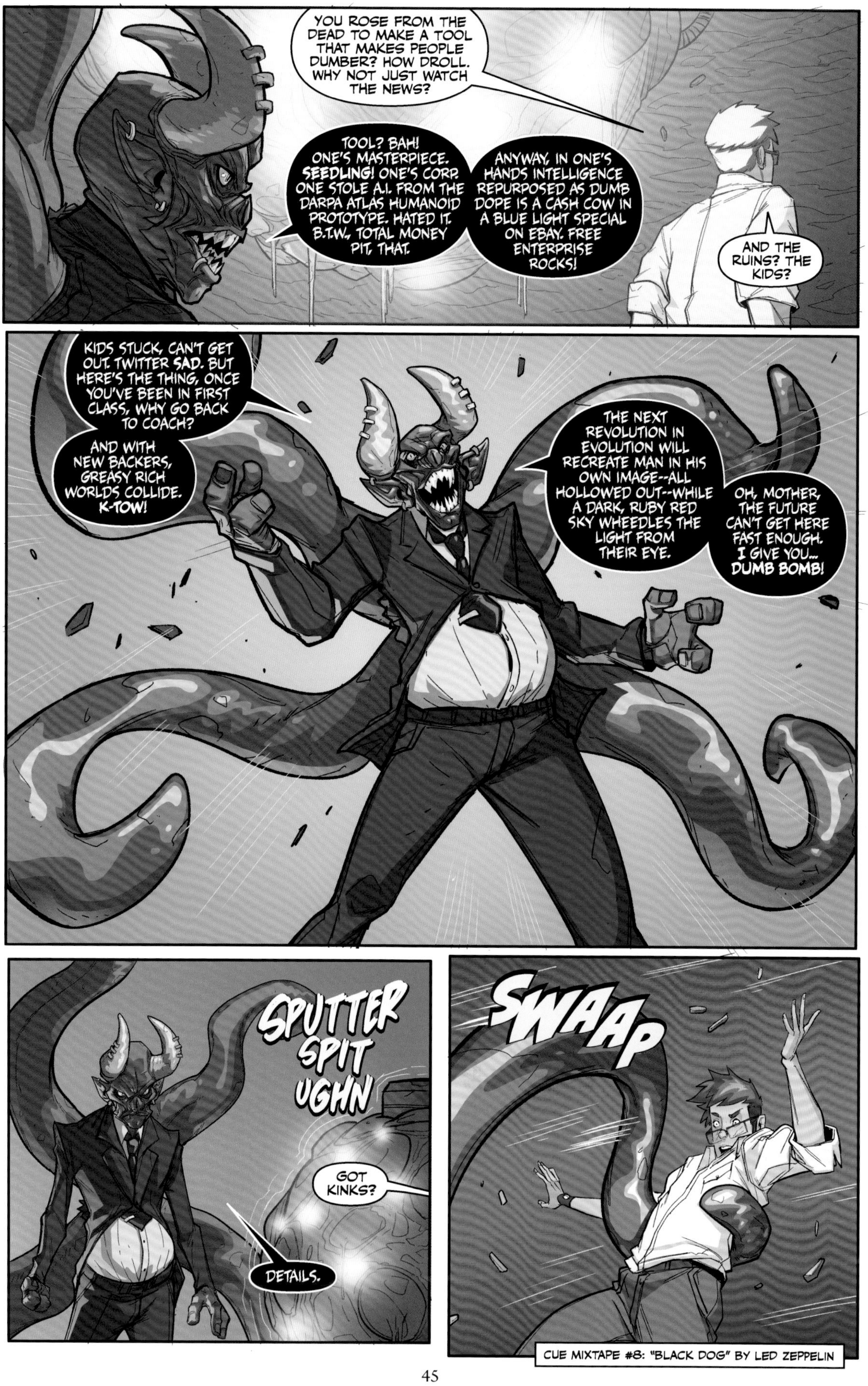
YOU ROSE FROM THE DEAD TO MAKE A TOOL THAT MAKES PEOPLE DUMBER? HOW DROLL. WHY NOT JUST WATCH THE NEWS?
TOOL? BAH! ONE'S MASTERPIECE. SEEDLING! ONE'S CORP. ONE STOLE A.I. FROM THE DARPA ATLAS HUMANOID PROTOTYPE. HATED IT. B.T.W., TOTAL MONEY PIT, THAT.
ANYWAY, IN ONE'S HANDS INTELLIGENCE REPURPOSED AS DUMB DOPE IS A CASH COW IN A BLUE LIGHT SPECIAL ON EBAY. FREE ENTERPRISE ROCKS!
AND THE RUINS? THE KIDS?
KIDS STUCK, CAN'T GET OUT. TWITTER SAD. BUT HERE'S THE THING, ONCE YOU'VE BEEN IN FIRST CLASS, WHY GO BACK TO COACH?
AND WITH NEW BACKERS, GREASY RICH WORLDS COLLIDE. K-TOW!
THE NEXT REVOLUTION IN EVOLUTION WILL RECREATE MAN IN HIS OWN IMAGE--ALL HOLLOWED OUT--WHILE A DARK, RUBY RED SKY WHEEDLES THE LIGHT FROM THEIR EYE.
OH, MOTHER, THE FUTURE CAN'T GET HERE FAST ENOUGH. I GIVE YOU... DUMB BOMB!
SPUTTER SPIT UGHN
GOT KINKS?
DETAILS.
SWAAAP
CUE MIXTAPE #8: "BLACK DOG" BY LED ZEPPELIN

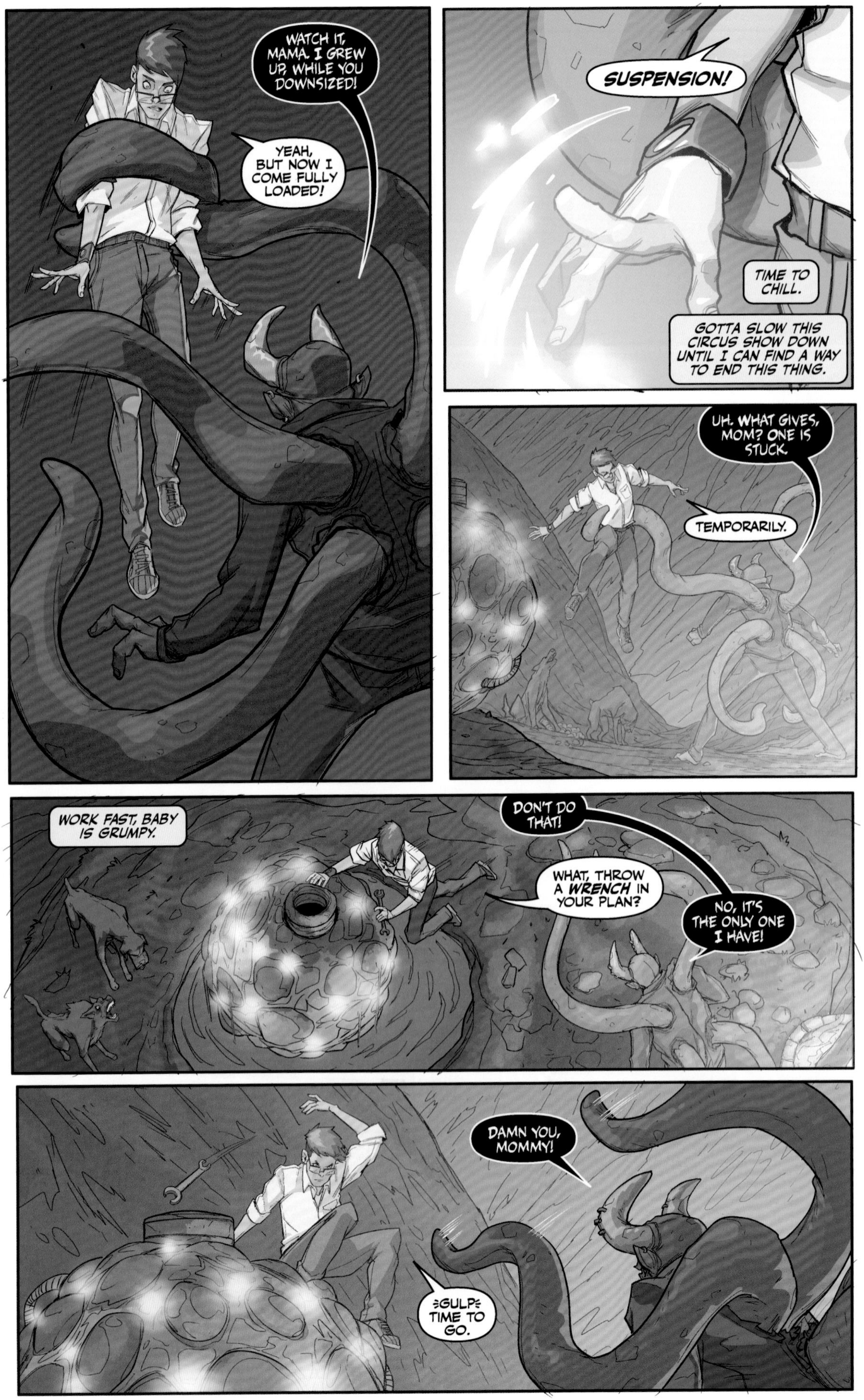
WATCH IT, MAMA. I GREW UP, WHILE YOU DOWNSIZED!
YEAH, BUT NOW I COME FULLY LOADED!
SUSPENSION!
TIME TO CHILL.
GOTTA SLOW THIS CIRCUS SHOW DOWN UNTIL I CAN FIND A WAY TO END THIS THING.
UH. WHAT GIVES, MOM? ONE IS STUCK.
TEMPORARILY.
WORK FAST, BABY IS GRUMPY.
DON'T DO THAT!
WHAT, THROW A WRENCH IN YOUR PLAN?
NO, IT'S THE ONLY ONE I HAVE!
DAMN YOU, MOMMY!
=GULP= TIME TO GO.

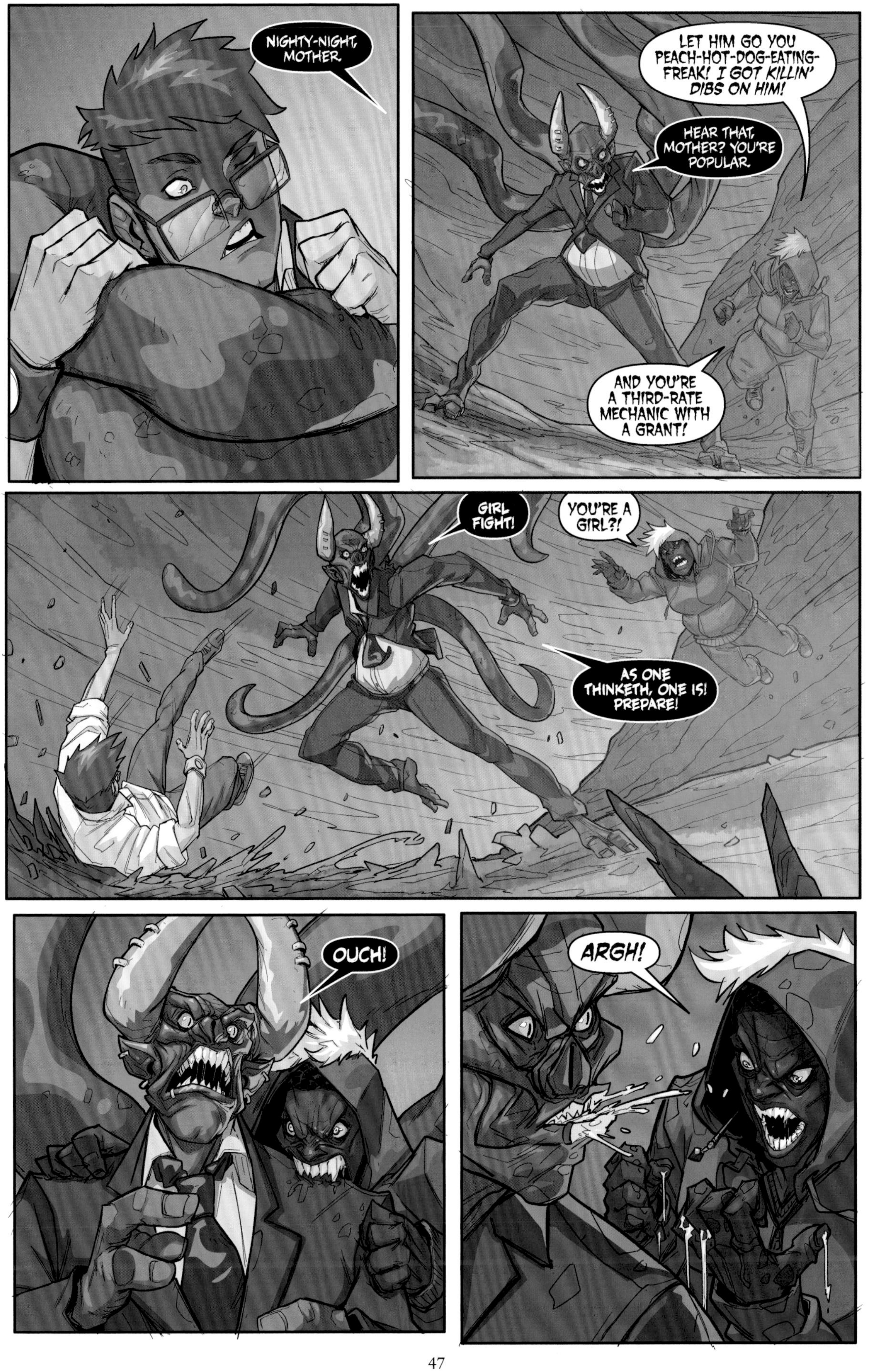
NIGHTY-NIGHT, MOTHER.
LET HIM GO YOU PEACH-HOT-DOG-EATING-FREAK! I GOT KILLIN' DIBS ON HIM!
HEAR THAT, MOTHER? YOU'RE POPULAR.
AND YOU'RE A THIRD-RATE MECHANIC WITH A GRANT!
GIRL FIGHT!
YOU'RE A GIRL?!
AS ONE THINKETH, ONE IS! PREPARE!
OUCH!
ARGH!

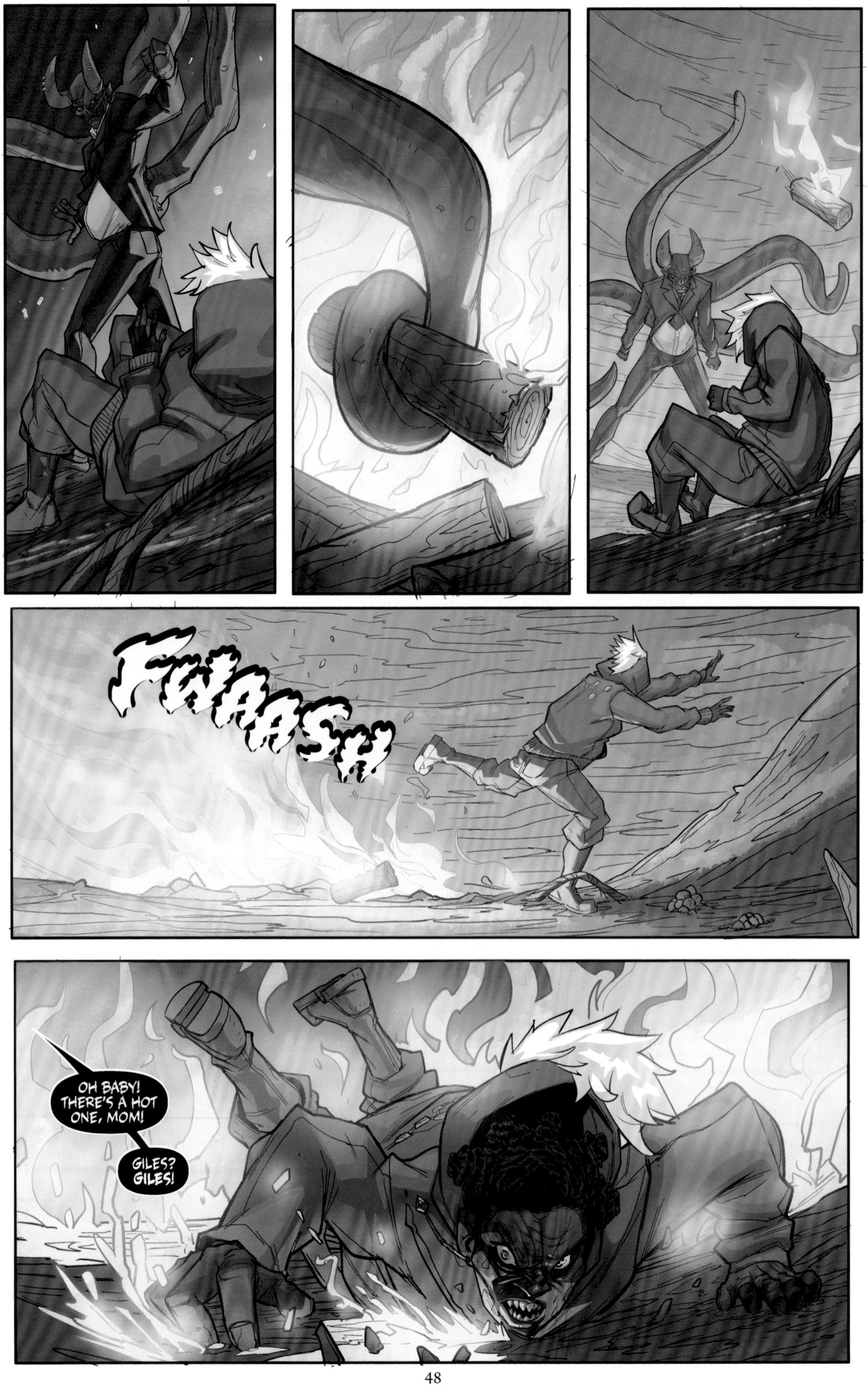
FWAASH
OH BABY! THERE'S A HOT ONE, MOM!
GILES? GILES!

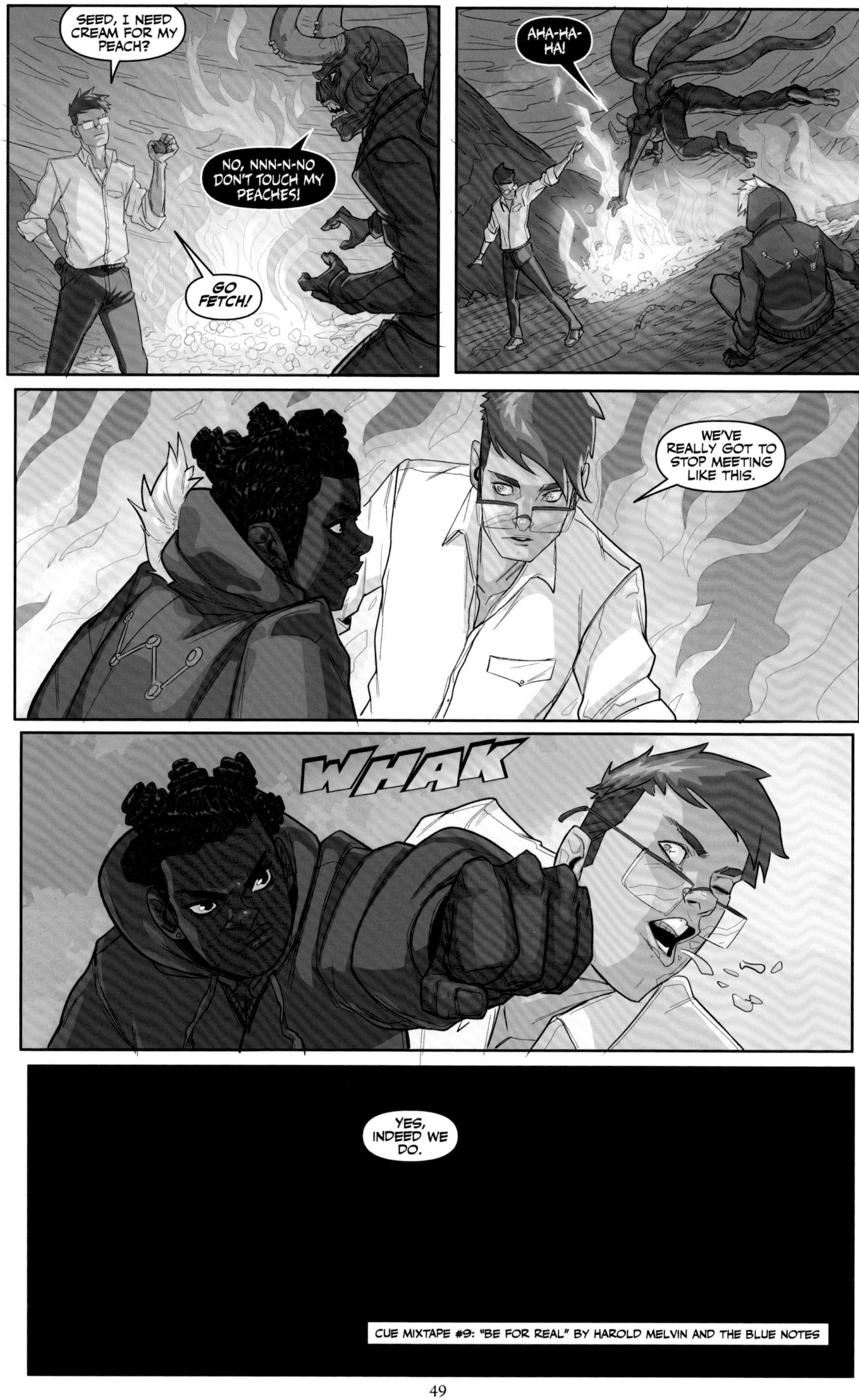
SEED, I NEED CREAM FOR MY PEACH?
NO, NNN-N-NO DON'T TOUCH MY PEACHES!
GO FETCH!
AHA-HA-HA!
WE'VE REALLY GOT TO STOP MEETING LIKE THIS.
WHAK
YES, INDEED WE DO.
CUE MIXTAPE #9: "BE FOR REAL" BY HAROLD MELVIN AND THE BLUE NOTES

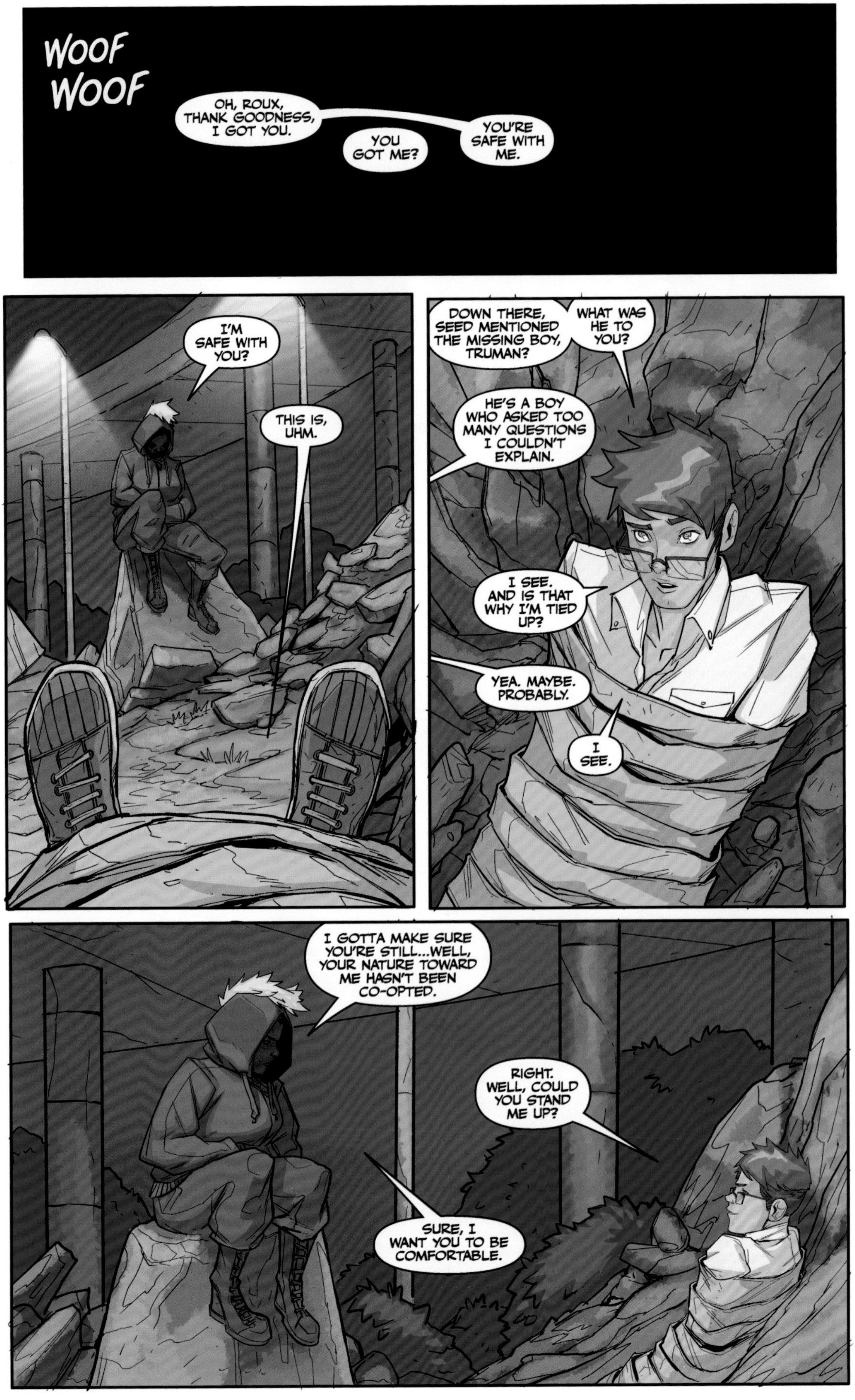

WOOF WOOF
OH, ROUX, THANK GOODNESS, I GOT YOU.
YOU GOT ME?
YOU'RE SAFE WITH ME.
I'M SAFE WITH YOU?
THIS IS, UHM.
DOWN THERE, SEED MENTIONED THE MISSING BOY, TRUMAN?
WHAT WAS HE TO YOU?
HE'S A BOY WHO ASKED TOO MANY QUESTIONS I COULDN'T EXPLAIN.
I SEE. AND IS THAT WHY I'M TIED UP?
YEA. MAYBE. PROBABLY.
I SEE.
I GOTTA MAKE SURE YOU'RE STILL...WELL, YOUR NATURE TOWARD ME HASN'T BEEN CO-OPTED.
RIGHT. WELL, COULD YOU STAND ME UP?
SURE, I WANT YOU TO BE COMFORTABLE.

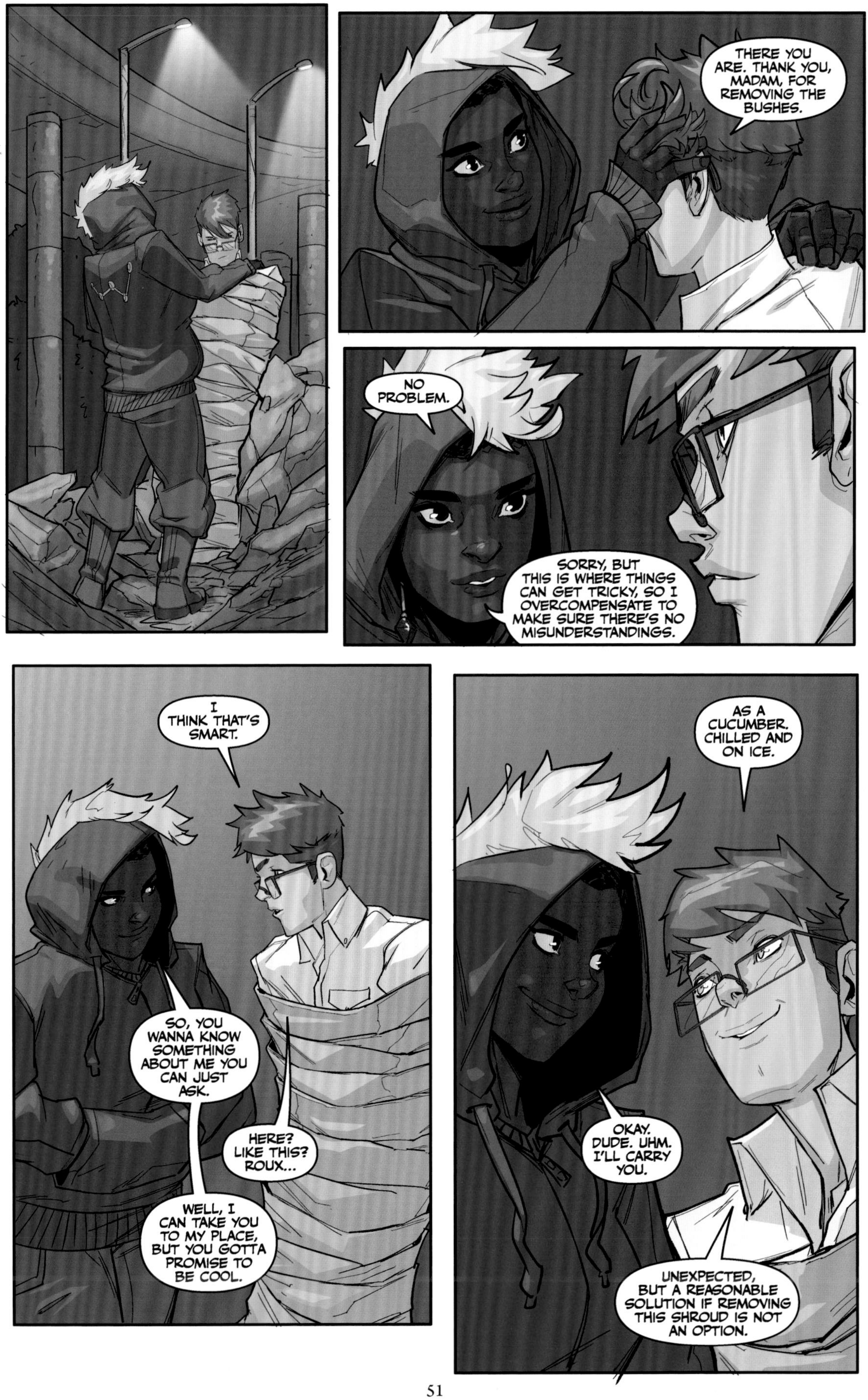
THERE YOU ARE. THANK YOU, MADAM, FOR REMOVING THE BUSHES.
NO PROBLEM.
SORRY, BUT THIS IS WHERE THINGS CAN GET TRICKY, SO I OVERCOMPENSATE TO MAKE SURE THERE'S NO MISUNDERSTANDINGS.
I THINK THAT'S SMART.
SO, YOU WANNA KNOW SOMETHING ABOUT ME YOU CAN JUST ASK.
HERE? LIKE THIS? ROUX...
WELL, I CAN TAKE YOU TO MY PLACE, BUT YOU GOTTA PROMISE TO BE COOL.
AS A CUCUMBER. CHILLED AND ON ICE.
OKAY. DUDE. UHM. I'LL CARRY YOU.
UNEXPECTED, BUT A REASONABLE SOLUTION IF REMOVING THIS SHROUD IS NOT AN OPTION.

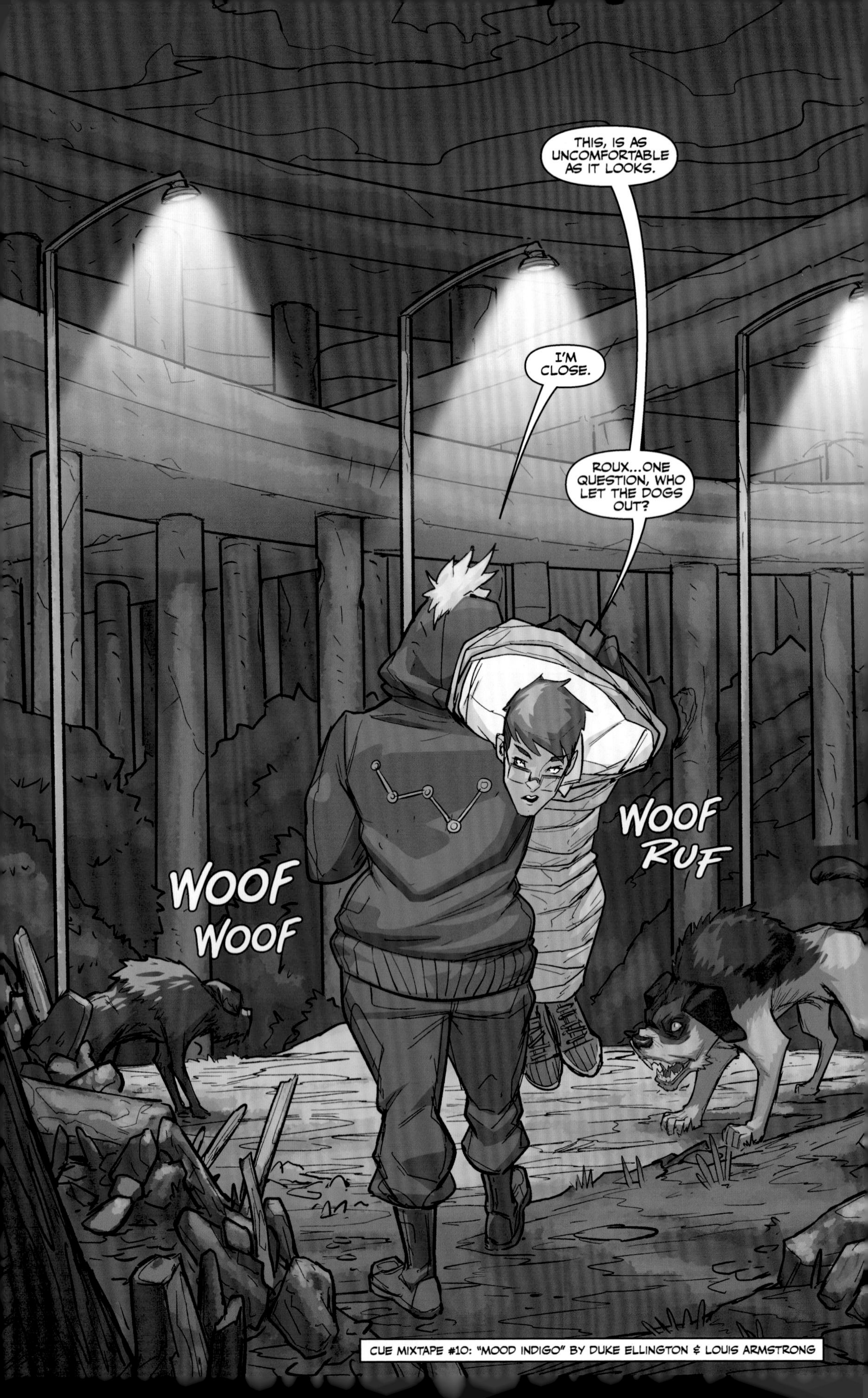
THIS, IS AS UNCOMFORTABLE AS IT LOOKS.
I'M CLOSE.
ROUX...ONE QUESTION, WHO LET THE DOGS OUT?
WOOF RUF
WOOF WOOF
CUE MIXTAPE #10: "MOOD INDIGO" BY DUKE ELLINGTON & LOUIS ARMSTRONG

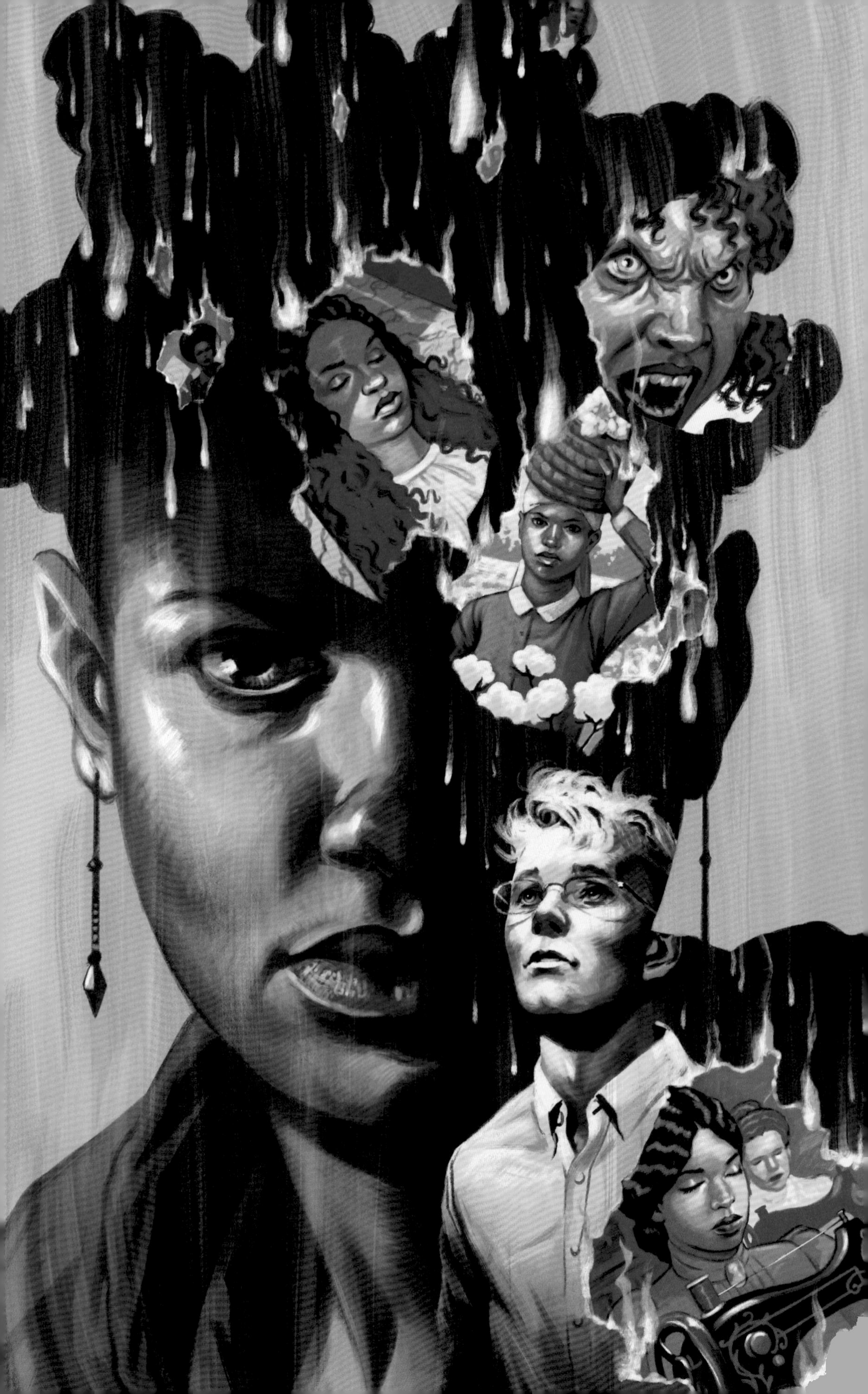

DAY. 1816. REMY PLANTATION, OWEN COUNTY, LOUISIANA--UPRIVER.

HELL ON EARTH.

HOOOOWWWLLL

SHHH. YA'LL MAKE IT HURT WORSE. EASY NOW. EASY...

"I WAS DEAD LONG BEFORE THEY KILLED ME...

"...BUT THEY SURE KILLED THE HELL OUTTA THE REST OF ME THAT NIGHT."

GIRL BLUE
PART THREE
YOU CAN'T BE TOLD

AS I LISTENED TO THE VAMPIRE ROUX, I REALIZED I WAS HER CAPTIVE, HER AUDIENCE, HER INTERROGATOR, **AND** HER BOYFRIEND.

MODERN DATING IS THORNY. NEXT TIME I'LL JUST SWIPE RIGHT.

CHIRP

CHIRP CHIRP

"SLAVERY BINDS FLESH AND CONCEALS ITS WOUNDS. THE OUTSIDE MAY SURVIVE, BUT THE SOUL, IF IT HAS GOOD SENSE, WILL RUN FOR ITS LIFE."

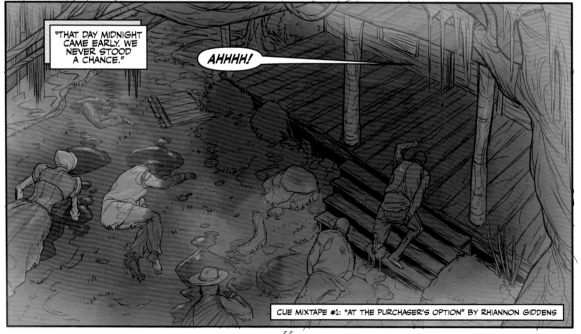

"THAT DAY MIDNIGHT CAME EARLY. WE NEVER STOOD A CHANCE."

AHHHH!

CUE MIXTAPE #1: "AT THE PURCHASER'S OPTION" BY RHIANNON GIDDENS

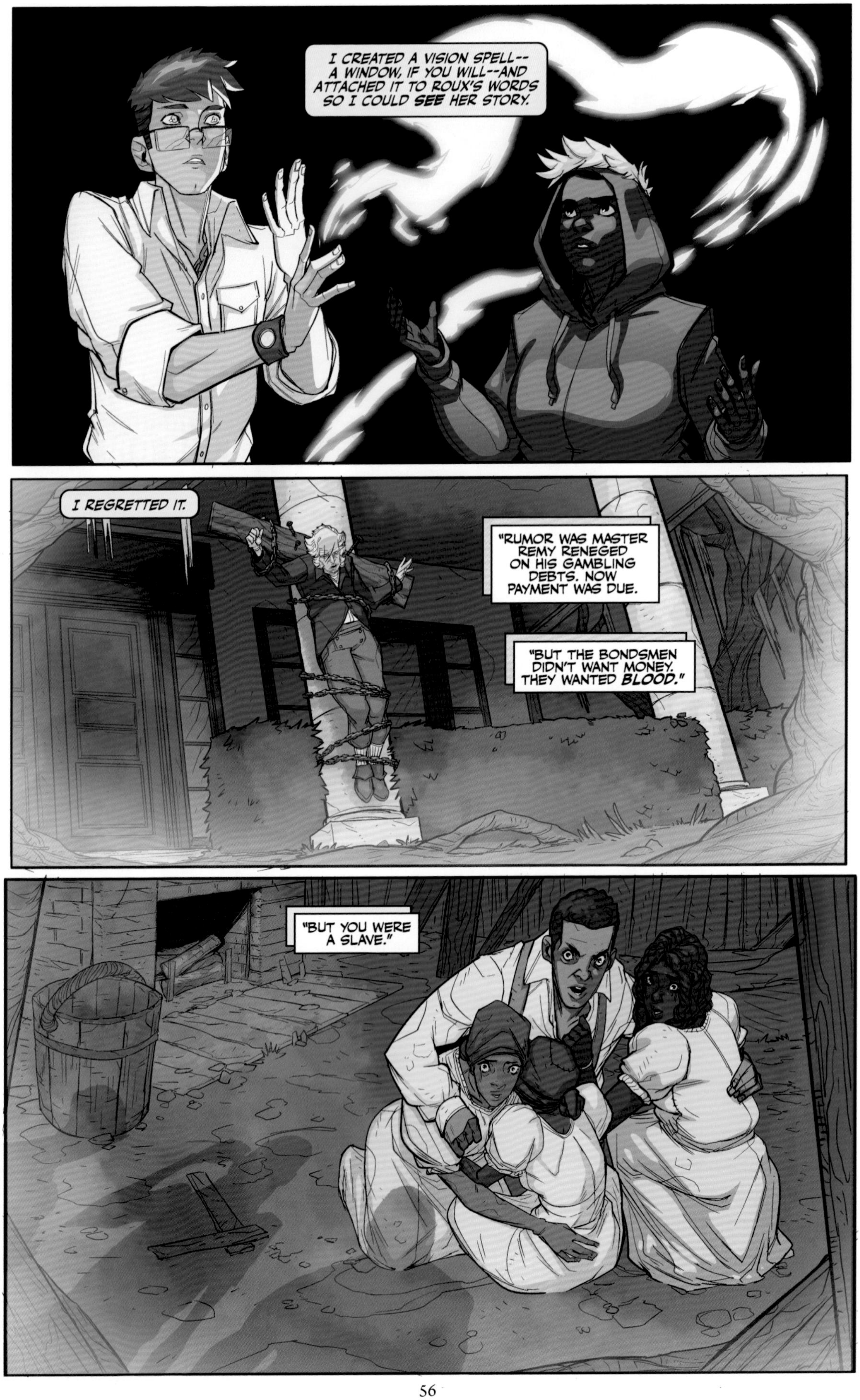
I CREATED A VISION SPELL-- A WINDOW, IF YOU WILL--AND ATTACHED IT TO ROUX'S WORDS SO I COULD SEE HER STORY.
I REGRETTED IT.
"RUMOR WAS MASTER REMY RENEGED ON HIS GAMBLING DEBTS. NOW PAYMENT WAS DUE.
"BUT THE BONDSMEN DIDN'T WANT MONEY. THEY WANTED BLOOD."
"BUT YOU WERE A SLAVE."

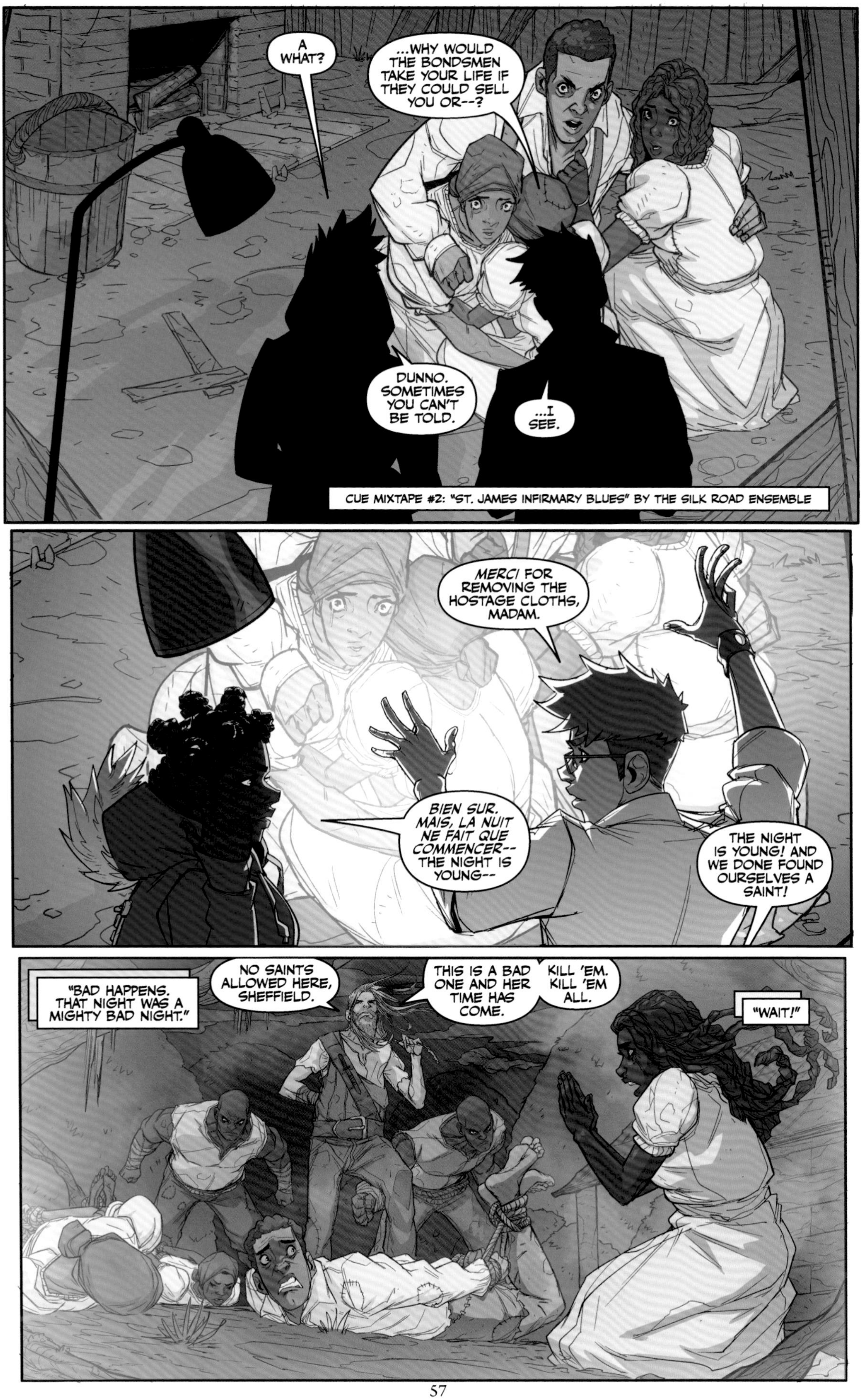
A WHAT?
...WHY WOULD THE BONDSMEN TAKE YOUR LIFE IF THEY COULD SELL YOU OR--?
DUNNO. SOMETIMES YOU CAN'T BE TOLD.
...I SEE.
CUE MIXTAPE #2: "ST. JAMES INFIRMARY BLUES" BY THE SILK ROAD ENSEMBLE
MERCI FOR REMOVING THE HOSTAGE CLOTHS, MADAM.
BIEN SUR. MAIS, LA NUIT NE FAIT QUE COMMENCER-- THE NIGHT IS YOUNG--
THE NIGHT IS YOUNG! AND WE DONE FOUND OURSELVES A SAINT!
"BAD HAPPENS. THAT NIGHT WAS A MIGHTY BAD NIGHT."
NO SAINTS ALLOWED HERE, SHEFFIELD.
THIS IS A BAD ONE AND HER TIME HAS COME.
KILL 'EM. KILL 'EM ALL.
"WAIT!"

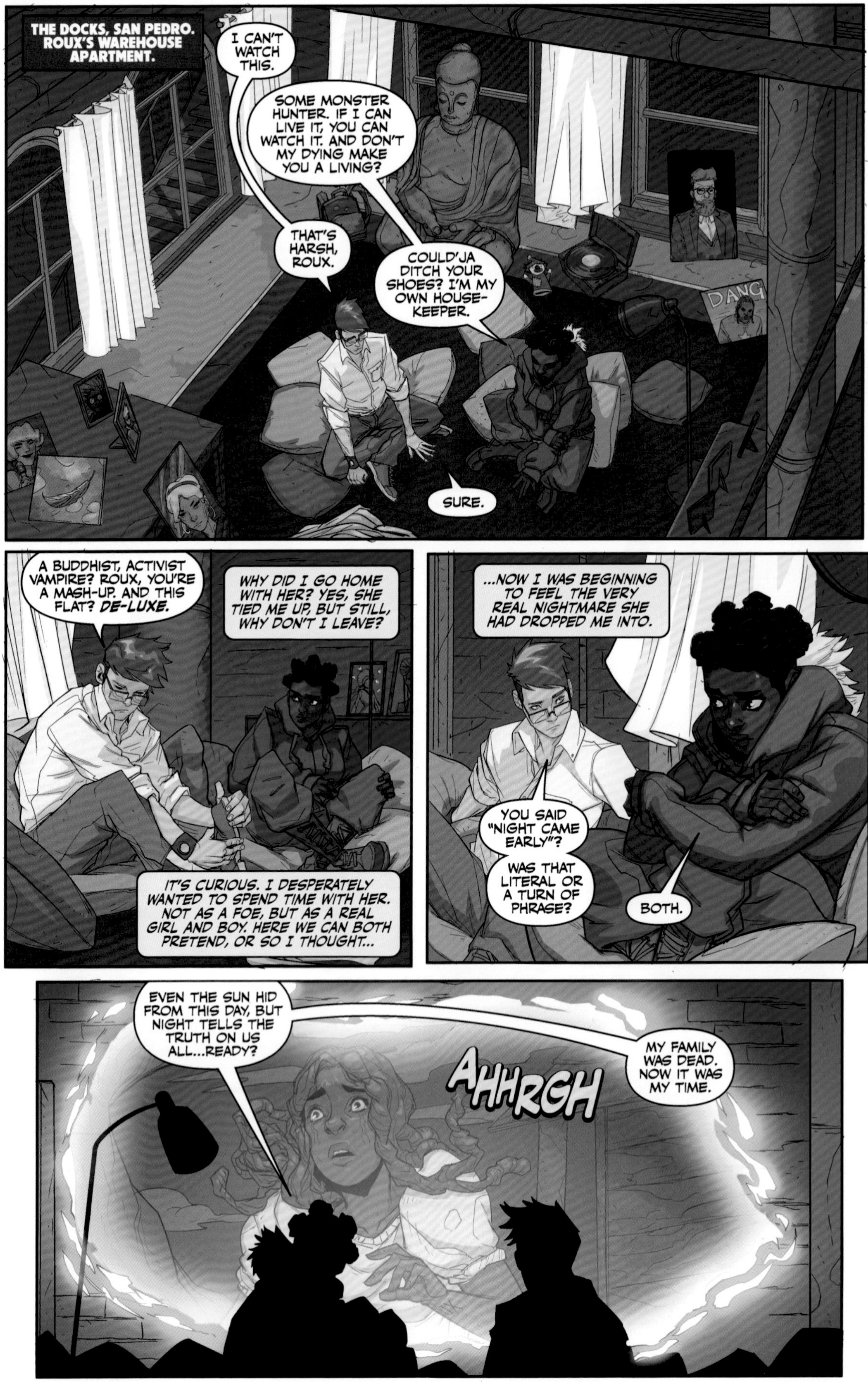
THE DOCKS, SAN PEDRO. ROUX'S WAREHOUSE APARTMENT.
I CAN'T WATCH THIS.
SOME MONSTER HUNTER. IF I CAN LIVE IT, YOU CAN WATCH IT. AND DON'T MY DYING MAKE YOU A LIVING?
THAT'S HARSH, ROUX.
COULD'JA DITCH YOUR SHOES? I'M MY OWN HOUSE-KEEPER.
SURE.
DANG
A BUDDHIST, ACTIVIST VAMPIRE? ROUX, YOU'RE A MASH-UP. AND THIS FLAT? DE-LUXE.
WHY DID I GO HOME WITH HER? YES, SHE TIED ME UP, BUT STILL, WHY DON'T I LEAVE?
IT'S CURIOUS. I DESPERATELY WANTED TO SPEND TIME WITH HER. NOT AS A FOE, BUT AS A REAL GIRL AND BOY. HERE WE CAN BOTH PRETEND, OR SO I THOUGHT...
...NOW I WAS BEGINNING TO FEEL THE VERY REAL NIGHTMARE SHE HAD DROPPED ME INTO.
YOU SAID "NIGHT CAME EARLY"?
WAS THAT LITERAL OR A TURN OF PHRASE?
BOTH.
EVEN THE SUN HID FROM THIS DAY, BUT NIGHT TELLS THE TRUTH ON US ALL...READY?
AHHRGH
MY FAMILY WAS DEAD. NOW IT WAS MY TIME.

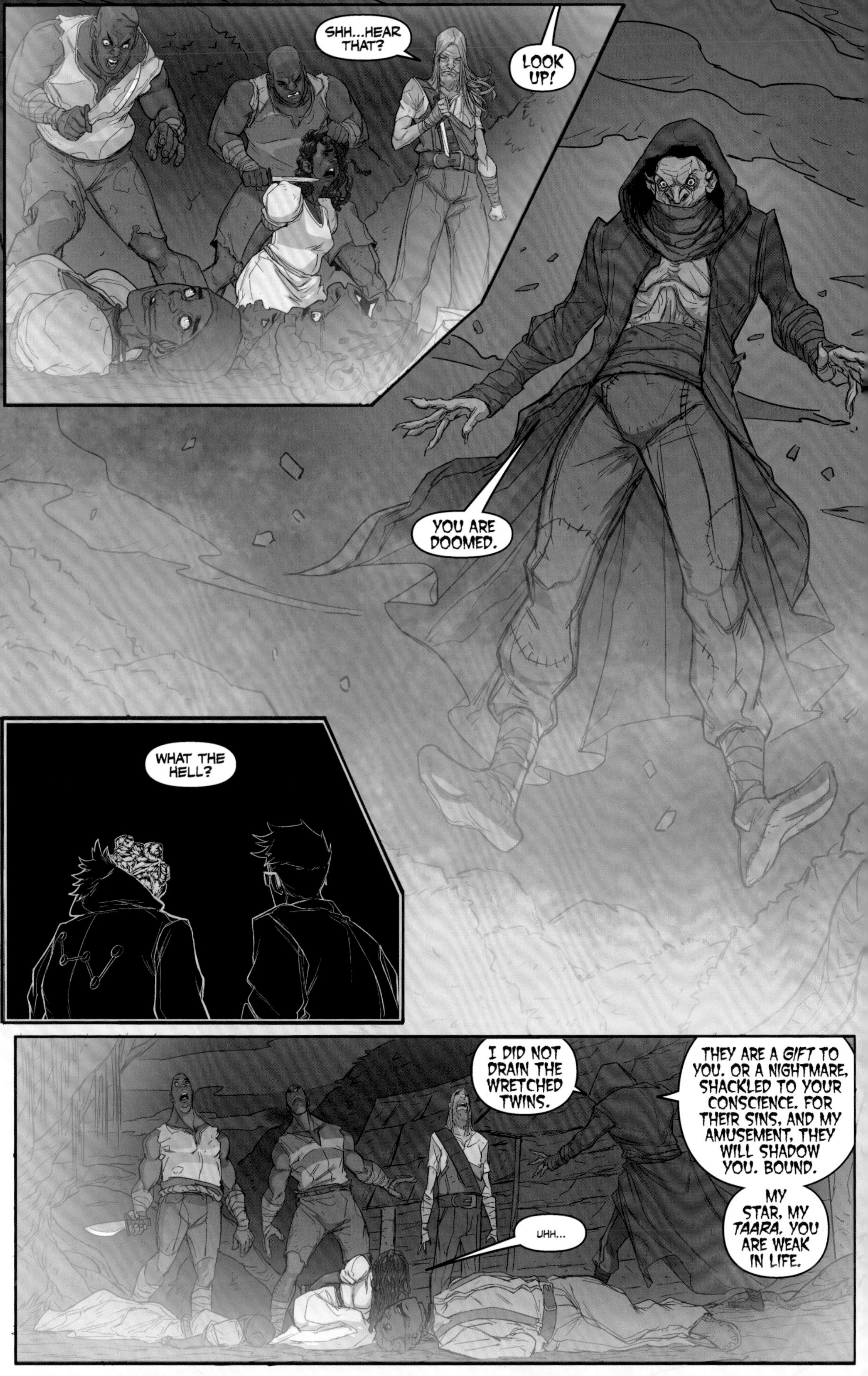

SHH...HEAR THAT?
LOOK UP!
YOU ARE DOOMED.
WHAT THE HELL?
I DID NOT DRAIN THE WRETCHED TWINS.
THEY ARE A *GIFT* TO YOU. OR A NIGHTMARE, SHACKLED TO YOUR CONSCIENCE. FOR THEIR SINS, AND MY AMUSEMENT, THEY WILL SHADOW YOU. BOUND.
MY STAR, MY *TAARA*. YOU ARE WEAK IN LIFE.
UHH...

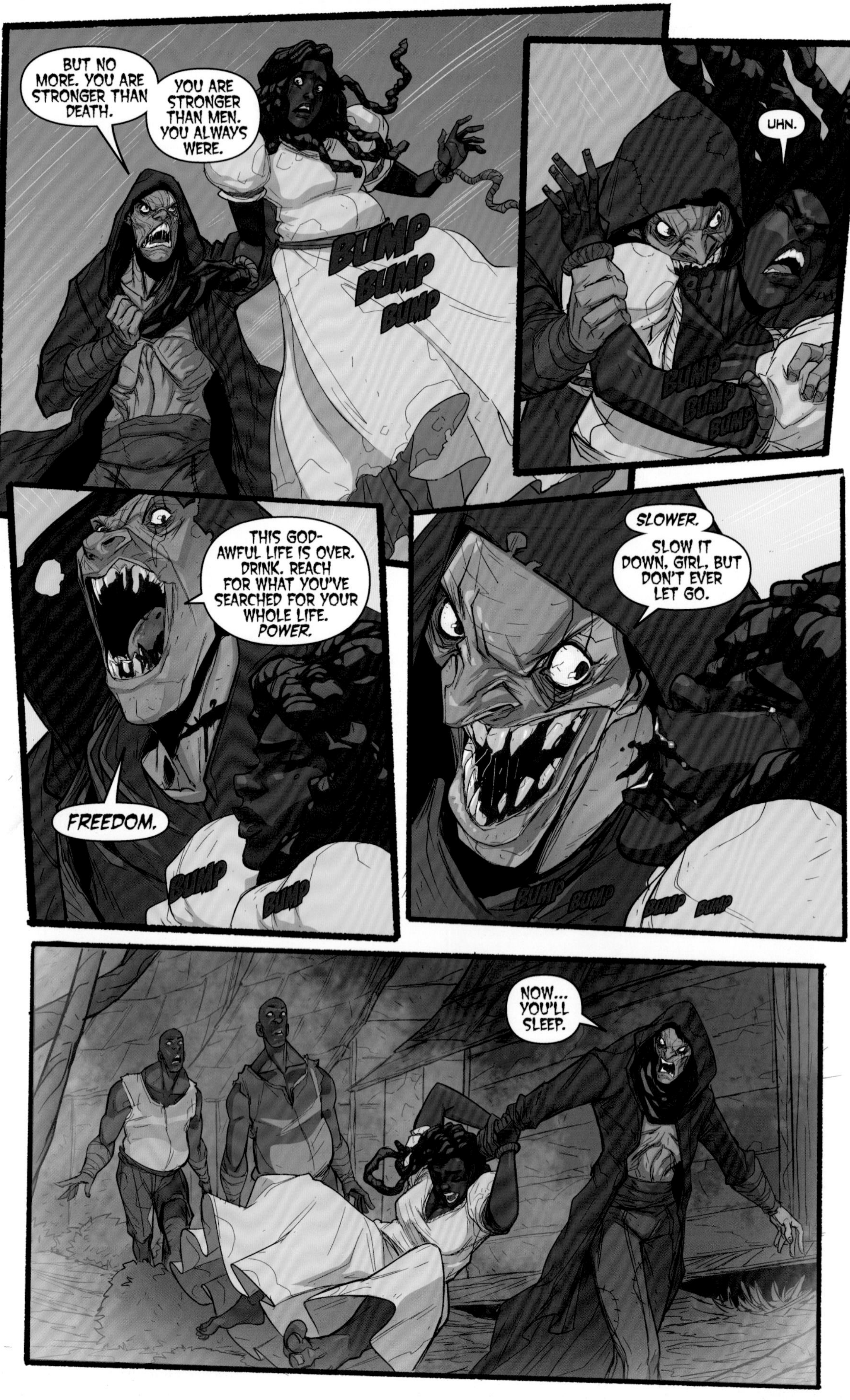

BUT NO MORE. YOU ARE STRONGER THAN DEATH.
YOU ARE STRONGER THAN MEN. YOU ALWAYS WERE.
BUMP BUMP BUMP
UHN.
BUMP BUMP BUMP
THIS GOD-AWFUL LIFE IS OVER. DRINK. REACH FOR WHAT YOU'VE SEARCHED FOR YOUR WHOLE LIFE. POWER.
FREEDOM.
BUMP BUMP
SLOWER.
SLOW IT DOWN, GIRL, BUT DON'T EVER LET GO.
BUMP BUMP BUMP BUMP
NOW... YOU'LL SLEEP.

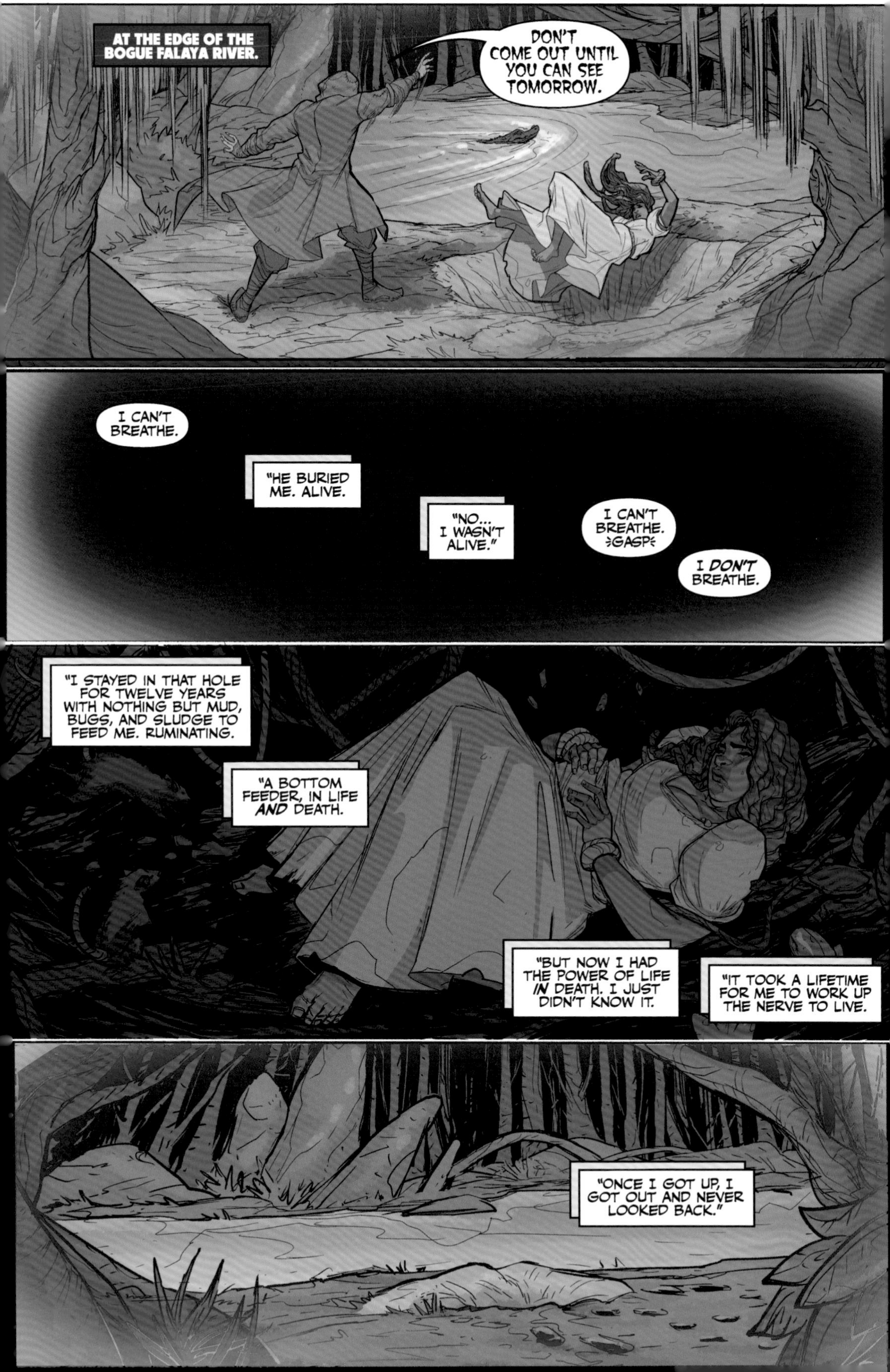
AT THE EDGE OF THE BOGUE FALAYA RIVER.
DON'T COME OUT UNTIL YOU CAN SEE TOMORROW.
I CAN'T BREATHE.
"HE BURIED ME. ALIVE.
"NO... I WASN'T ALIVE."
I CAN'T BREATHE. *GASP*
I DON'T BREATHE.
"I STAYED IN THAT HOLE FOR TWELVE YEARS WITH NOTHING BUT MUD, BUGS, AND SLUDGE TO FEED ME. RUMINATING.
"A BOTTOM FEEDER, IN LIFE AND DEATH.
"BUT NOW I HAD THE POWER OF LIFE IN DEATH. I JUST DIDN'T KNOW IT.
"IT TOOK A LIFETIME FOR ME TO WORK UP THE NERVE TO LIVE.
"ONCE I GOT UP, I GOT OUT AND NEVER LOOKED BACK."

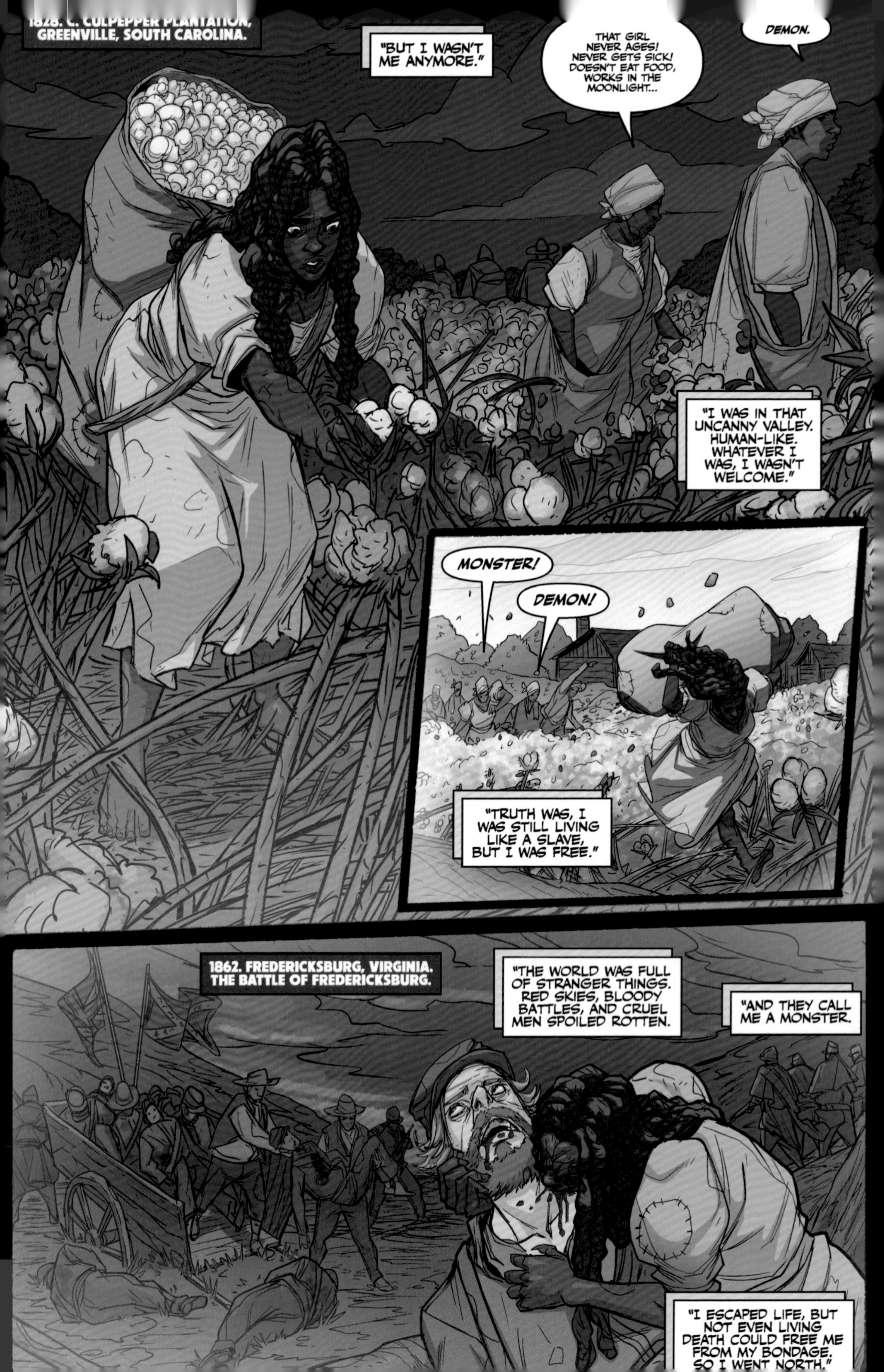
1828. C. CULPEPPER PLANTATION, GREENVILLE, SOUTH CAROLINA.
"BUT I WASN'T ME ANYMORE."
THAT GIRL NEVER AGES! NEVER GETS SICK! DOESN'T EAT FOOD, WORKS IN THE MOONLIGHT...
DEMON.
"I WAS IN THAT UNCANNY VALLEY. HUMAN-LIKE. WHATEVER I WAS, I WASN'T WELCOME."
MONSTER!
DEMON!
"TRUTH WAS, I WAS STILL LIVING LIKE A SLAVE, BUT I WAS FREE."
1862. FREDERICKSBURG, VIRGINIA. THE BATTLE OF FREDERICKSBURG.
"THE WORLD WAS FULL OF STRANGER THINGS. RED SKIES, BLOODY BATTLES, AND CRUEL MEN SPOILED ROTTEN.
"AND THEY CALL ME A MONSTER.
"I ESCAPED LIFE, BUT NOT EVEN LIVING DEATH COULD FREE ME FROM MY BONDAGE. SO I WENT NORTH."

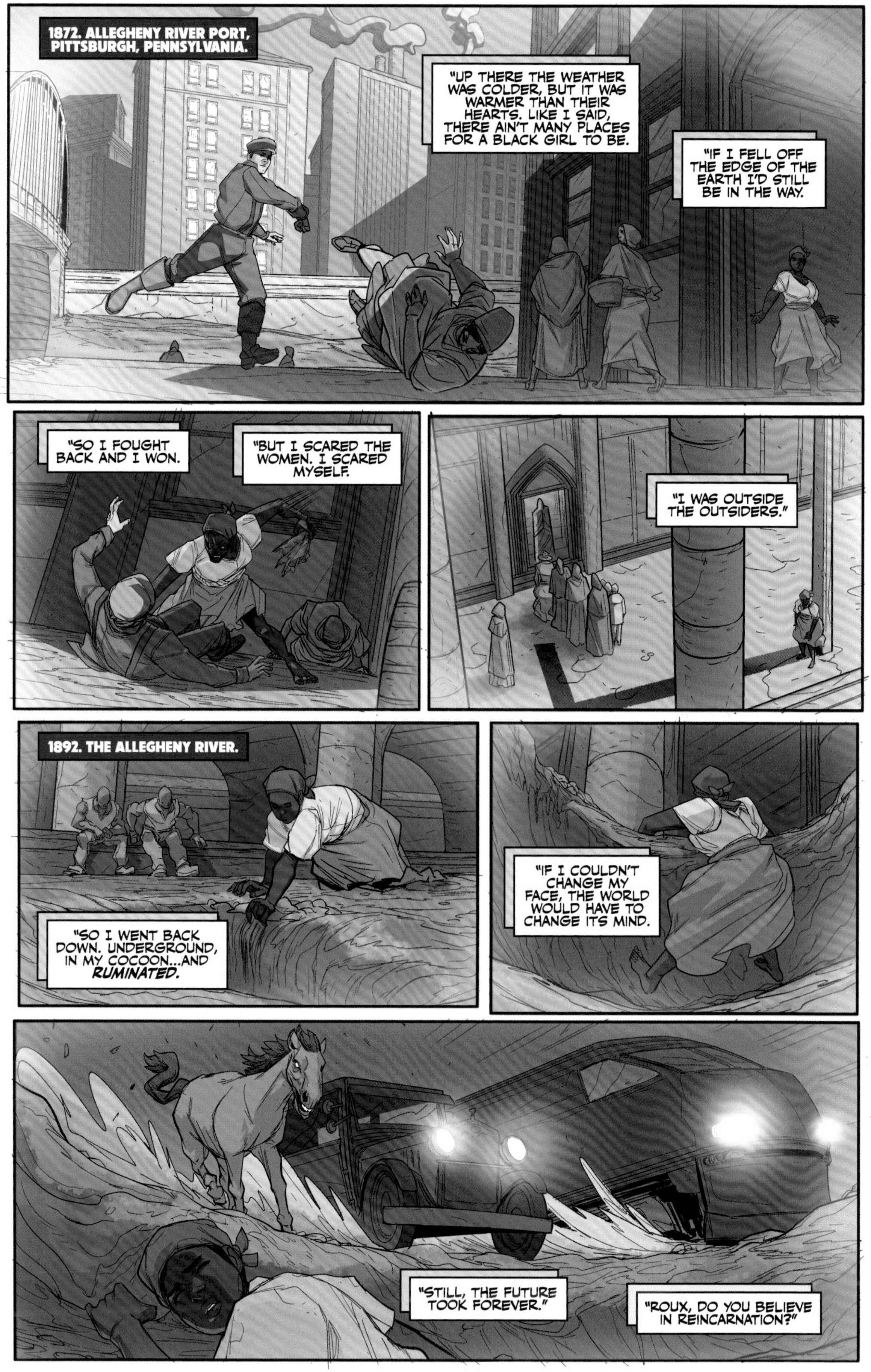
1872. ALLEGHENY RIVER PORT, PITTSBURGH, PENNSYLVANIA.
"UP THERE THE WEATHER WAS COLDER, BUT IT WAS WARMER THAN THEIR HEARTS. LIKE I SAID, THERE AIN'T MANY PLACES FOR A BLACK GIRL TO BE.
"IF I FELL OFF THE EDGE OF THE EARTH I'D STILL BE IN THE WAY.
"SO I FOUGHT BACK AND I WON.
"BUT I SCARED THE WOMEN. I SCARED MYSELF.
"I WAS OUTSIDE THE OUTSIDERS."
1892. THE ALLEGHENY RIVER.
"SO I WENT BACK DOWN. UNDERGROUND, IN MY COCOON...AND *RUMINATED.*
"IF I COULDN'T CHANGE MY FACE, THE WORLD WOULD HAVE TO CHANGE ITS MIND.
"STILL, THE FUTURE TOOK FOREVER."
"ROUX, DO YOU BELIEVE IN REINCARNATION?"

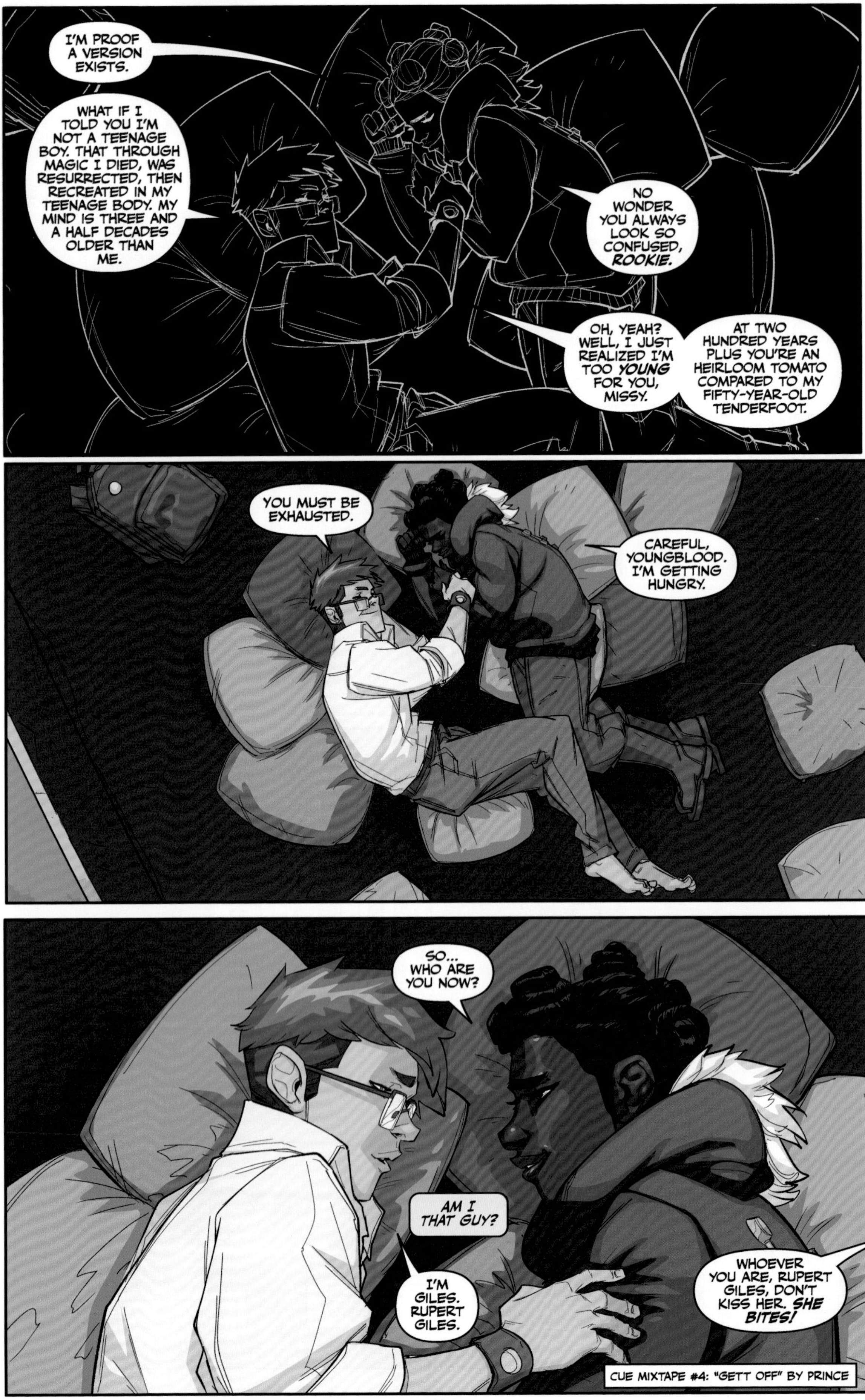
I'M PROOF A VERSION EXISTS.
WHAT IF I TOLD YOU I'M NOT A TEENAGE BOY. THAT THROUGH MAGIC I DIED, WAS RESURRECTED, THEN RECREATED IN MY TEENAGE BODY. MY MIND IS THREE AND A HALF DECADES OLDER THAN ME.
NO WONDER YOU ALWAYS LOOK SO CONFUSED, ROOKIE.
OH, YEAH? WELL, I JUST REALIZED I'M TOO YOUNG FOR YOU, MISSY.
AT TWO HUNDRED YEARS PLUS YOU'RE AN HEIRLOOM TOMATO COMPARED TO MY FIFTY-YEAR-OLD TENDERFOOT.
YOU MUST BE EXHAUSTED.
CAREFUL, YOUNGBLOOD. I'M GETTING HUNGRY.
SO... WHO ARE YOU NOW?
AM I THAT GUY?
I'M GILES. RUPERT GILES.
WHOEVER YOU ARE, RUPERT GILES, DON'T KISS HER. SHE BITES!
CUE MIXTAPE #4: "GETT OFF" BY PRINCE

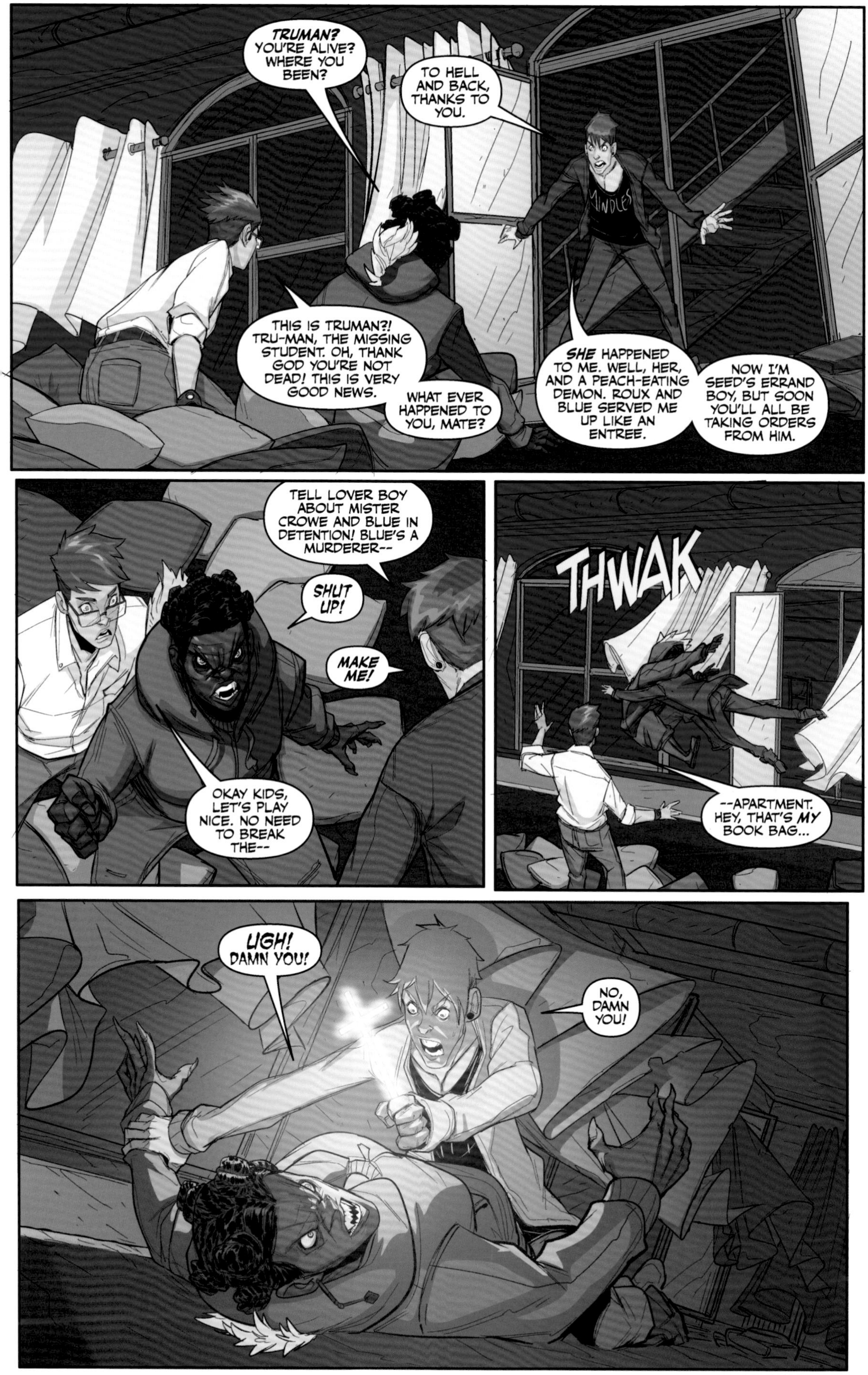
TRUMAN? YOU'RE ALIVE? WHERE YOU BEEN?
TO HELL AND BACK, THANKS TO YOU.
MINDLESS
THIS IS TRUMAN?! TRU-MAN, THE MISSING STUDENT. OH, THANK GOD YOU'RE NOT DEAD! THIS IS VERY GOOD NEWS.
WHAT EVER HAPPENED TO YOU, MATE?
SHE HAPPENED TO ME. WELL, HER, AND A PEACH-EATING DEMON. ROUX AND BLUE SERVED ME UP LIKE AN ENTREE.
NOW I'M SEED'S ERRAND BOY, BUT SOON YOU'LL ALL BE TAKING ORDERS FROM HIM.
TELL LOVER BOY ABOUT MISTER CROWE AND BLUE IN DETENTION! BLUE'S A MURDERER--
SHUT UP!
MAKE ME!
OKAY KIDS, LET'S PLAY NICE. NO NEED TO BREAK THE--
THWAK
--APARTMENT. HEY, THAT'S MY BOOK BAG...
UGH! DAMN YOU!
NO, DAMN YOU!

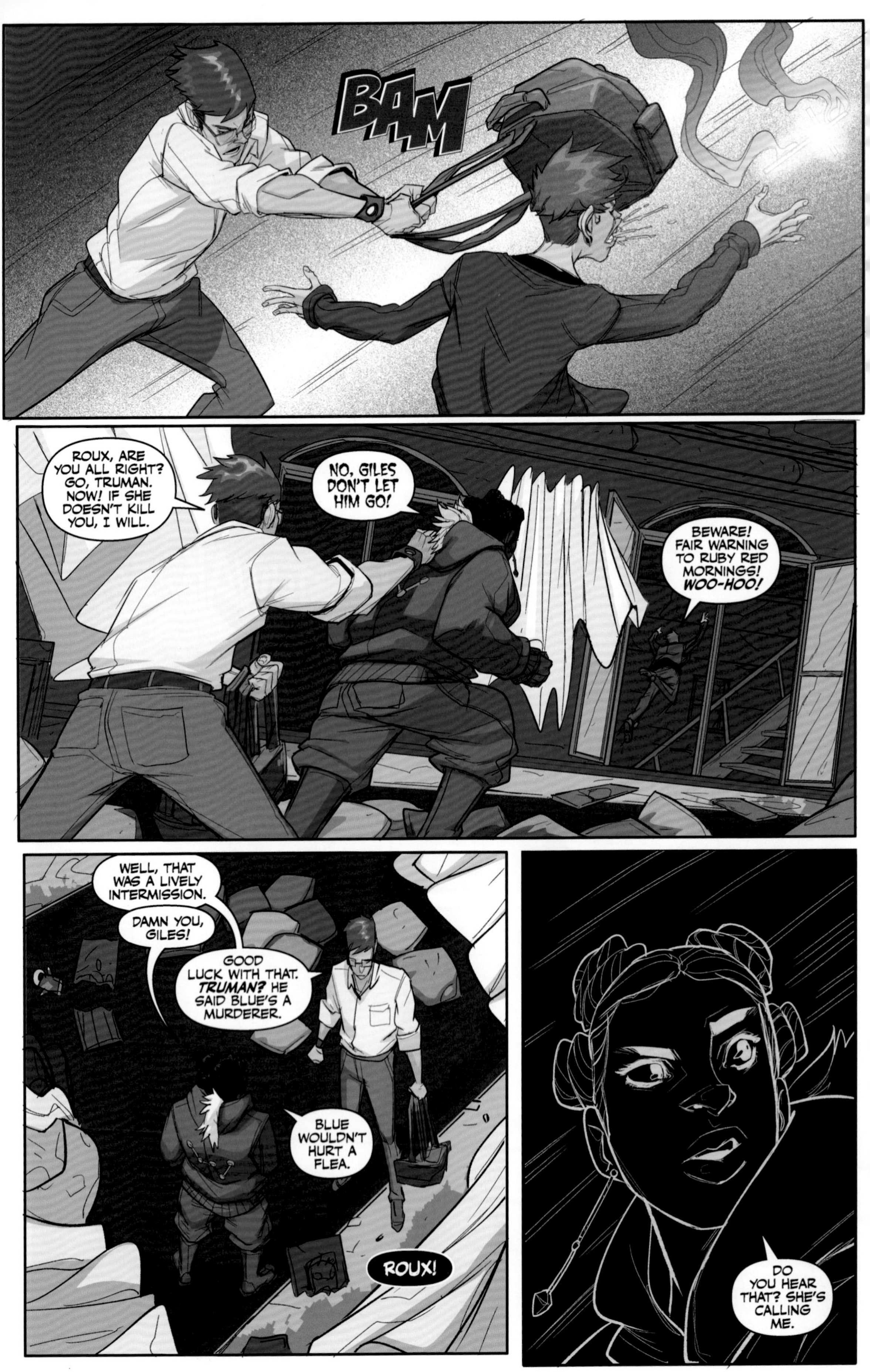
BAM
ROUX, ARE YOU ALL RIGHT? GO, TRUMAN. NOW! IF SHE DOESN'T KILL YOU, I WILL.
NO, GILES DON'T LET HIM GO!
BEWARE! FAIR WARNING TO RUBY RED MORNINGS! WOO-HOO!
WELL, THAT WAS A LIVELY INTERMISSION.
DAMN YOU, GILES!
GOOD LUCK WITH THAT. TRUMAN? HE SAID BLUE'S A MURDERER.
BLUE WOULDN'T HURT A FLEA.
ROUX!
DO YOU HEAR THAT? SHE'S CALLING ME.

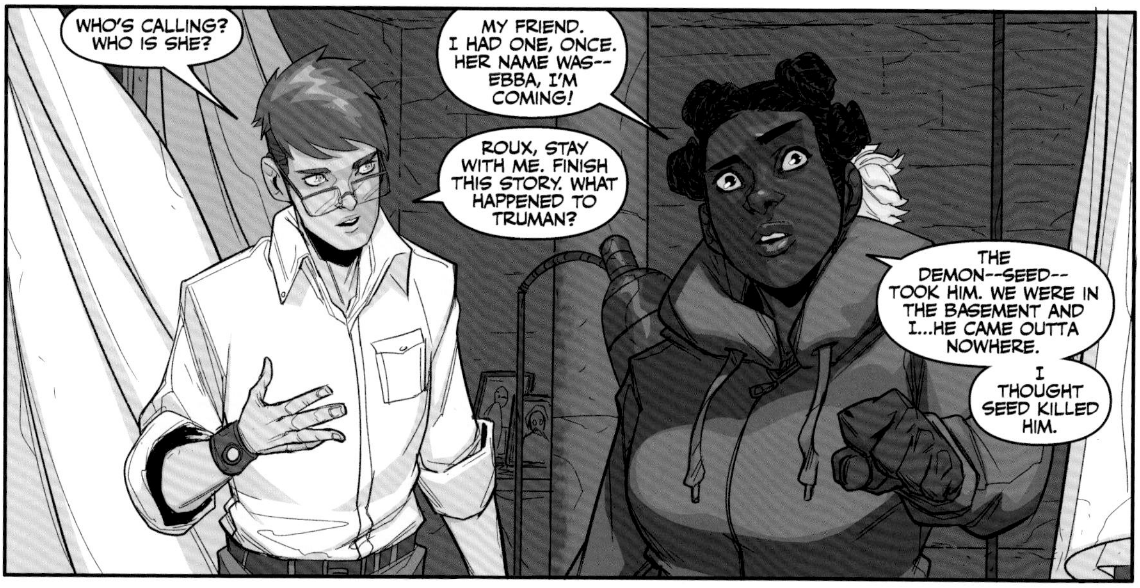
WHO'S CALLING? WHO IS SHE?
MY FRIEND. I HAD ONE, ONCE. HER NAME WAS-- EBBA, I'M COMING!
ROUX, STAY WITH ME. FINISH THIS STORY. WHAT HAPPENED TO TRUMAN?
THE DEMON--SEED-- TOOK HIM. WE WERE IN THE BASEMENT AND I...HE CAME OUTTA NOWHERE.
I THOUGHT SEED KILLED HIM.

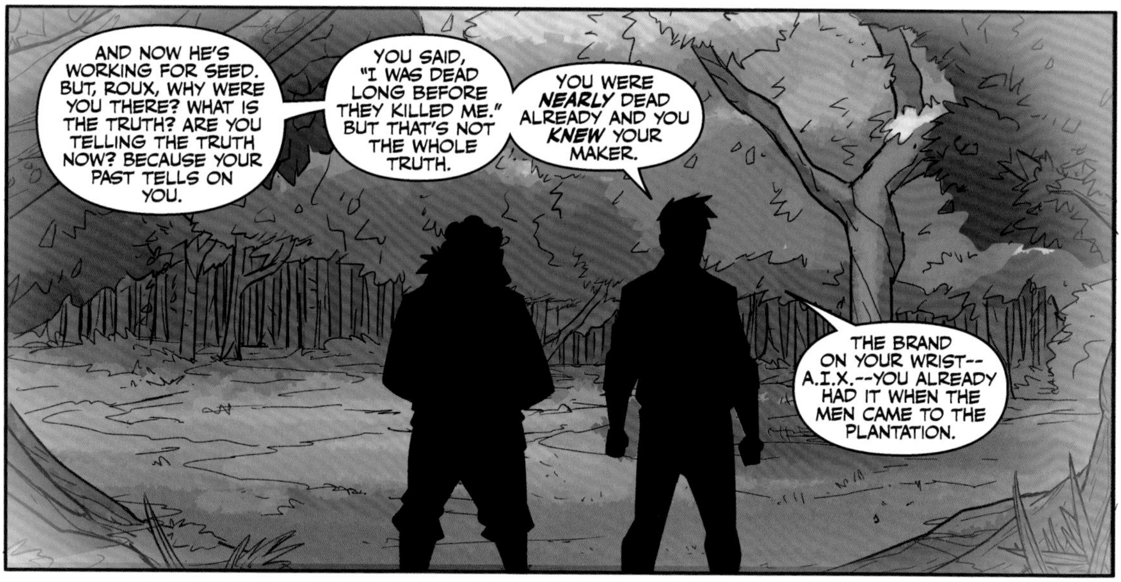
AND NOW HE'S WORKING FOR SEED. BUT, ROUX, WHY WERE YOU THERE? WHAT IS THE TRUTH? ARE YOU TELLING THE TRUTH NOW? BECAUSE YOUR PAST TELLS ON YOU.
YOU SAID, "I WAS DEAD LONG BEFORE THEY KILLED ME." BUT THAT'S NOT THE WHOLE TRUTH.
YOU WERE NEARLY DEAD ALREADY AND YOU KNEW YOUR MAKER.
THE BRAND ON YOUR WRIST-- A.I.X.--YOU ALREADY HAD IT WHEN THE MEN CAME TO THE PLANTATION.

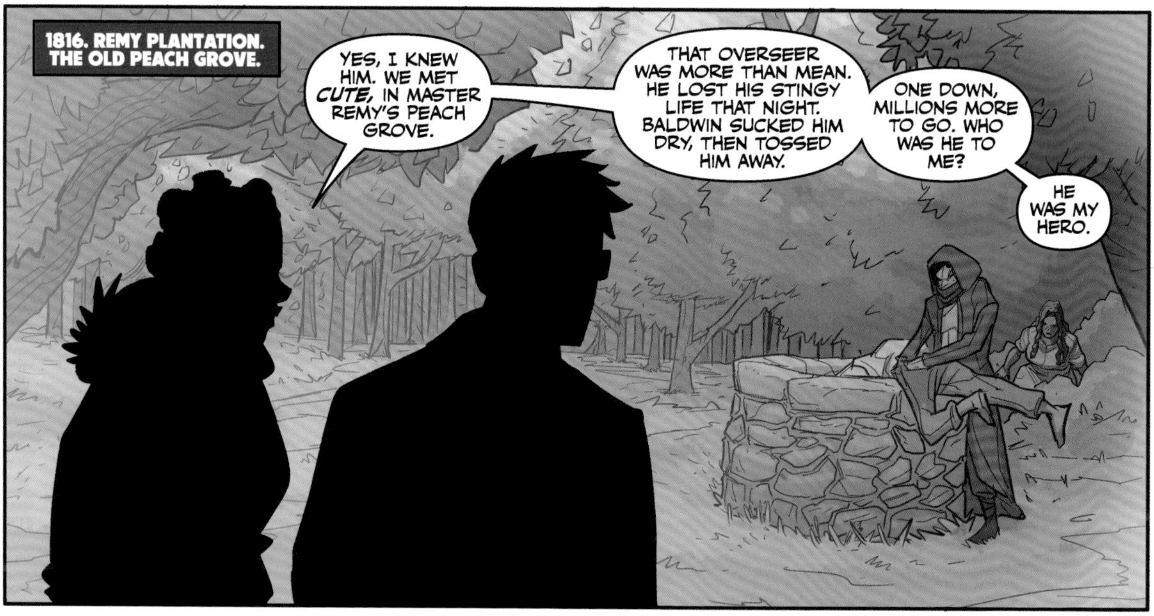
1816. REMY PLANTATION. THE OLD PEACH GROVE.
YES, I KNEW HIM. WE MET CUTE, IN MASTER REMY'S PEACH GROVE.
THAT OVERSEER WAS MORE THAN MEAN. HE LOST HIS STINGY LIFE THAT NIGHT. BALDWIN SUCKED HIM DRY, THEN TOSSED HIM AWAY.
ONE DOWN, MILLIONS MORE TO GO. WHO WAS HE TO ME?
HE WAS MY HERO.

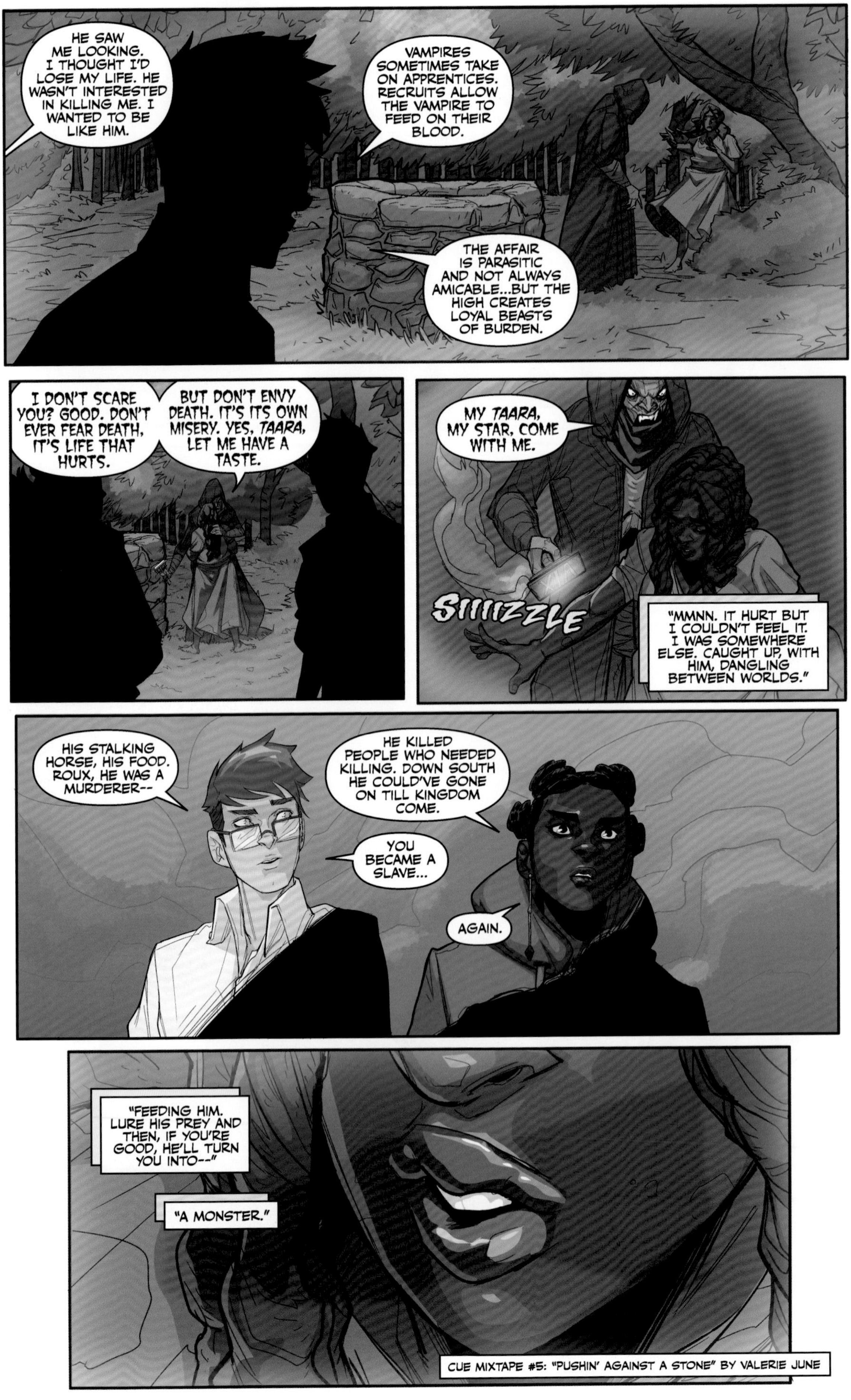
HE SAW ME LOOKING. I THOUGHT I'D LOSE MY LIFE. HE WASN'T INTERESTED IN KILLING ME. I WANTED TO BE LIKE HIM.
VAMPIRES SOMETIMES TAKE ON APPRENTICES. RECRUITS ALLOW THE VAMPIRE TO FEED ON THEIR BLOOD.
THE AFFAIR IS PARASITIC AND NOT ALWAYS AMICABLE...BUT THE HIGH CREATES LOYAL BEASTS OF BURDEN.
I DON'T SCARE YOU? GOOD. DON'T EVER FEAR DEATH, IT'S LIFE THAT HURTS.
BUT DON'T ENVY DEATH. IT'S ITS OWN MISERY. YES, *TAARA*, LET ME HAVE A TASTE.
MY *TAARA*, MY STAR, COME WITH ME.
SIIIIZZLE
"MMNN. IT HURT BUT I COULDN'T FEEL IT. I WAS SOMEWHERE ELSE. CAUGHT UP, WITH HIM, DANGLING BETWEEN WORLDS."
HIS STALKING HORSE, HIS FOOD. ROUX, HE WAS A MURDERER--
HE KILLED PEOPLE WHO NEEDED KILLING. DOWN SOUTH HE COULD'VE GONE ON TILL KINGDOM COME.
YOU BECAME A SLAVE...
AGAIN.
"FEEDING HIM. LURE HIS PREY AND THEN, IF YOU'RE GOOD, HE'LL TURN YOU INTO--"
"A MONSTER."
CUE MIXTAPE #5: "PUSHIN' AGAINST A STONE" BY VALERIE JUNE

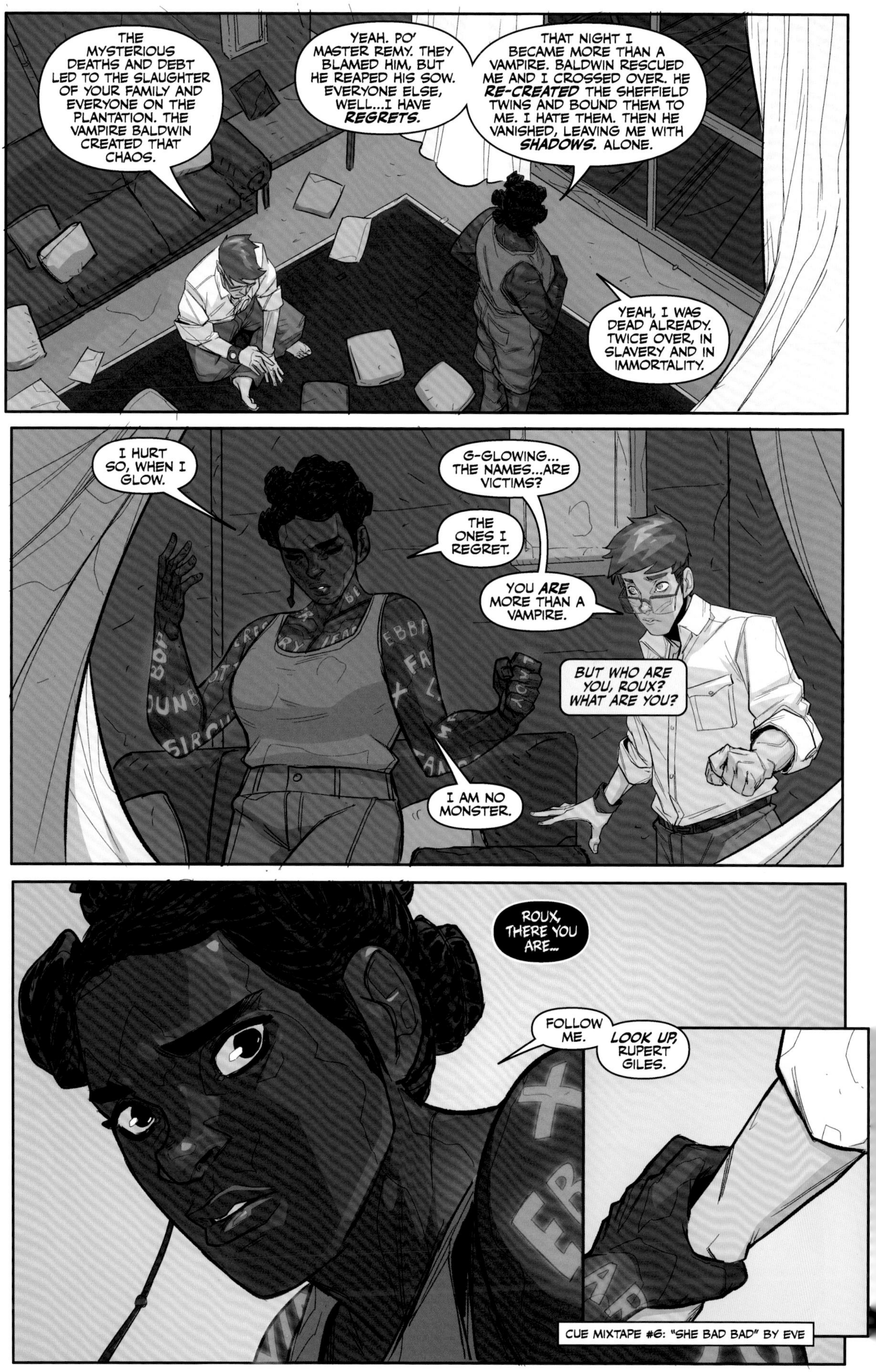
THE MYSTERIOUS DEATHS AND DEBT LED TO THE SLAUGHTER OF YOUR FAMILY AND EVERYONE ON THE PLANTATION. THE VAMPIRE BALDWIN CREATED THAT CHAOS.
YEAH. PO' MASTER REMY. THEY BLAMED HIM, BUT HE REAPED HIS SOW. EVERYONE ELSE, WELL...I HAVE REGRETS.
THAT NIGHT I BECAME MORE THAN A VAMPIRE. BALDWIN RESCUED ME AND I CROSSED OVER. HE RE-CREATED THE SHEFFIELD TWINS AND BOUND THEM TO ME. I HATE THEM. THEN HE VANISHED, LEAVING ME WITH SHADOWS. ALONE.
YEAH, I WAS DEAD ALREADY. TWICE OVER, IN SLAVERY AND IN IMMORTALITY.
I HURT SO, WHEN I GLOW.
G-GLOWING... THE NAMES...ARE VICTIMS?
THE ONES I REGRET.
YOU ARE MORE THAN A VAMPIRE.
BUT WHO ARE YOU, ROUX? WHAT ARE YOU?
I AM NO MONSTER.
ROUX, THERE YOU ARE...
FOLLOW ME.
LOOK UP, RUPERT GILES.
CUE MIXTAPE #6: "SHE BAD BAD" BY EVE

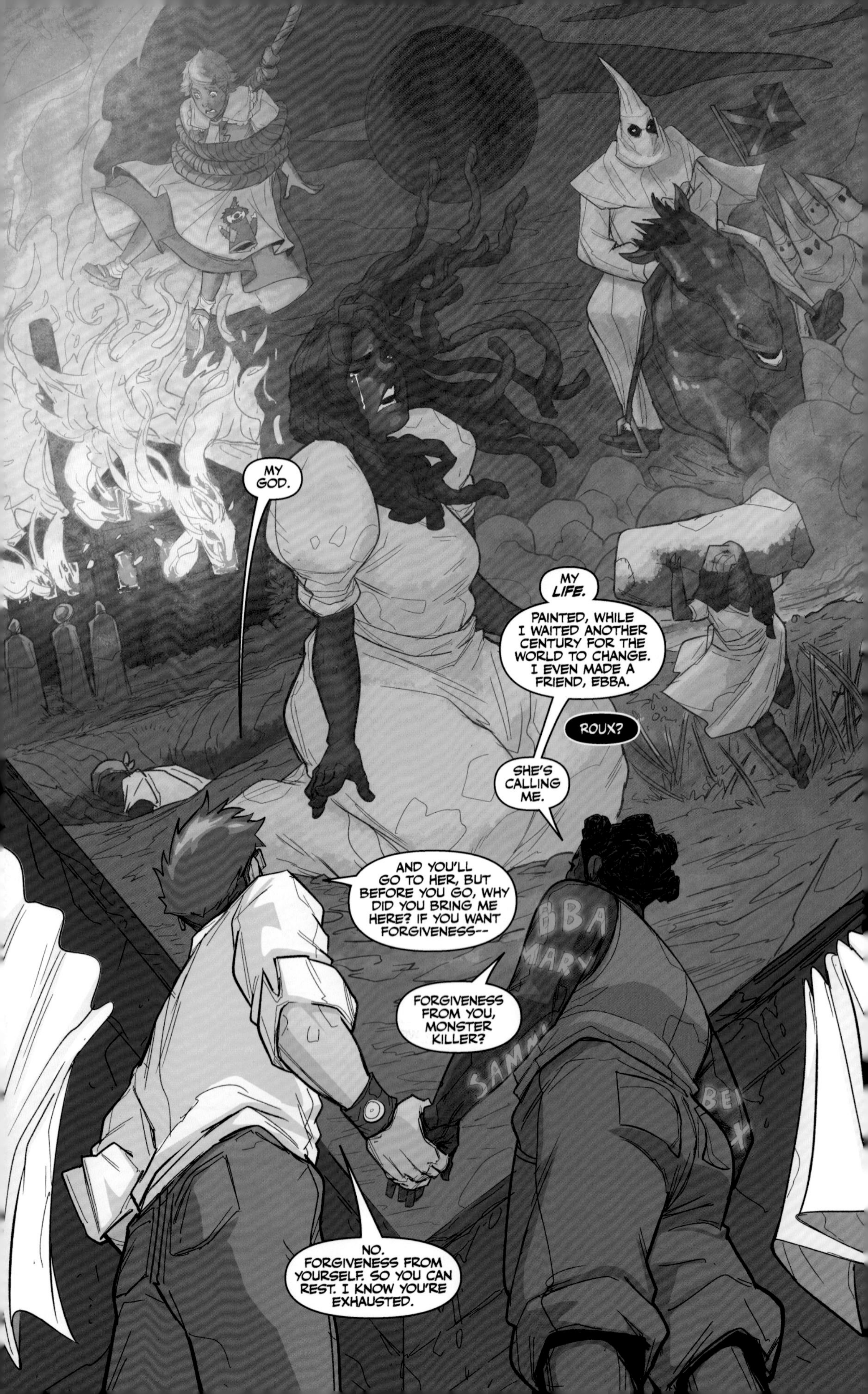
MY GOD.
MY ***LIFE.***
PAINTED, WHILE I WAITED ANOTHER CENTURY FOR THE WORLD TO CHANGE. I EVEN MADE A FRIEND, EBBA.
ROUX?
SHE'S CALLING ME.
AND YOU'LL GO TO HER, BUT BEFORE YOU GO, WHY DID YOU BRING ME HERE? IF YOU WANT FORGIVENESS--
FORGIVENESS FROM YOU, MONSTER KILLER?
NO. FORGIVENESS FROM YOURSELF. SO YOU CAN REST. I KNOW YOU'RE EXHAUSTED.

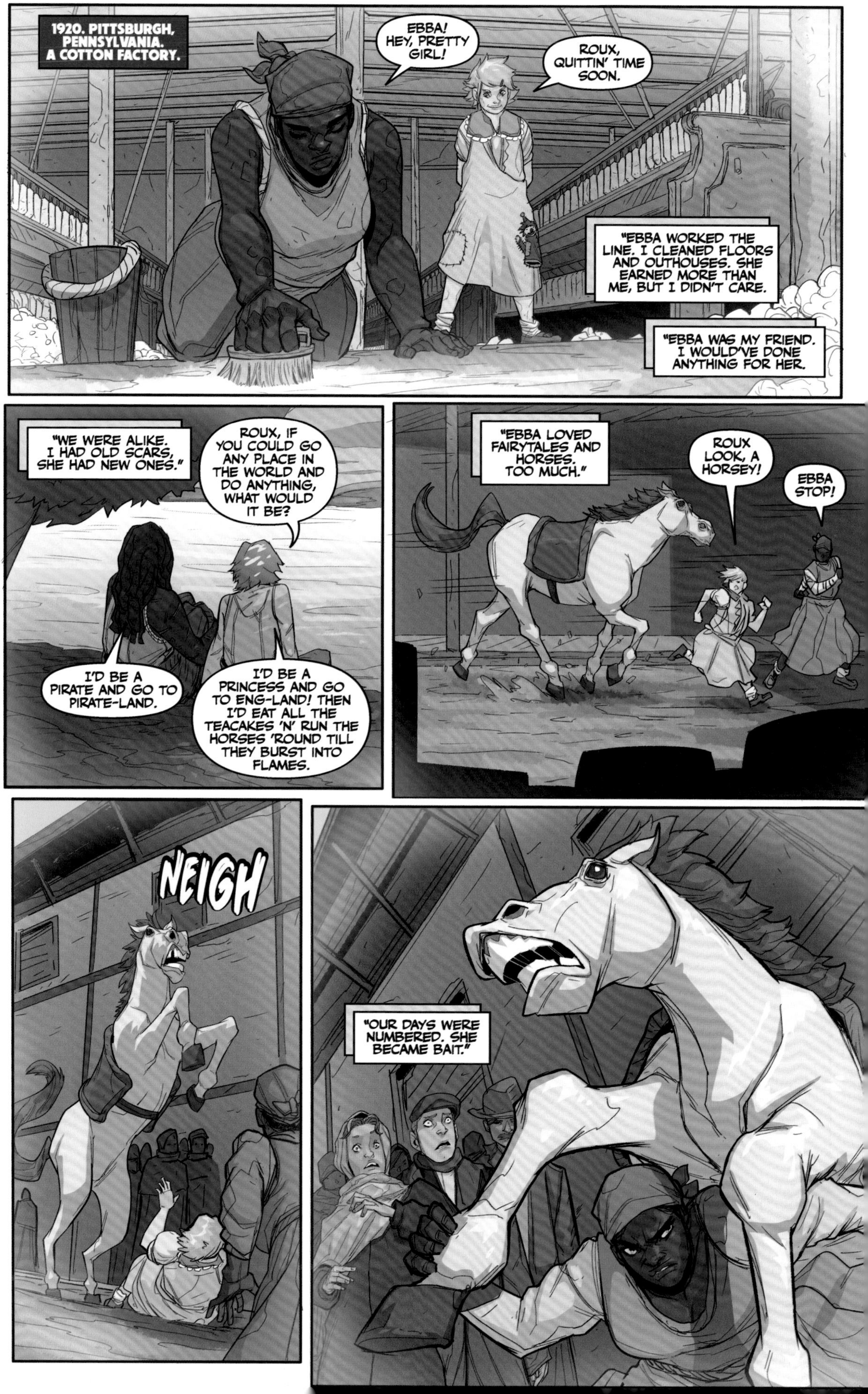
1920. PITTSBURGH, PENNSYLVANIA. A COTTON FACTORY.
EBBA! HEY, PRETTY GIRL!
ROUX, QUITTIN' TIME SOON.
"EBBA WORKED THE LINE. I CLEANED FLOORS AND OUTHOUSES. SHE EARNED MORE THAN ME, BUT I DIDN'T CARE.
"EBBA WAS MY FRIEND. I WOULD'VE DONE ANYTHING FOR HER.
"WE WERE ALIKE. I HAD OLD SCARS, SHE HAD NEW ONES."
ROUX, IF YOU COULD GO ANY PLACE IN THE WORLD AND DO ANYTHING, WHAT WOULD IT BE?
I'D BE A PIRATE AND GO TO PIRATE-LAND.
I'D BE A PRINCESS AND GO TO ENG-LAND! THEN I'D EAT ALL THE TEACAKES 'N' RUN THE HORSES 'ROUND TILL THEY BURST INTO FLAMES.
"EBBA LOVED FAIRYTALES AND HORSES. TOO MUCH."
ROUX LOOK, A HORSEY!
EBBA STOP!
NEIGH
"OUR DAYS WERE NUMBERED. SHE BECAME BAIT."

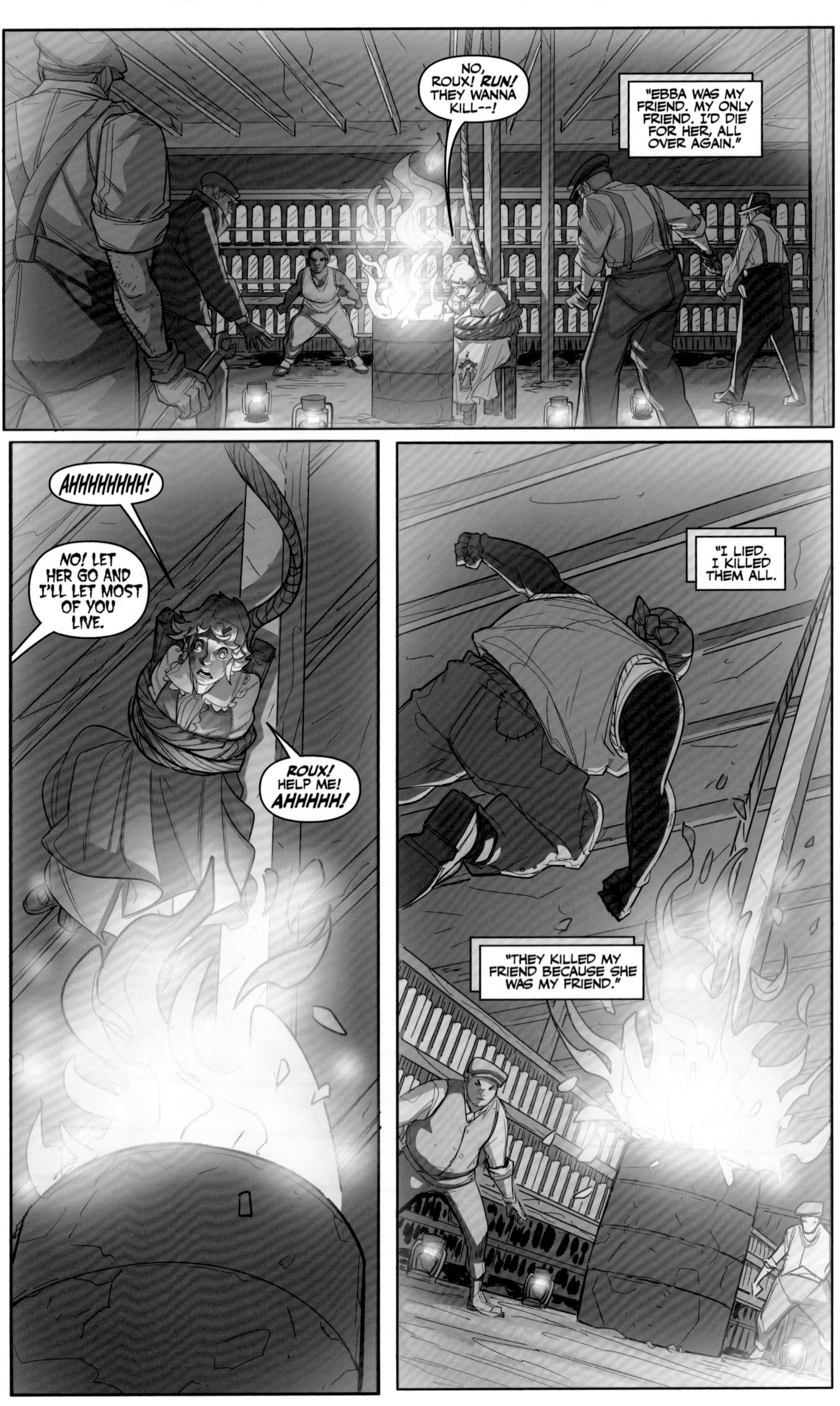
NO, ROUX! RUN! THEY WANNA KILL--!
"EBBA WAS MY FRIEND. MY ONLY FRIEND. I'D DIE FOR HER, ALL OVER AGAIN."
AHHHHHHHH!
NO! LET HER GO AND I'LL LET MOST OF YOU LIVE.
ROUX! HELP ME! AHHHHH!
"I LIED. I KILLED THEM ALL.
"THEY KILLED MY FRIEND BECAUSE SHE WAS MY FRIEND."

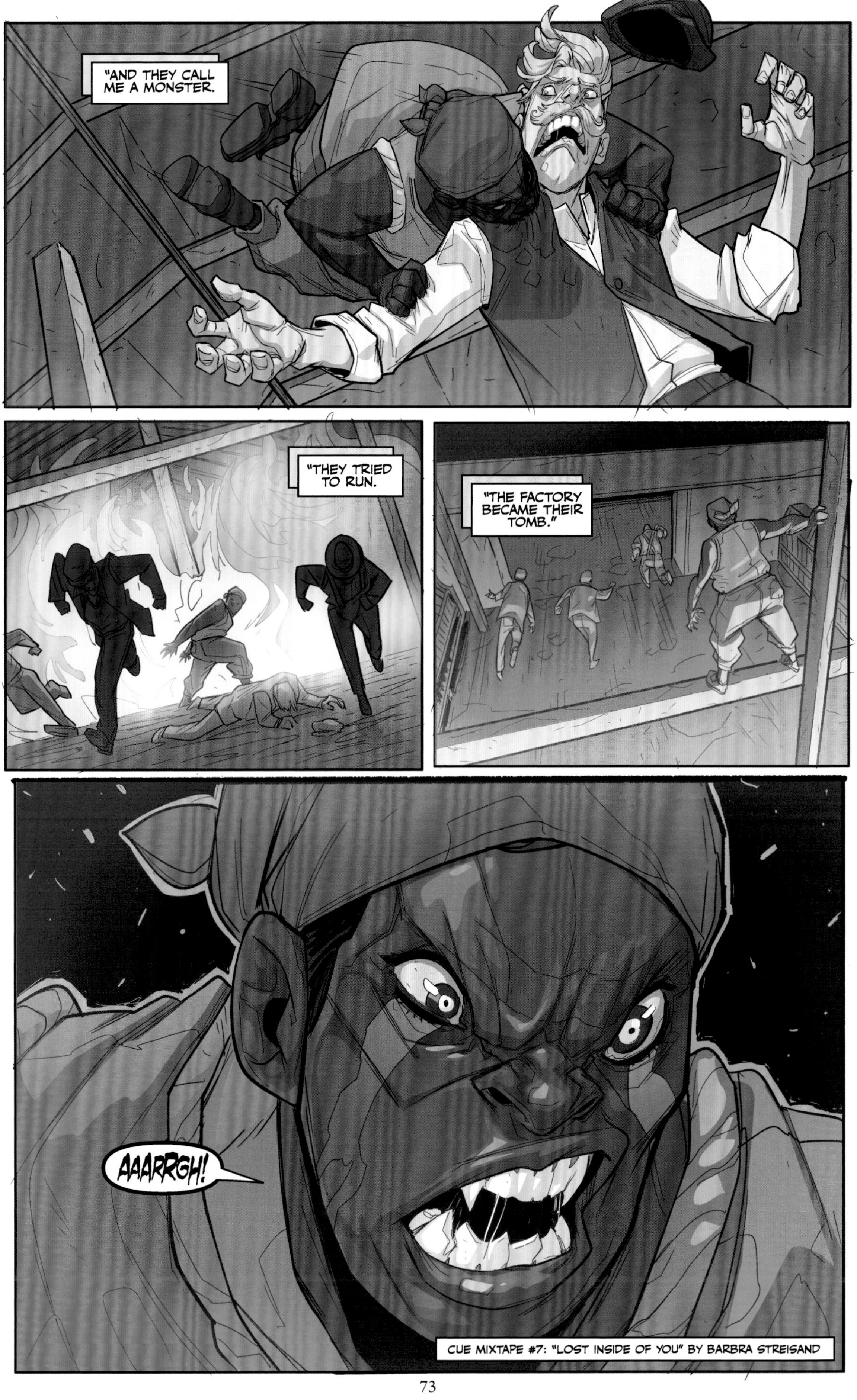
"AND THEY CALL ME A MONSTER.
"THEY TRIED TO RUN.
"THE FACTORY BECAME THEIR TOMB."
AAARRGH!
CUE MIXTAPE #7: "LOST INSIDE OF YOU" BY BARBRA STREISAND

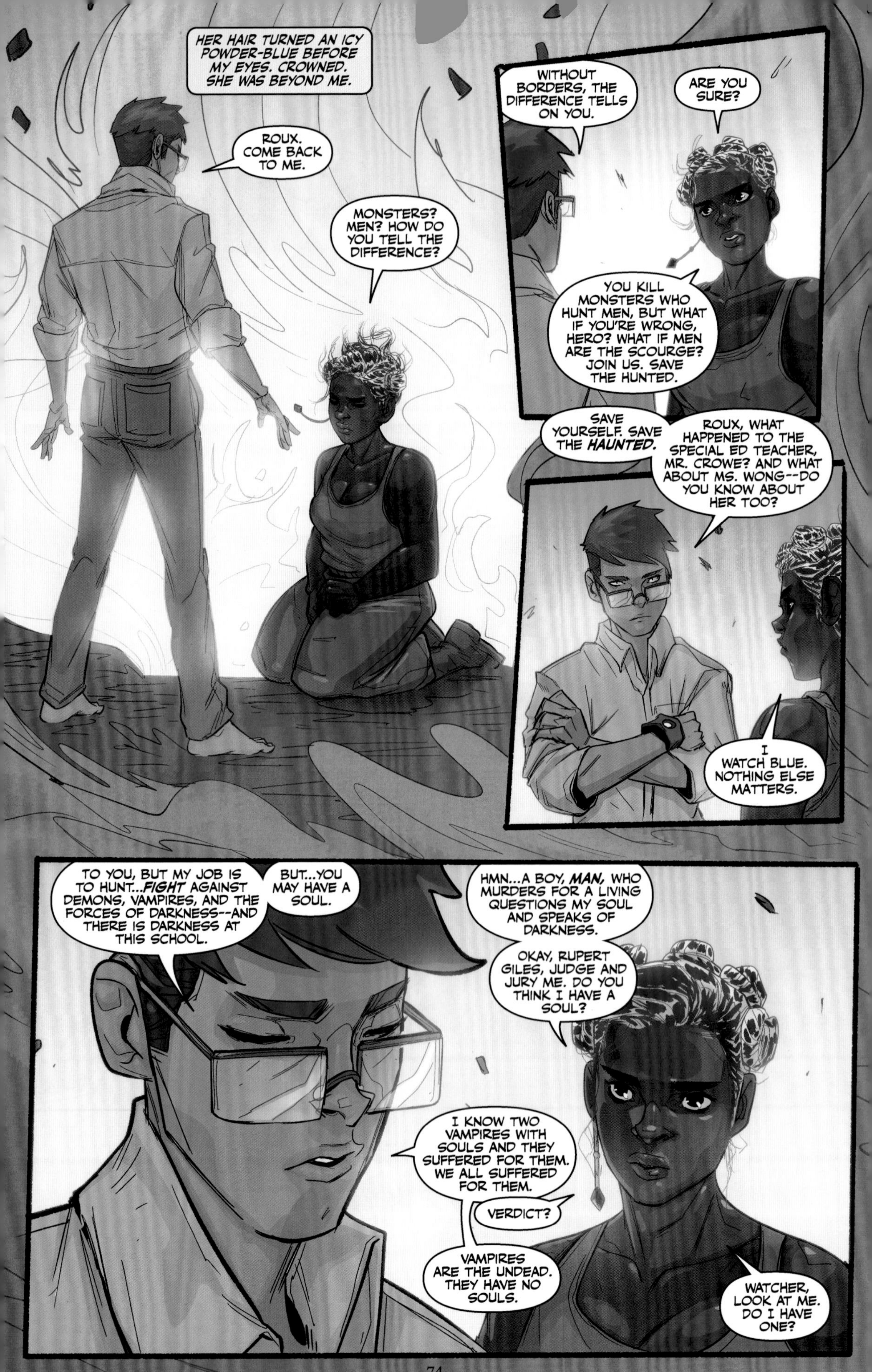
HER HAIR TURNED AN ICY POWDER-BLUE BEFORE MY EYES. CROWNED. SHE WAS BEYOND ME.
ROUX. COME BACK TO ME.
MONSTERS? MEN? HOW DO YOU TELL THE DIFFERENCE?
WITHOUT BORDERS, THE DIFFERENCE TELLS ON YOU.
ARE YOU SURE?
YOU KILL MONSTERS WHO HUNT MEN, BUT WHAT IF YOU'RE WRONG, HERO? WHAT IF MEN ARE THE SCOURGE? JOIN US. SAVE THE HUNTED.
SAVE YOURSELF. SAVE THE *HAUNTED.*
ROUX, WHAT HAPPENED TO THE SPECIAL ED TEACHER, MR. CROWE? AND WHAT ABOUT MS. WONG--DO YOU KNOW ABOUT HER TOO?
I WATCH BLUE. NOTHING ELSE MATTERS.
TO YOU, BUT MY JOB IS TO HUNT...*FIGHT* AGAINST DEMONS, VAMPIRES, AND THE FORCES OF DARKNESS--AND THERE IS DARKNESS AT THIS SCHOOL.
BUT...YOU MAY HAVE A SOUL.
HMN...A BOY, ***MAN,*** WHO MURDERS FOR A LIVING QUESTIONS MY SOUL AND SPEAKS OF DARKNESS.
OKAY, RUPERT GILES, JUDGE AND JURY ME. DO YOU THINK I HAVE A SOUL?
I KNOW TWO VAMPIRES WITH SOULS AND THEY SUFFERED FOR THEM. WE ALL SUFFERED FOR THEM.
VERDICT?
VAMPIRES ARE THE UNDEAD. THEY HAVE NO SOULS.
WATCHER, LOOK AT ME. DO I HAVE ONE?

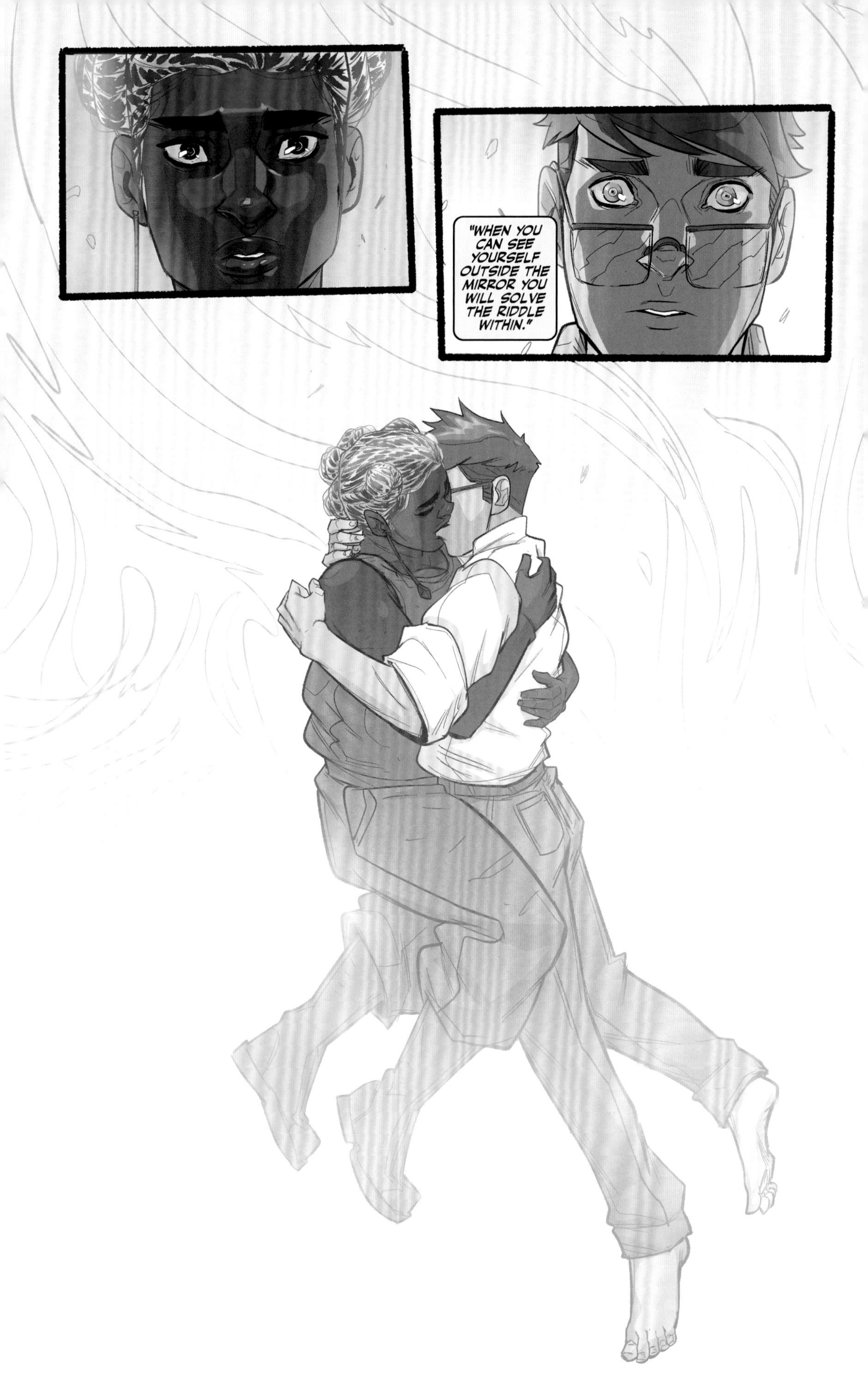
"WHEN YOU CAN SEE YOURSELF OUTSIDE THE MIRROR YOU WILL SOLVE THE RIDDLE WITHIN."

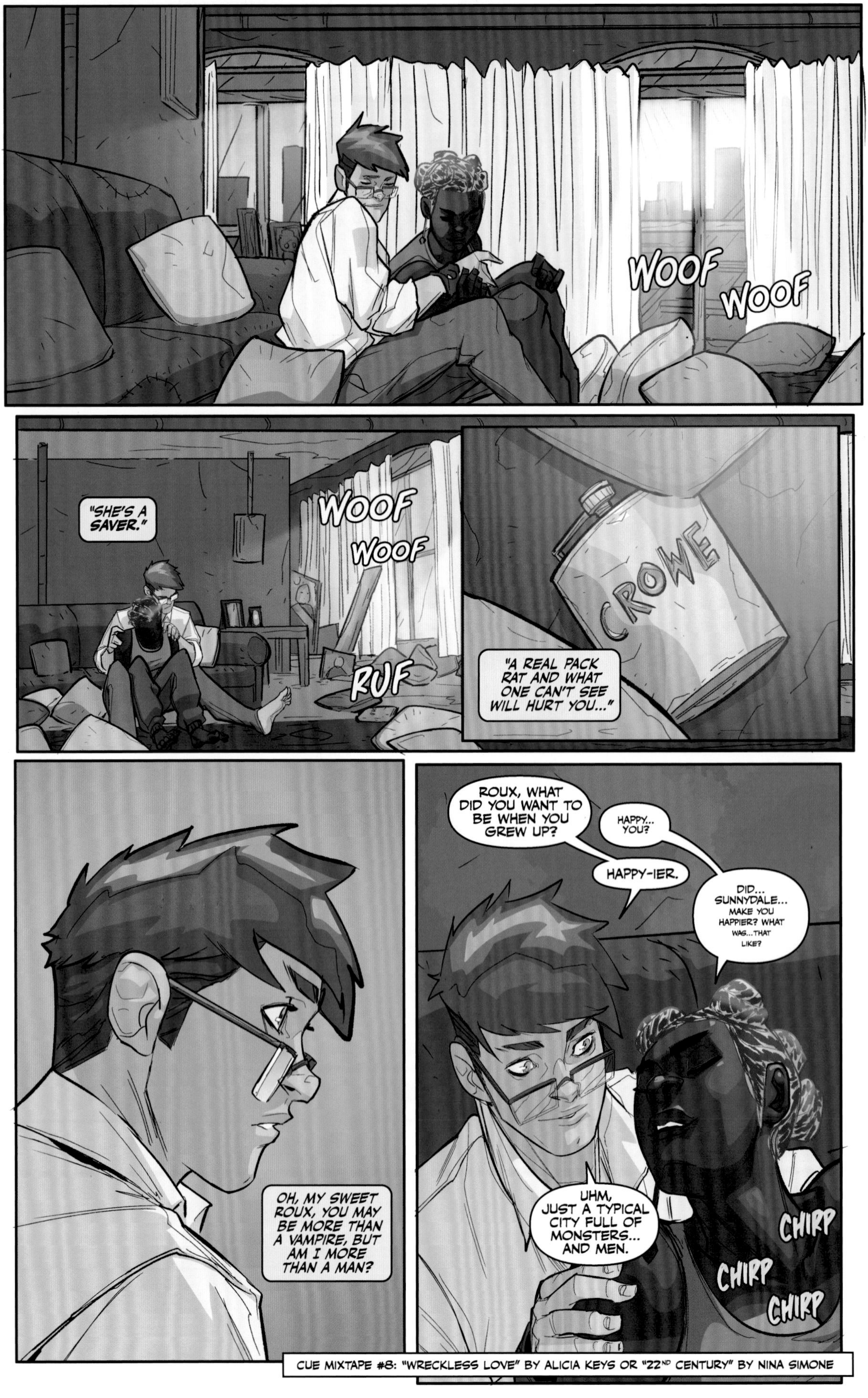

WOOF
WOOF
"SHE'S A SAVER."
WOOF
WOOF
RUF
CROWE
"A REAL PACK RAT AND WHAT ONE CAN'T SEE WILL HURT YOU..."
OH, MY SWEET ROUX, YOU MAY BE MORE THAN A VAMPIRE, BUT AM I MORE THAN A MAN?
ROUX, WHAT DID YOU WANT TO BE WHEN YOU GREW UP?
HAPPY... YOU?
HAPPY-IER.
DID... SUNNYDALE... MAKE YOU HAPPIER? WHAT WAS...THAT LIKE?
UHM, JUST A TYPICAL CITY FULL OF MONSTERS... AND MEN.
CHIRP
CHIRP
CHIRP
CUE MIXTAPE #8: "WRECKLESS LOVE" BY ALICIA KEYS OR "22ND CENTURY" BY NINA SIMONE

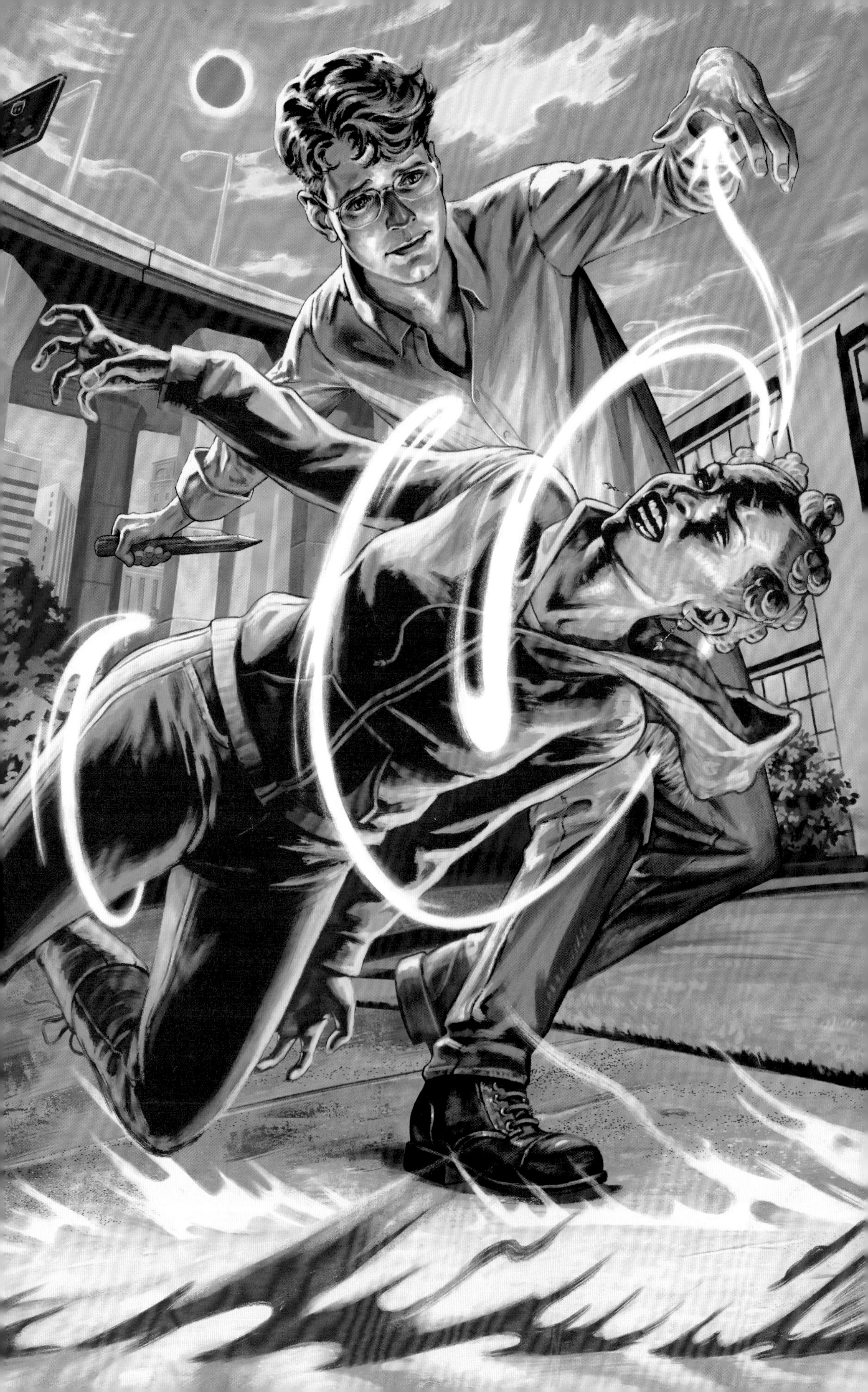

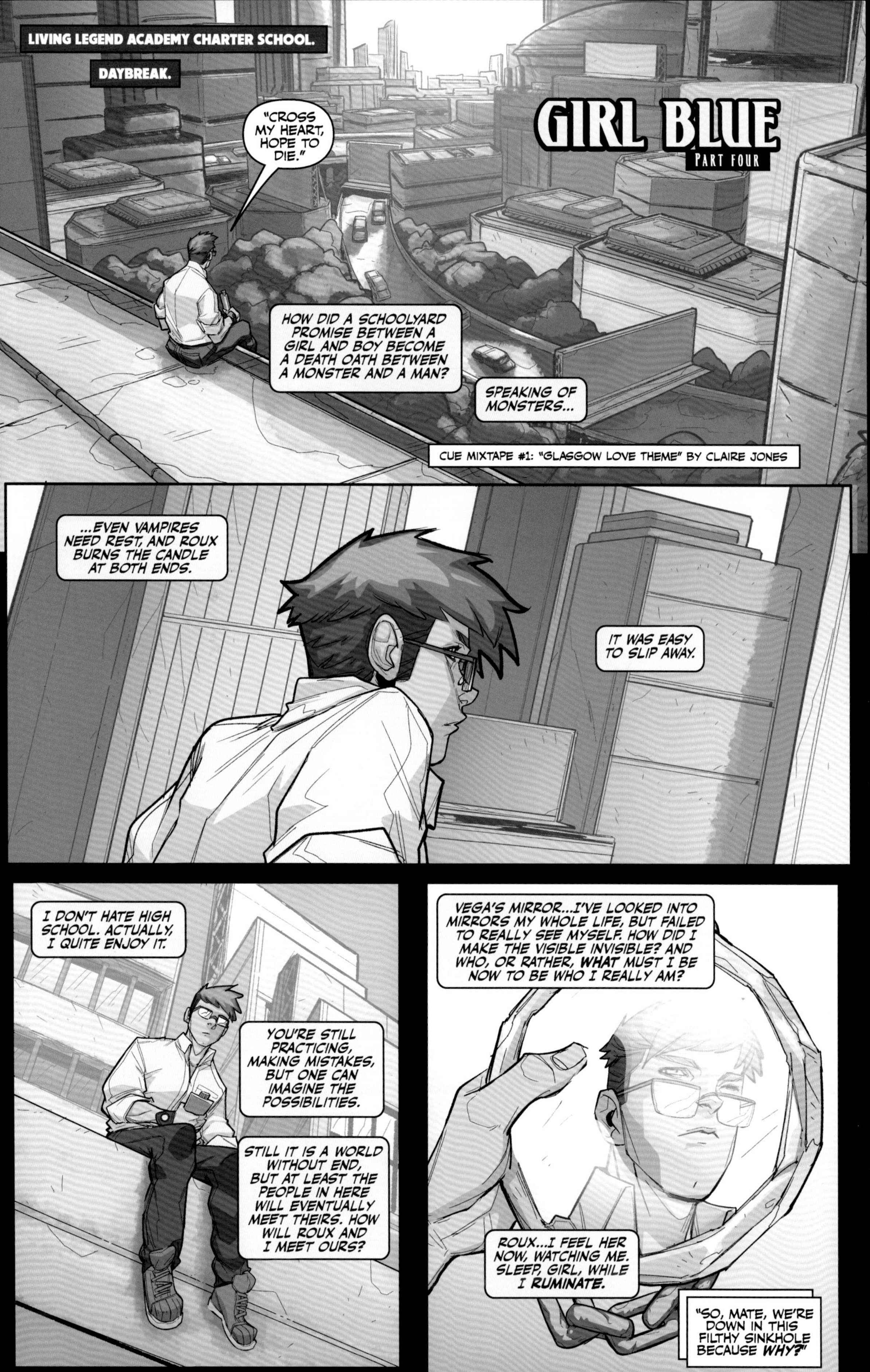

LIVING LEGEND ACADEMY CHARTER SCHOOL.
DAYBREAK.
"CROSS MY HEART, HOPE TO DIE."
GIRL BLUE
PART FOUR
HOW DID A SCHOOLYARD PROMISE BETWEEN A GIRL AND BOY BECOME A DEATH OATH BETWEEN A MONSTER AND A MAN?
SPEAKING OF MONSTERS...
CUE MIXTAPE #1: "GLASGOW LOVE THEME" BY CLAIRE JONES
...EVEN VAMPIRES NEED REST, AND ROUX BURNS THE CANDLE AT BOTH ENDS.
IT WAS EASY TO SLIP AWAY.
I DON'T HATE HIGH SCHOOL. ACTUALLY, I QUITE ENJOY IT.
YOU'RE STILL PRACTICING, MAKING MISTAKES, BUT ONE CAN IMAGINE THE POSSIBILITIES.
STILL IT IS A WORLD WITHOUT END, BUT AT LEAST THE PEOPLE IN HERE WILL EVENTUALLY MEET THEIRS. HOW WILL ROUX AND I MEET OURS?
VEGA'S MIRROR...I'VE LOOKED INTO MIRRORS MY WHOLE LIFE, BUT FAILED TO REALLY SEE MYSELF. HOW DID I MAKE THE VISIBLE INVISIBLE? AND WHO, OR RATHER, WHAT MUST I BE NOW TO BE WHO I REALLY AM?
ROUX...I FEEL HER NOW, WATCHING ME. SLEEP, GIRL, WHILE I RUMINATE.
"SO, MATE, WE'RE DOWN IN THIS FILTHY SINKHOLE BECAUSE WHY?"

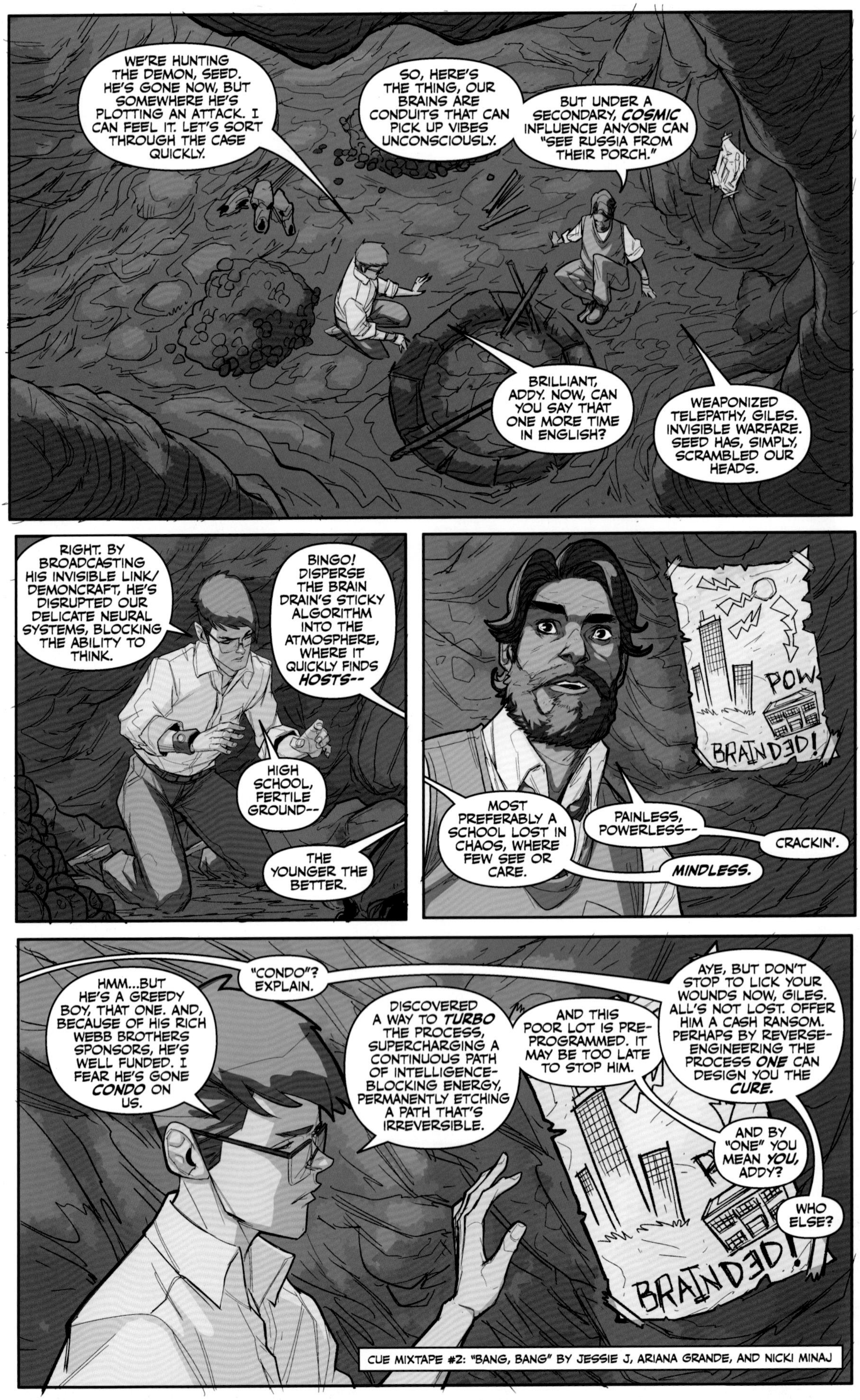
WE'RE HUNTING THE DEMON, SEED. HE'S GONE NOW, BUT SOMEWHERE HE'S PLOTTING AN ATTACK. I CAN FEEL IT. LET'S SORT THROUGH THE CASE QUICKLY.
SO, HERE'S THE THING, OUR BRAINS ARE CONDUITS THAT CAN PICK UP VIBES UNCONSCIOUSLY.
BUT UNDER A SECONDARY, COSMIC INFLUENCE ANYONE CAN "SEE RUSSIA FROM THEIR PORCH."
BRILLIANT, ADDY. NOW, CAN YOU SAY THAT ONE MORE TIME IN ENGLISH?
WEAPONIZED TELEPATHY, GILES. INVISIBLE WARFARE. SEED HAS, SIMPLY, SCRAMBLED OUR HEADS.
RIGHT. BY BROADCASTING HIS INVISIBLE LINK/ DEMONCRAFT, HE'S DISRUPTED OUR DELICATE NEURAL SYSTEMS, BLOCKING THE ABILITY TO THINK.
BINGO! DISPERSE THE BRAIN DRAIN'S STICKY ALGORITHM INTO THE ATMOSPHERE, WHERE IT QUICKLY FINDS HOSTS--
HIGH SCHOOL, FERTILE GROUND--
THE YOUNGER THE BETTER.
POW
BRAINDED!
MOST PREFERABLY A SCHOOL LOST IN CHAOS, WHERE FEW SEE OR CARE.
PAINLESS, POWERLESS--
CRACKIN'.
MINDLESS.
HMM...BUT HE'S A GREEDY BOY, THAT ONE. AND, BECAUSE OF HIS RICH WEBB BROTHERS SPONSORS, HE'S WELL FUNDED. I FEAR HE'S GONE CONDO ON US.
"CONDO"? EXPLAIN.
DISCOVERED A WAY TO TURBO THE PROCESS, SUPERCHARGING A CONTINUOUS PATH OF INTELLIGENCE-BLOCKING ENERGY, PERMANENTLY ETCHING A PATH THAT'S IRREVERSIBLE.
AND THIS POOR LOT IS PRE-PROGRAMMED. IT MAY BE TOO LATE TO STOP HIM.
AYE, BUT DON'T STOP TO LICK YOUR WOUNDS NOW, GILES. ALL'S NOT LOST. OFFER HIM A CASH RANSOM. PERHAPS BY REVERSE-ENGINEERING THE PROCESS ONE CAN DESIGN YOU THE CURE.
AND BY "ONE" YOU MEAN YOU, ADDY?
WHO ELSE?
BRAINDED!
CUE MIXTAPE #2: "BANG, BANG" BY JESSIE J, ARIANA GRANDE, AND NICKI MINAJ

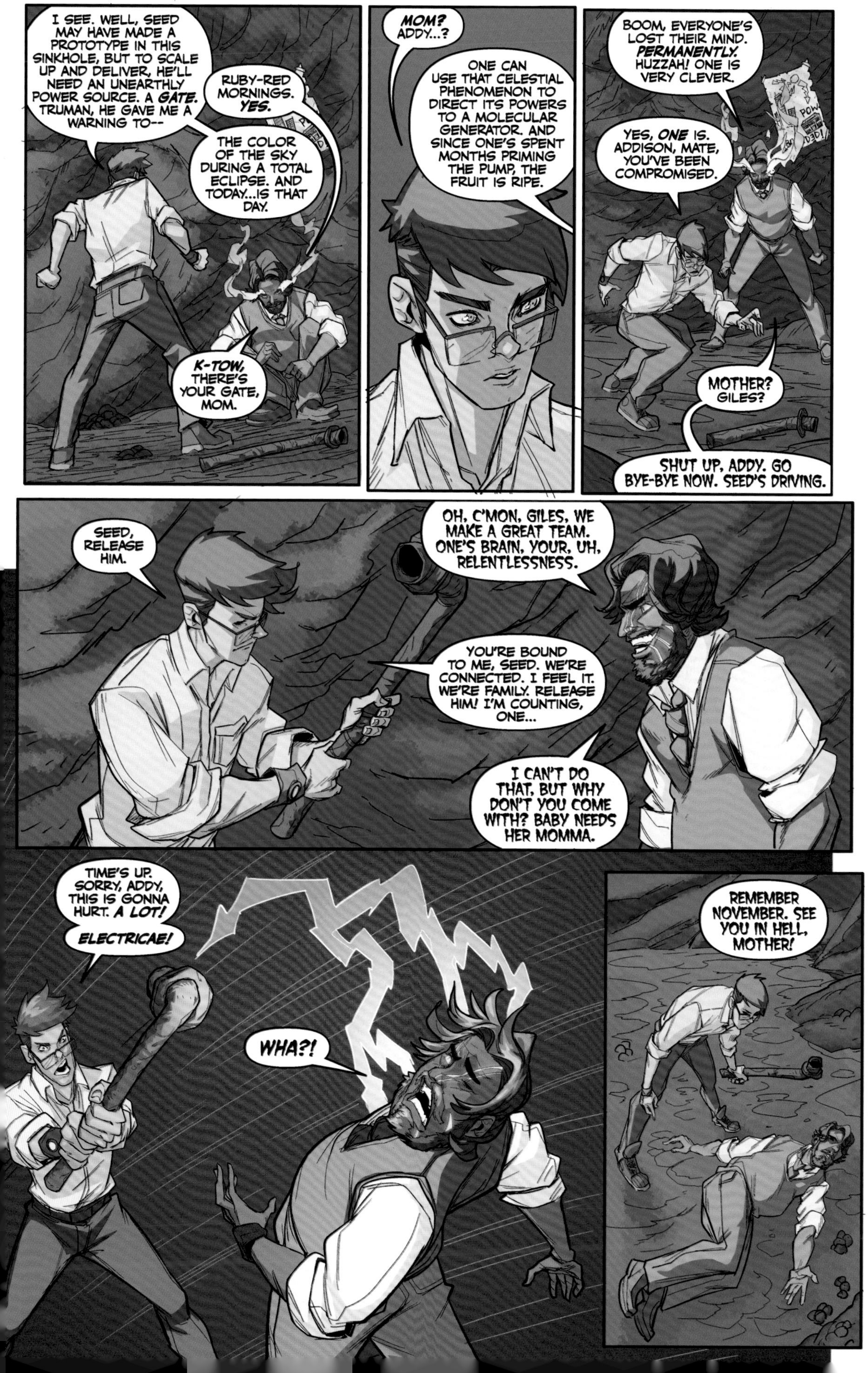

I SEE. WELL, SEED MAY HAVE MADE A PROTOTYPE IN THIS SINKHOLE, BUT TO SCALE UP AND DELIVER, HE'LL NEED AN UNEARTHLY POWER SOURCE. A GATE. TRUMAN, HE GAVE ME A WARNING TO--
RUBY-RED MORNINGS. YES.
THE COLOR OF THE SKY DURING A TOTAL ECLIPSE. AND TODAY...IS THAT DAY.
K-TOW, THERE'S YOUR GATE, MOM.
MOM? ADDY...?
ONE CAN USE THAT CELESTIAL PHENOMENON TO DIRECT ITS POWERS TO A MOLECULAR GENERATOR. AND SINCE ONE'S SPENT MONTHS PRIMING THE PUMP, THE FRUIT IS RIPE.
BOOM, EVERYONE'S LOST THEIR MIND. PERMANENTLY. HUZZAH! ONE IS VERY CLEVER.
YES, ONE IS. ADDISON, MATE, YOU'VE BEEN COMPROMISED.
MOTHER? GILES?
SHUT UP, ADDY. GO BYE-BYE NOW. SEED'S DRIVING.
SEED, RELEASE HIM.
OH, C'MON, GILES, WE MAKE A GREAT TEAM. ONE'S BRAIN, YOUR, UH, RELENTLESSNESS.
YOU'RE BOUND TO ME, SEED. WE'RE CONNECTED. I FEEL IT. WE'RE FAMILY. RELEASE HIM! I'M COUNTING, ONE...
I CAN'T DO THAT, BUT WHY DON'T YOU COME WITH? BABY NEEDS HER MOMMA.
TIME'S UP. SORRY, ADDY, THIS IS GONNA HURT. A LOT!
ELECTRICAE!
WHA?!
REMEMBER NOVEMBER. SEE YOU IN HELL, MOTHER!

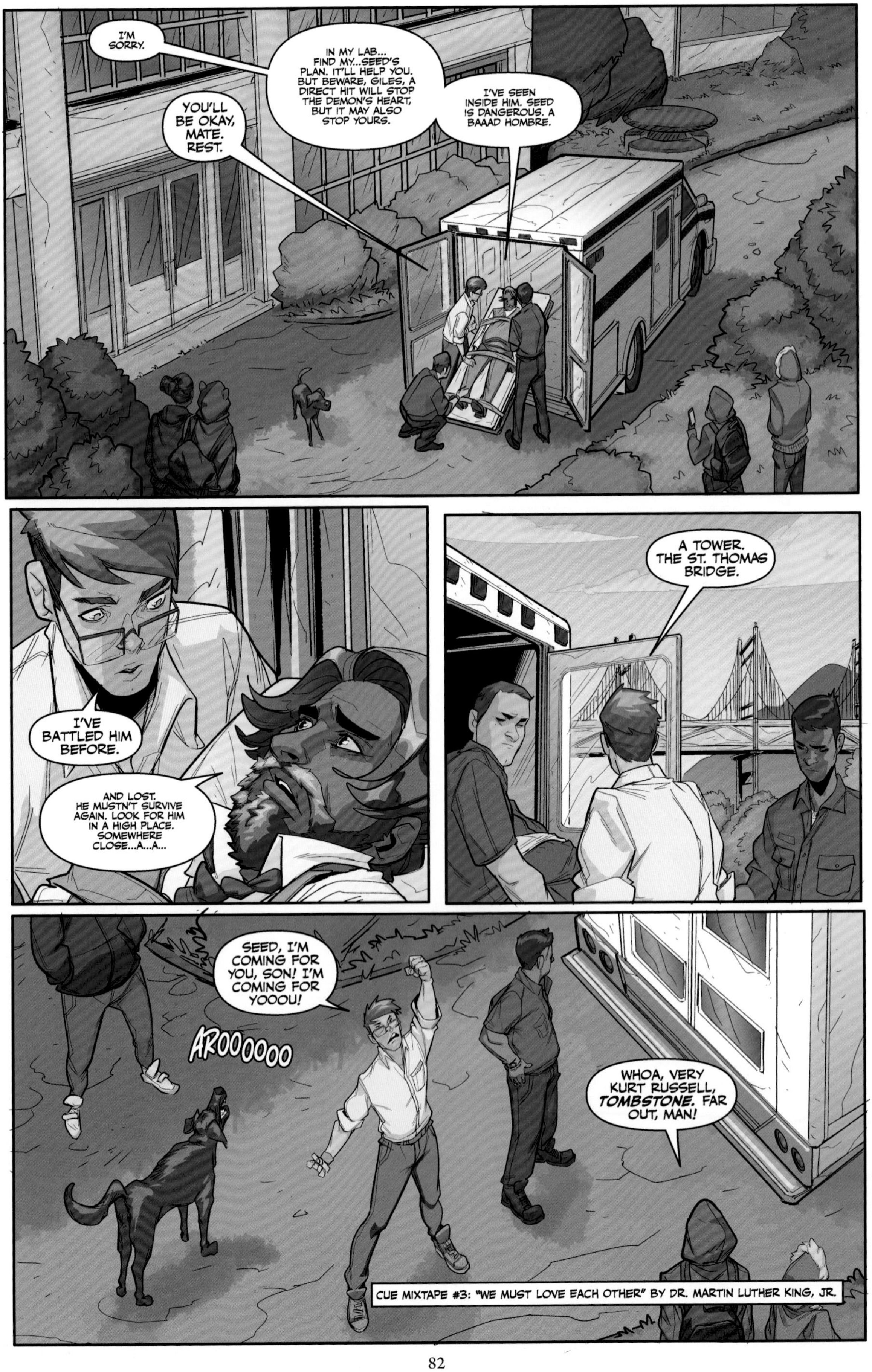
I'M SORRY.
IN MY LAB... FIND MY...SEED'S PLAN. IT'LL HELP YOU. BUT BEWARE, GILES, A DIRECT HIT WILL STOP THE DEMON'S HEART, BUT IT MAY ALSO STOP YOURS.
YOU'LL BE OKAY, MATE. REST.
I'VE SEEN INSIDE HIM. SEED IS DANGEROUS. A BAAAD HOMBRE.
I'VE BATTLED HIM BEFORE.
AND LOST. HE MUSTN'T SURVIVE AGAIN. LOOK FOR HIM IN A HIGH PLACE. SOMEWHERE CLOSE...A...A...
A TOWER. THE ST. THOMAS BRIDGE.
SEED, I'M COMING FOR YOU, SON! I'M COMING FOR YOOOU!
AROOOOOO
WHOA, VERY KURT RUSSELL, TOMBSTONE. FAR OUT, MAN!
CUE MIXTAPE #3: "WE MUST LOVE EACH OTHER" BY DR. MARTIN LUTHER KING, JR.

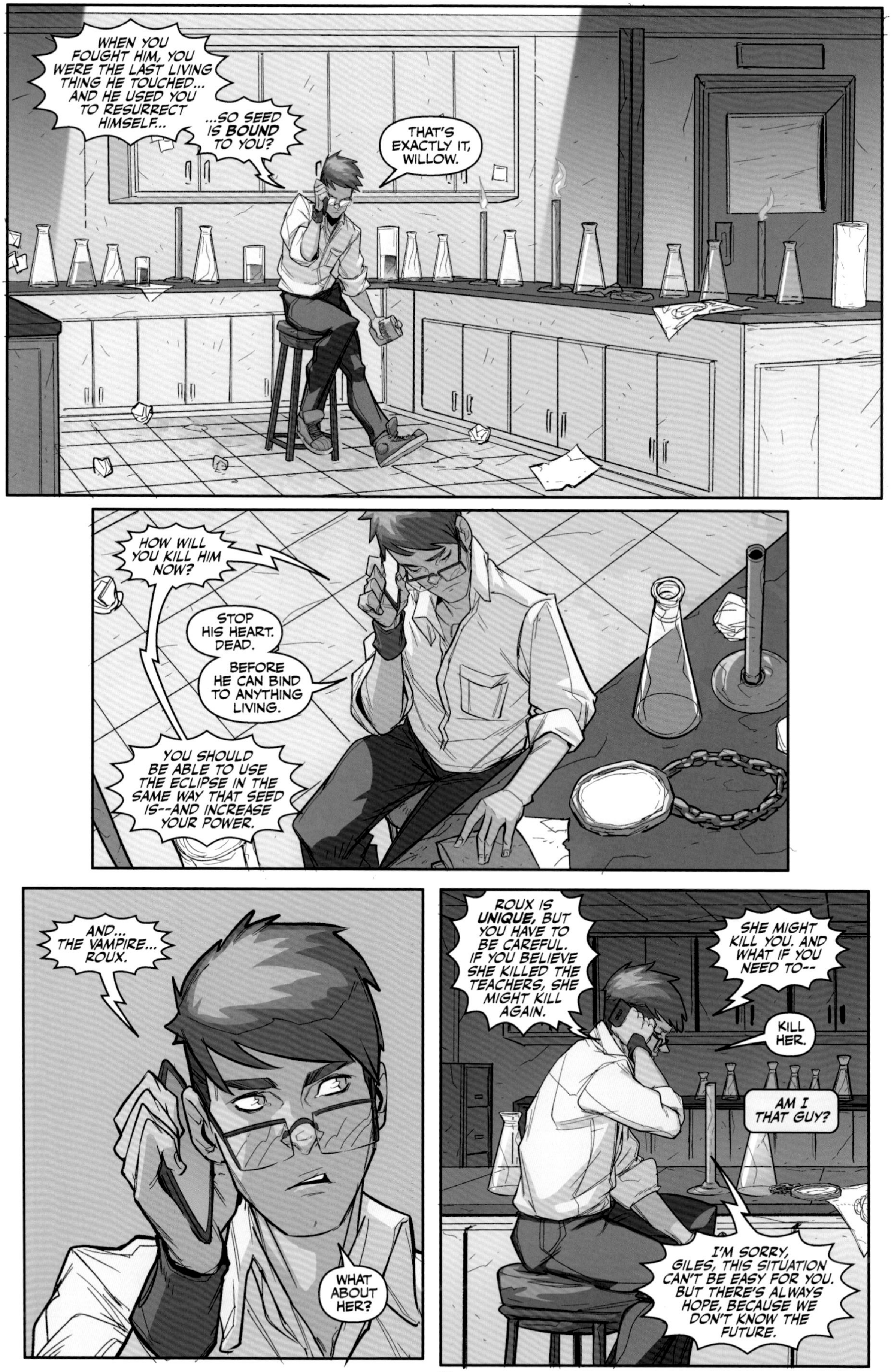
WHEN YOU FOUGHT HIM, YOU WERE THE LAST LIVING THING HE TOUCHED... AND HE USED YOU TO RESURRECT HIMSELF...
...SO SEED IS BOUND TO YOU?
THAT'S EXACTLY IT, WILLOW.
HOW WILL YOU KILL HIM NOW?
STOP HIS HEART. DEAD.
BEFORE HE CAN BIND TO ANYTHING LIVING.
YOU SHOULD BE ABLE TO USE THE ECLIPSE IN THE SAME WAY THAT SEED IS--AND INCREASE YOUR POWER.
AND... THE VAMPIRE... ROUX.
WHAT ABOUT HER?
ROUX IS UNIQUE, BUT YOU HAVE TO BE CAREFUL. IF YOU BELIEVE SHE KILLED THE TEACHERS, SHE MIGHT KILL AGAIN.
SHE MIGHT KILL YOU. AND WHAT IF YOU NEED TO--
KILL HER.
AM I THAT GUY?
I'M SORRY, GILES, THIS SITUATION CAN'T BE EASY FOR YOU. BUT THERE'S ALWAYS HOPE, BECAUSE WE DON'T KNOW THE FUTURE.

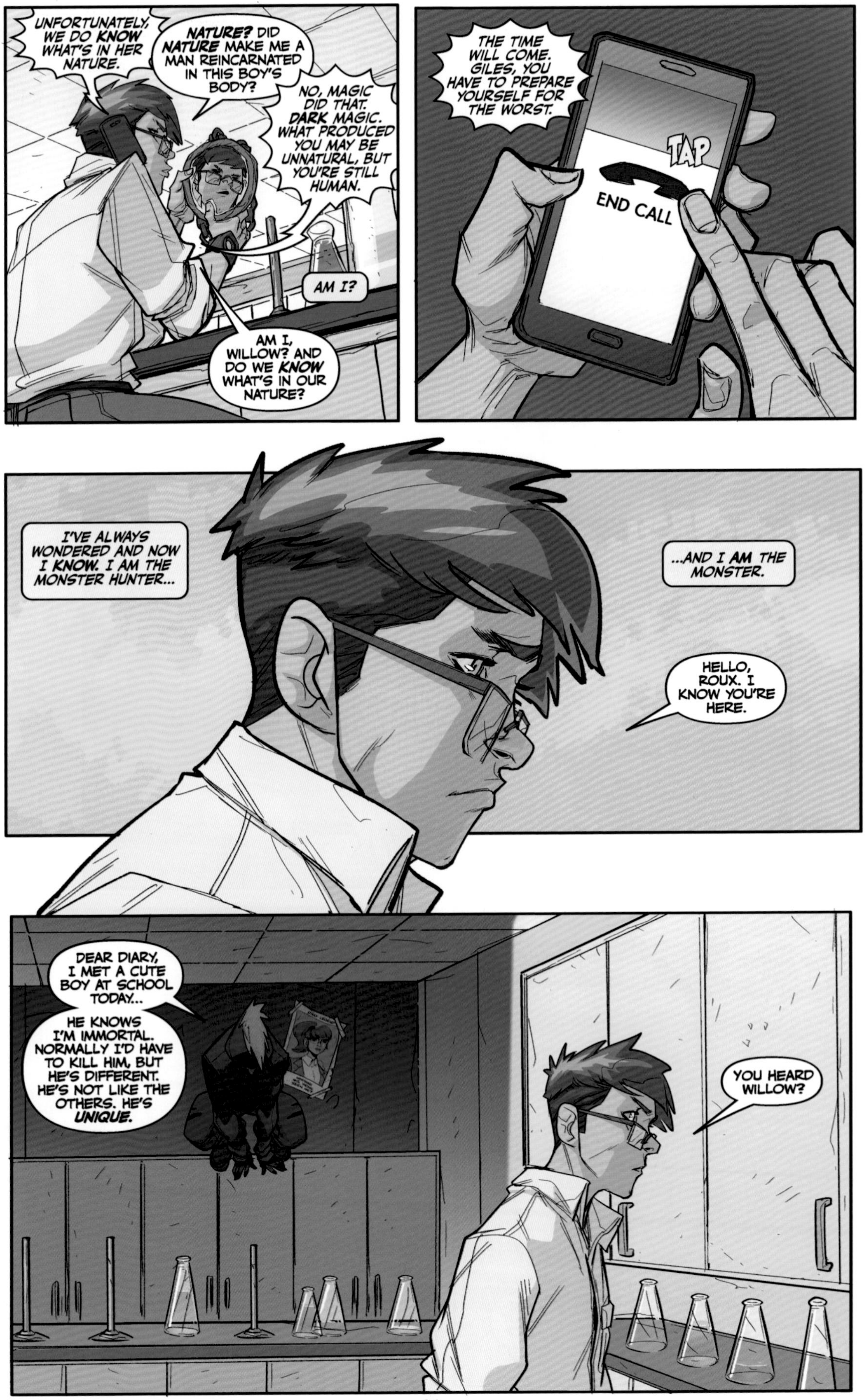
UNFORTUNATELY, WE DO KNOW WHAT'S IN HER NATURE.
NATURE? DID NATURE MAKE ME A MAN REINCARNATED IN THIS BOY'S BODY?
NO, MAGIC DID THAT. DARK MAGIC. WHAT PRODUCED YOU MAY BE UNNATURAL, BUT YOU'RE STILL HUMAN.
AM I?
AM I, WILLOW? AND DO WE KNOW WHAT'S IN OUR NATURE?
THE TIME WILL COME. GILES, YOU HAVE TO PREPARE YOURSELF FOR THE WORST.
TAP
END CALL
I'VE ALWAYS WONDERED AND NOW I KNOW. I AM THE MONSTER HUNTER...
...AND I AM THE MONSTER.
HELLO, ROUX. I KNOW YOU'RE HERE.
DEAR DIARY, I MET A CUTE BOY AT SCHOOL TODAY...
HE KNOWS I'M IMMORTAL. NORMALLY I'D HAVE TO KILL HIM, BUT HE'S DIFFERENT. HE'S NOT LIKE THE OTHERS. HE'S UNIQUE.
YOU HEARD WILLOW?

I HEARD *YOU*. ECLIPSE; KILL DEMON; KILL ROUX...

YOU THINK I SHOULD?

KILL ME? I'M DEAD ALREADY. NO MATTER WHAT YOU DO, I CAN'T COME OUT OF THIS ALIVE.

BUT HEADS UP, ROOKIE, I'M UNDEFEATED IN DEATH. YOU SHOULD SAVE ALL YOUR STRENGTH FOR THE DEMON WHO CARRIES YOUR D.N.A.

WHY DID YOU DO IT? WHY DID YOU KILL CROWE?

I WAS HUNGRY. GILES, WHAT DO YOU THINK ABOUT MY NEW 'DO? BLUE SUITS ME--

ROUX...

CROWE WAS A MENACE TO *ALL* THE STUDENTS, BUT ESPECIALLY TO BLUE. HIS END WAS INEVITABLE.

"DETENTION. A SKETCHY HOUR IN A ROOM DESIGNED TO STEAL YOUR SOUL AND MAKE YOU SAY UNCLE.

"THAT DAY BLUE COULDN'T THINK. THE DUMB BOMB HAD TAKEN HOLD OF HER MIND.

NO WORK NO REWARD

"BLUE WAS CONFUSED. CROWE WAS FRUSTRATED. AND BANG.

"SHE SNAPPED."

CUE MIXTAPE #4: "DREAMS" BY GIRL BLUE

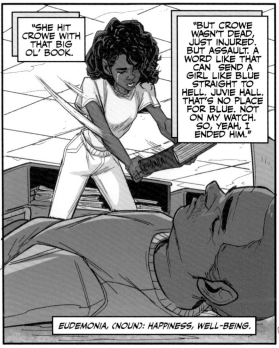

"SHE HIT CROWE WITH THAT BIG OL' BOOK.

"BUT CROWE WASN'T DEAD, JUST INJURED. BUT ASSAULT. A WORD LIKE THAT CAN SEND A GIRL LIKE BLUE STRAIGHT TO HELL. JUVIE HALL. THAT'S NO PLACE FOR BLUE. NOT ON MY WATCH. SO, YEAH, I ENDED HIM."

EUDEMONIA, (NOUN): HAPPINESS, WELL-BEING.

"I WAS THE CLEANUP CREW. I SAVED HER FROM A LIVING DEATH.

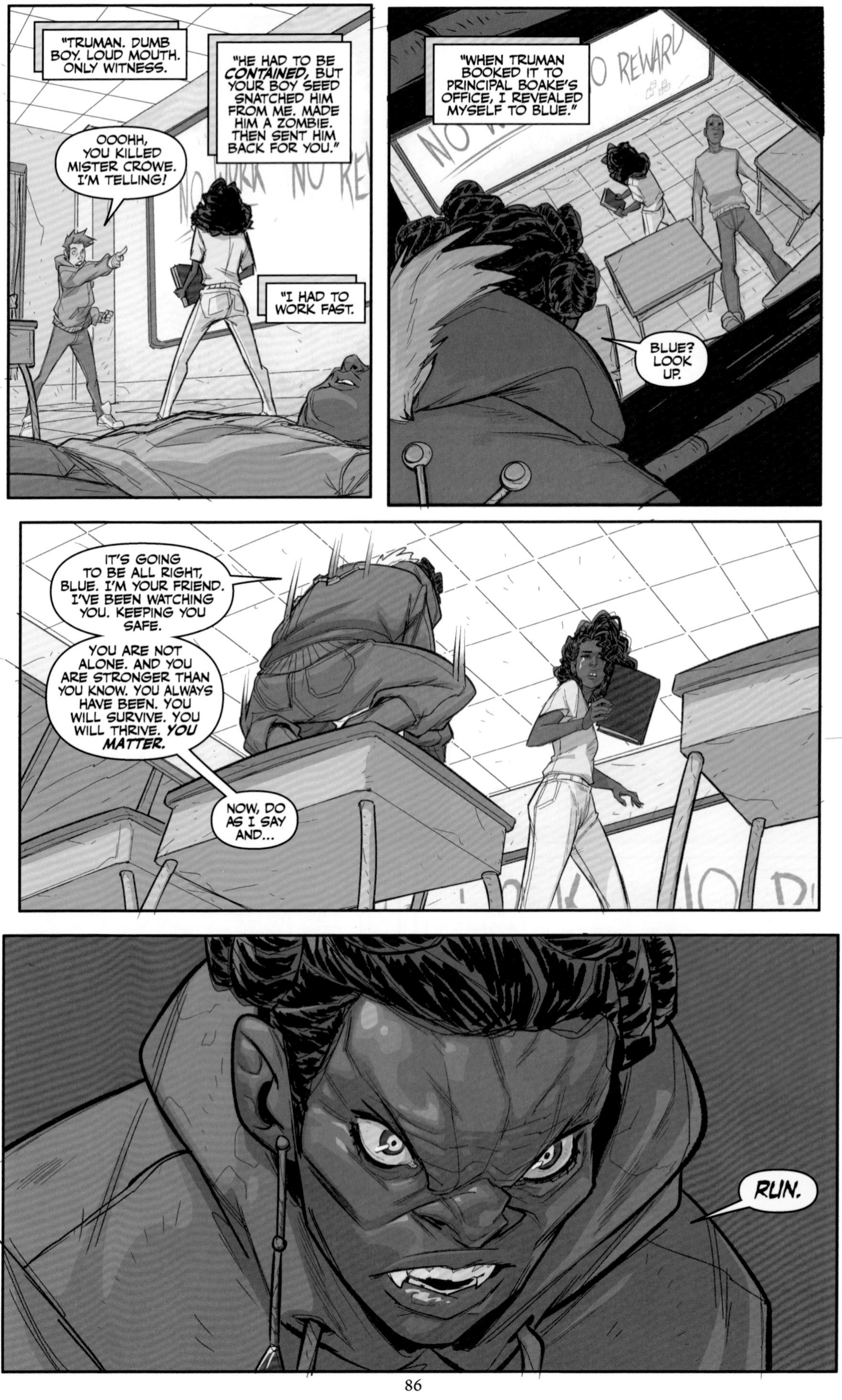
"TRUMAN. DUMB BOY. LOUD MOUTH. ONLY WITNESS.
OOOHH, YOU KILLED MISTER CROWE. I'M TELLING!
"HE HAD TO BE *CONTAINED,* BUT YOUR BOY SEED SNATCHED HIM FROM ME. MADE HIM A ZOMBIE. THEN SENT HIM BACK FOR YOU."
"I HAD TO WORK FAST.
"WHEN TRUMAN BOOKED IT TO PRINCIPAL BOAKE'S OFFICE, I REVEALED MYSELF TO BLUE."
NO WORK NO REWARD
BLUE? LOOK UP.
IT'S GOING TO BE ALL RIGHT, BLUE. I'M YOUR FRIEND. I'VE BEEN WATCHING YOU. KEEPING YOU SAFE.
YOU ARE NOT ALONE. AND YOU ARE STRONGER THAN YOU KNOW. YOU ALWAYS HAVE BEEN. YOU WILL SURVIVE. YOU WILL THRIVE. ***YOU MATTER.***
NOW, DO AS I SAY AND...
RUN.

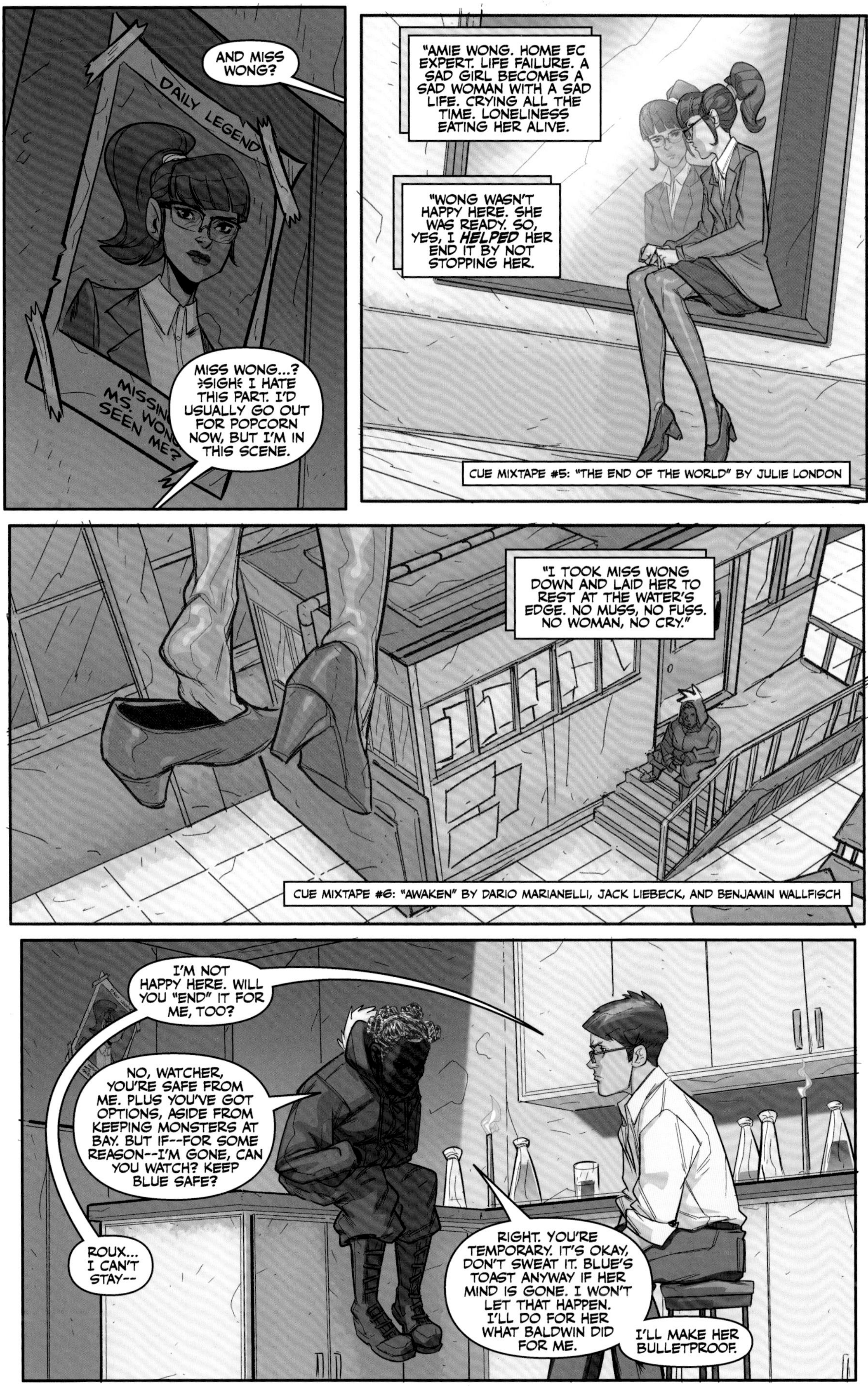
AND MISS WONG?
DAILY LEGEND
MISSIN
MS. WON
SEEN ME?
MISS WONG...? ≶SIGH≷ I HATE THIS PART. I'D USUALLY GO OUT FOR POPCORN NOW, BUT I'M IN THIS SCENE.
"AMIE WONG. HOME EC EXPERT. LIFE FAILURE. A SAD GIRL BECOMES A SAD WOMAN WITH A SAD LIFE. CRYING ALL THE TIME. LONELINESS EATING HER ALIVE.
"WONG WASN'T HAPPY HERE. SHE WAS READY. SO, YES, I *HELPED* HER END IT BY NOT STOPPING HER.
CUE MIXTAPE #5: "THE END OF THE WORLD" BY JULIE LONDON
"I TOOK MISS WONG DOWN AND LAID HER TO REST AT THE WATER'S EDGE. NO MUSS, NO FUSS. NO WOMAN, NO CRY."
CUE MIXTAPE #6: "AWAKEN" BY DARIO MARIANELLI, JACK LIEBECK, AND BENJAMIN WALLFISCH
I'M NOT HAPPY HERE. WILL YOU "END" IT FOR ME, TOO?
NO, WATCHER, YOU'RE SAFE FROM ME. PLUS YOU'VE GOT OPTIONS, ASIDE FROM KEEPING MONSTERS AT BAY. BUT IF--FOR SOME REASON--I'M GONE, CAN YOU WATCH? KEEP BLUE SAFE?
ROUX... I CAN'T STAY--
RIGHT. YOU'RE TEMPORARY. IT'S OKAY, DON'T SWEAT IT. BLUE'S TOAST ANYWAY IF HER MIND IS GONE. I WON'T LET THAT HAPPEN. I'LL DO FOR HER WHAT BALDWIN DID FOR ME.
I'LL MAKE HER BULLETPROOF.

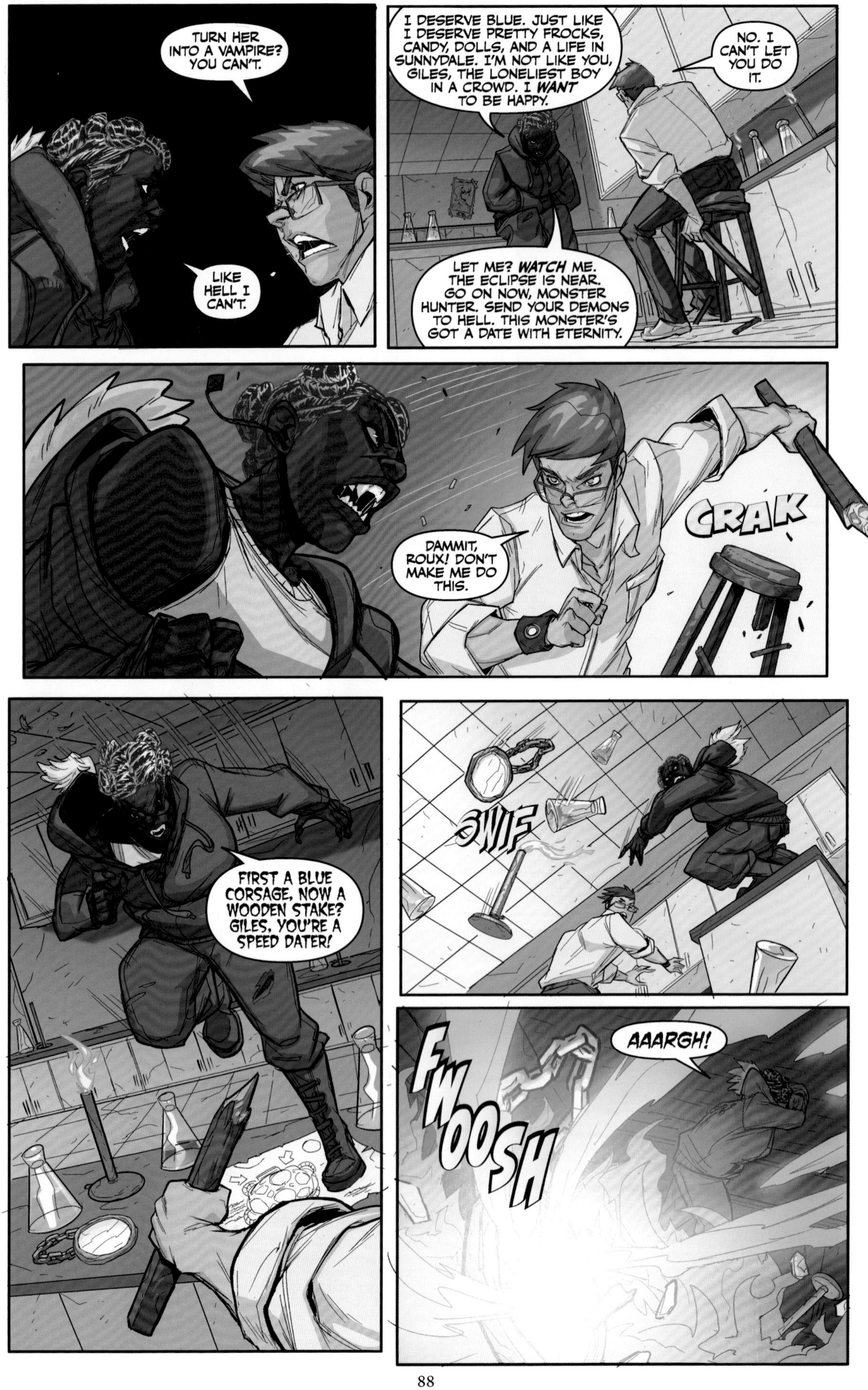
TURN HER INTO A VAMPIRE? YOU CAN'T.
LIKE HELL I CAN'T.
I DESERVE BLUE. JUST LIKE I DESERVE PRETTY FROCKS, CANDY, DOLLS, AND A LIFE IN SUNNYDALE. I'M NOT LIKE YOU, GILES, THE LONELIEST BOY IN A CROWD. I *WANT* TO BE HAPPY.
NO. I CAN'T LET YOU DO IT.
LET ME? *WATCH* ME. THE ECLIPSE IS NEAR. GO ON NOW, MONSTER HUNTER. SEND YOUR DEMONS TO HELL. THIS MONSTER'S GOT A DATE WITH ETERNITY.
DAMMIT, ROUX! DON'T MAKE ME DO THIS.
CRAK
FIRST A BLUE CORSAGE, NOW A WOODEN STAKE? GILES. YOU'RE A SPEED DATER!
SWIF
AAARGH!
FWOOSH

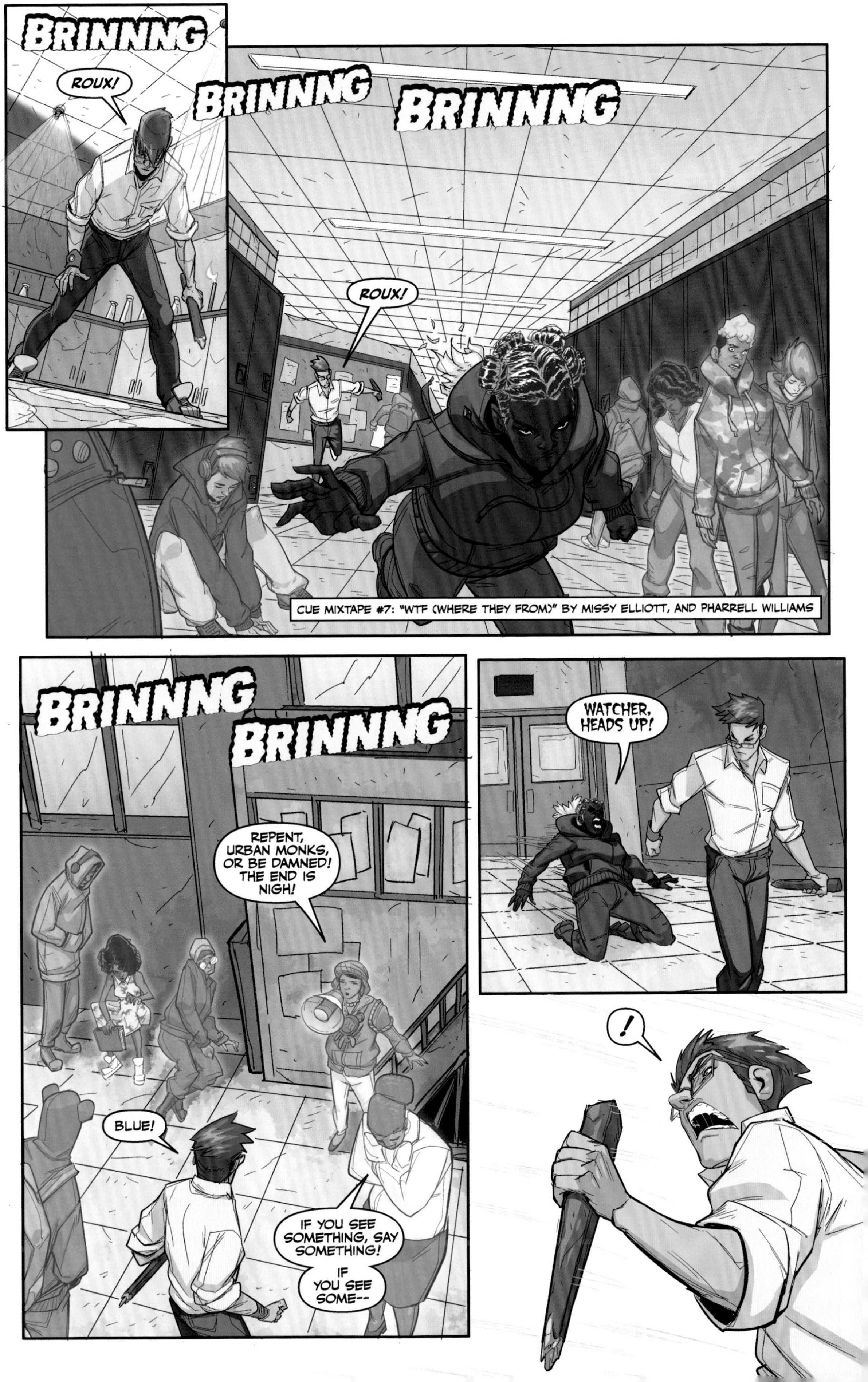
BRINNNG
ROUX!
BRINNNG
BRINNNG
ROUX!
CUE MIXTAPE #7: "WTF (WHERE THEY FROM)" BY MISSY ELLIOTT, AND PHARRELL WILLIAMS
BRINNNG
BRINNNG
REPENT, URBAN MONKS, OR BE DAMNED! THE END IS NIGH!
BLUE!
IF YOU SEE SOMETHING, SAY SOMETHING!
IF YOU SEE SOME--
WATCHER, HEADS UP!
!

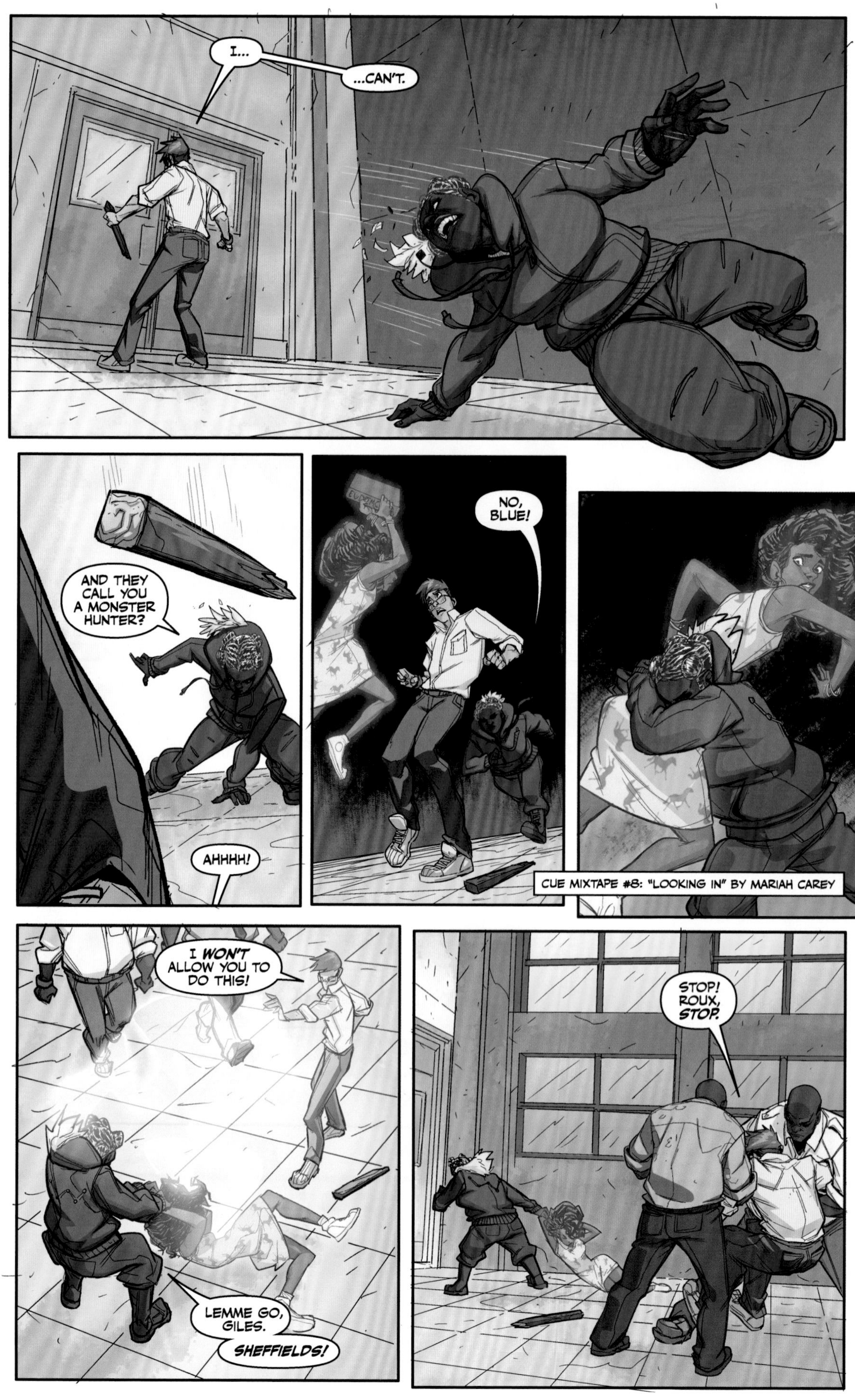
I...
...CAN'T.
AND THEY CALL YOU A MONSTER HUNTER?
AHHHH!
NO, BLUE!
CUE MIXTAPE #8: "LOOKING IN" BY MARIAH CAREY
I *WON'T* ALLOW YOU TO DO THIS!
LEMME GO, GILES.
SHEFFIELDS!
STOP! ROUX, *STOP.*

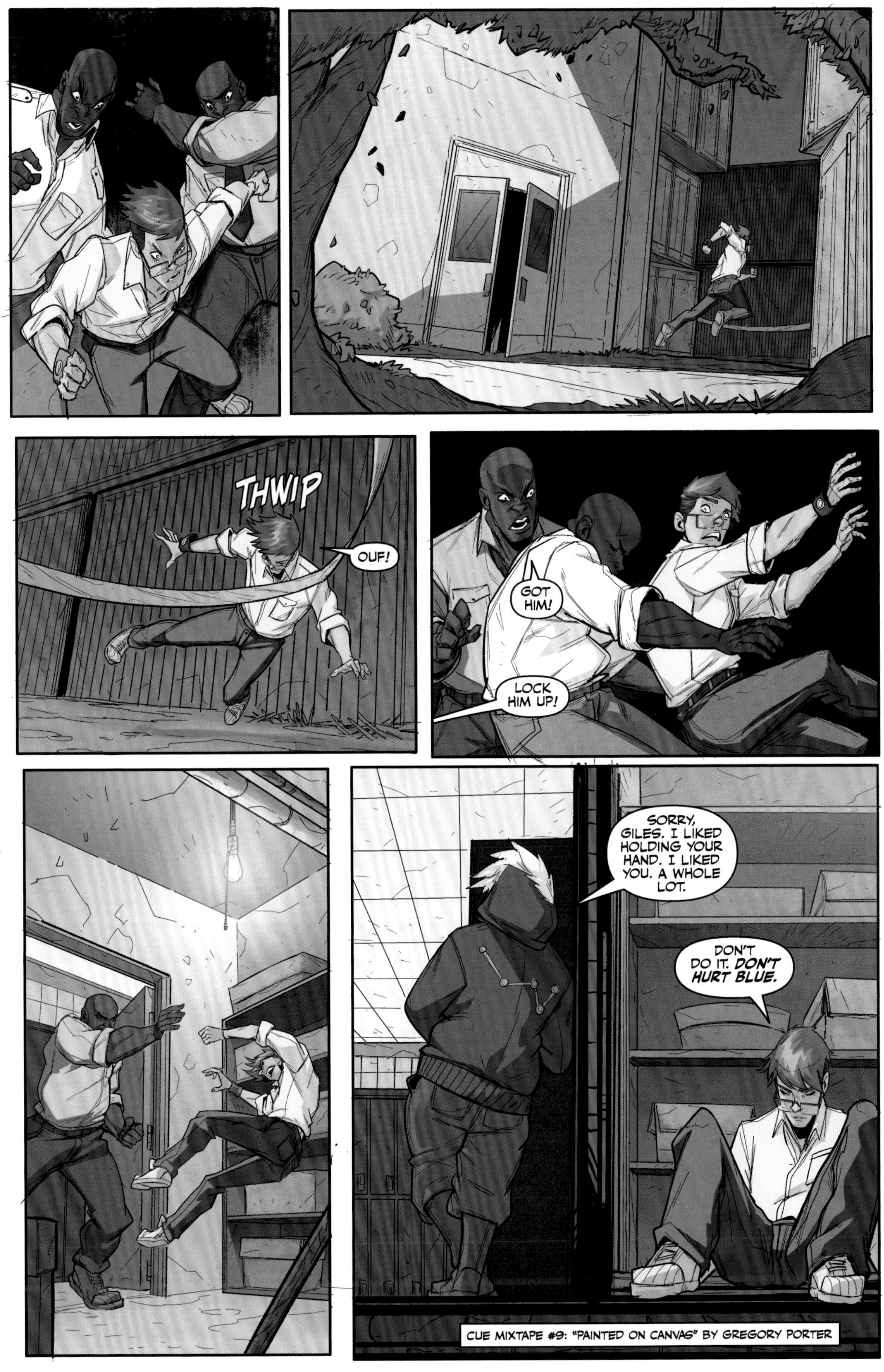
THWIP
OUF!
GOT HIM!
LOCK HIM UP!
SORRY, GILES. I LIKED HOLDING YOUR HAND. I LIKED YOU. A WHOLE LOT.
DON'T DO IT. DON'T HURT BLUE.
CUE MIXTAPE #9: "PAINTED ON CANVAS" BY GREGORY PORTER

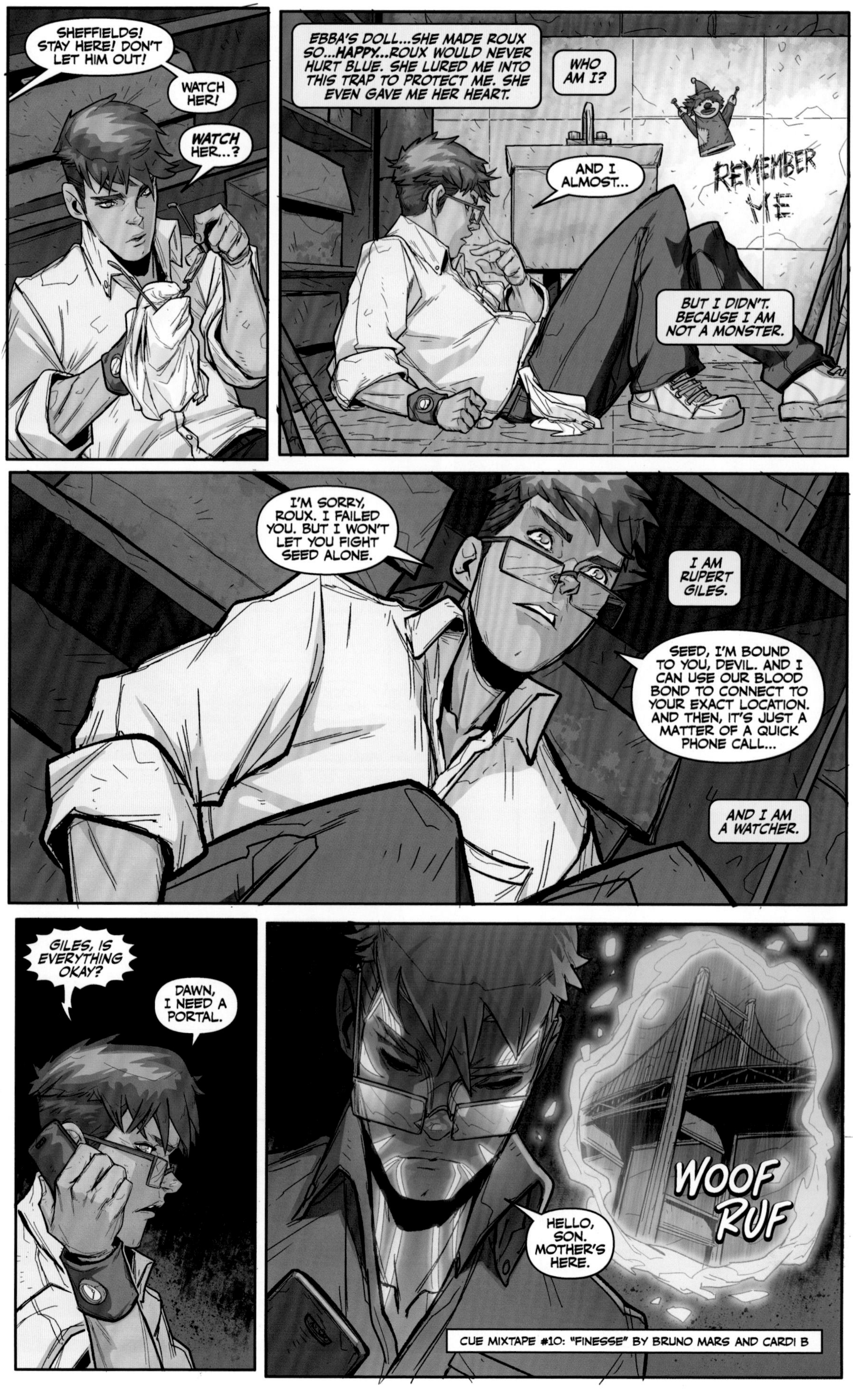
SHEFFIELDS! STAY HERE! DON'T LET HIM OUT!
WATCH HER!
WATCH HER...?
EBBA'S DOLL...SHE MADE ROUX SO...HAPPY...ROUX WOULD NEVER HURT BLUE. SHE LURED ME INTO THIS TRAP TO PROTECT ME. SHE EVEN GAVE ME HER HEART.
WHO AM I?
AND I ALMOST...
REMEMBER ME
BUT I DIDN'T. BECAUSE I AM NOT A MONSTER.
I'M SORRY, ROUX. I FAILED YOU. BUT I WON'T LET YOU FIGHT SEED ALONE.
I AM RUPERT GILES.
SEED, I'M BOUND TO YOU, DEVIL. AND I CAN USE OUR BLOOD BOND TO CONNECT TO YOUR EXACT LOCATION. AND THEN, IT'S JUST A MATTER OF A QUICK PHONE CALL...
AND I AM A WATCHER.
GILES, IS EVERYTHING OKAY?
DAWN, I NEED A PORTAL.
WOOF RUF
HELLO, SON. MOTHER'S HERE.
CUE MIXTAPE #10: "FINESSE" BY BRUNO MARS AND CARDI B

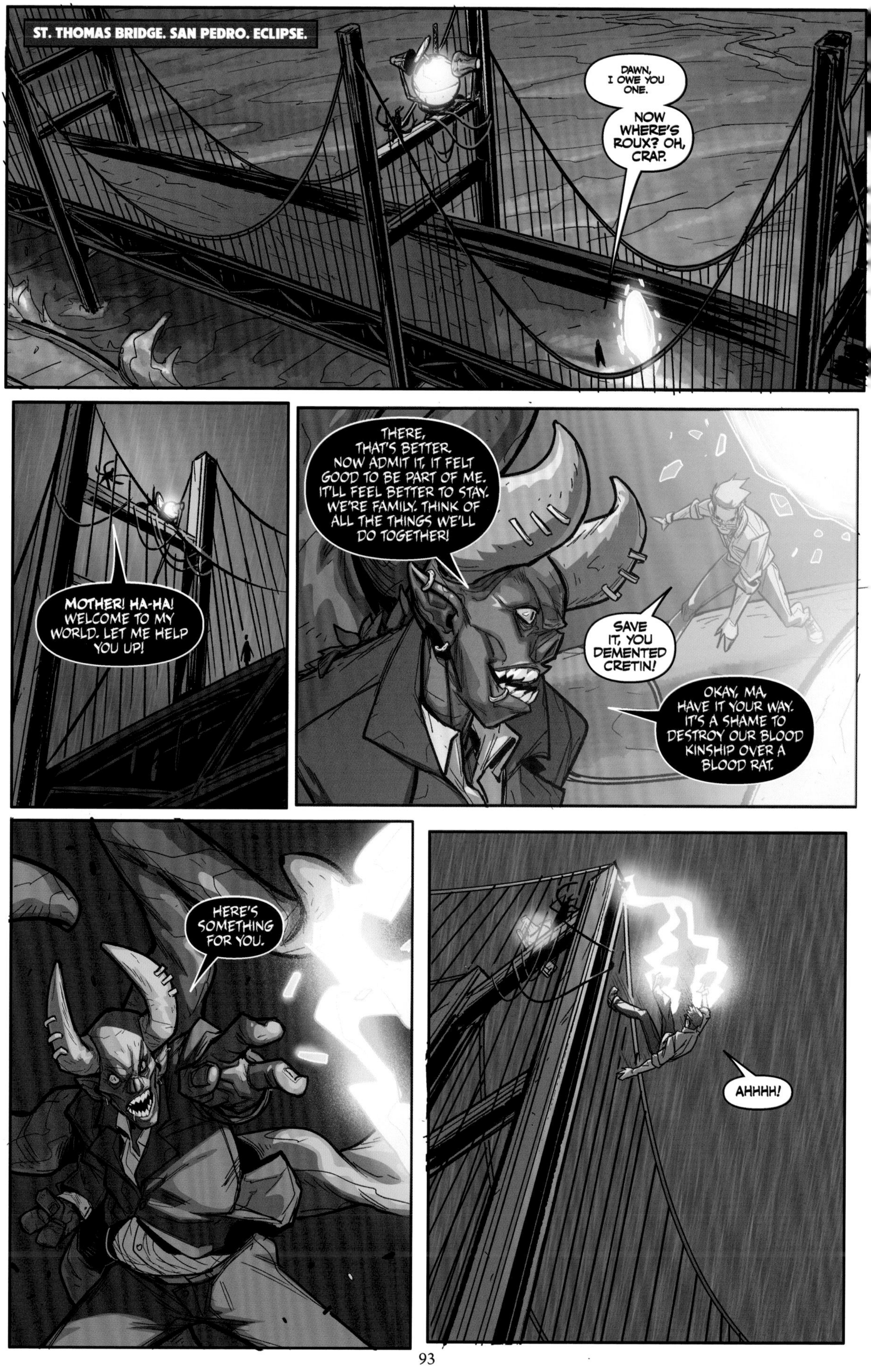
ST. THOMAS BRIDGE. SAN PEDRO. ECLIPSE.
DAWN, I OWE YOU ONE.
NOW WHERE'S ROUX? OH, CRAP.
MOTHER! HA-HA! WELCOME TO MY WORLD. LET ME HELP YOU UP!
THERE, THAT'S BETTER. NOW ADMIT IT, IT FELT GOOD TO BE PART OF ME. IT'LL FEEL BETTER TO STAY. WE'RE FAMILY. THINK OF ALL THE THINGS WE'LL DO TOGETHER!
SAVE IT, YOU DEMENTED CRETIN!
OKAY, MA, HAVE IT YOUR WAY. IT'S A SHAME TO DESTROY OUR BLOOD KINSHIP OVER A BLOOD RAT.
HERE'S SOMETHING FOR YOU.
AHHHH!

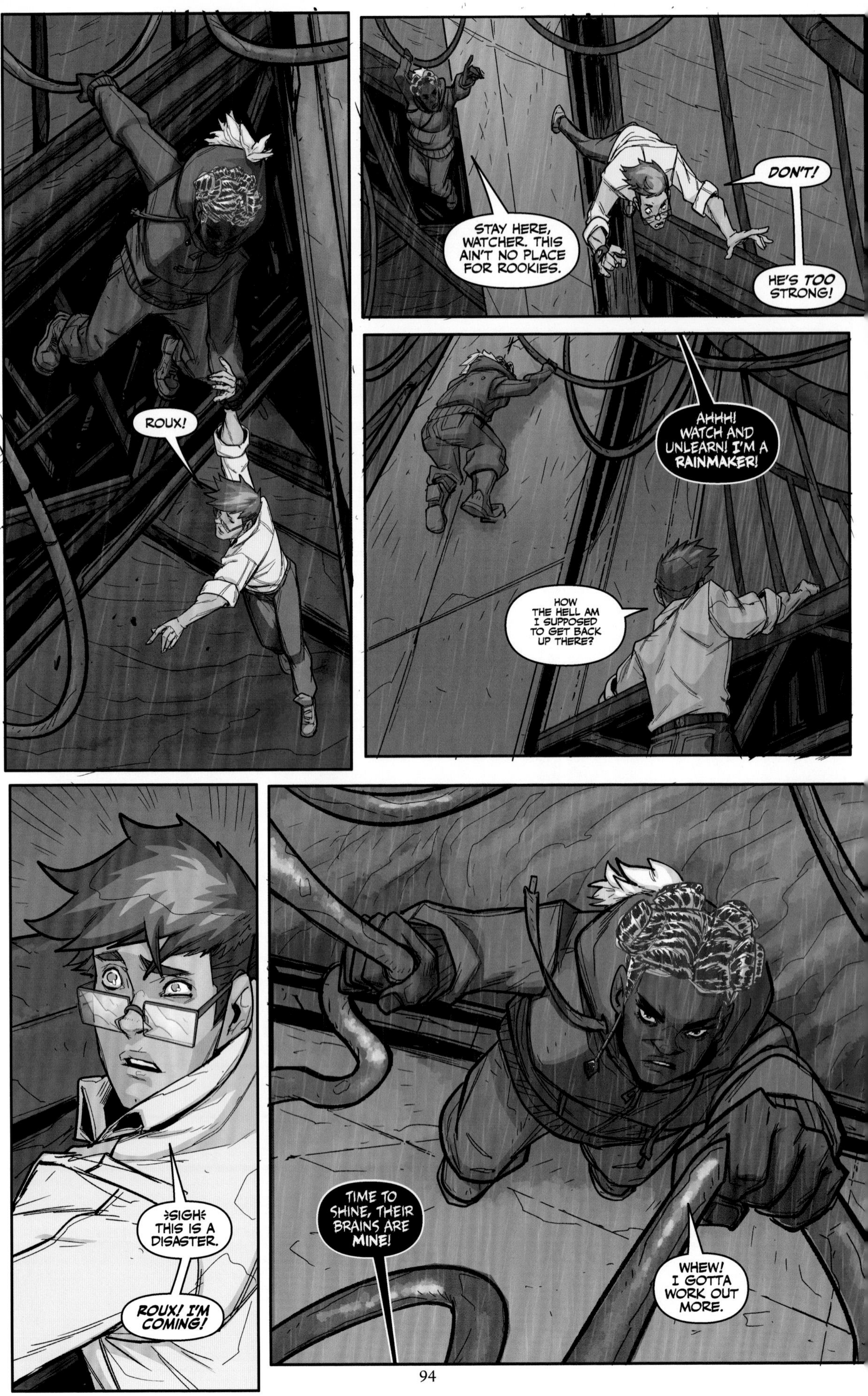
ROUX!
STAY HERE, WATCHER. THIS AIN'T NO PLACE FOR ROOKIES.
DON'T!
HE'S TOO STRONG!
AHHH! WATCH AND UNLEARN! I'M A RAINMAKER!
HOW THE HELL AM I SUPPOSED TO GET BACK UP THERE?
SIGH THIS IS A DISASTER.
ROUX! I'M COMING!
TIME TO SHINE, THEIR BRAINS ARE MINE!
WHEW! I GOTTA WORK OUT MORE.

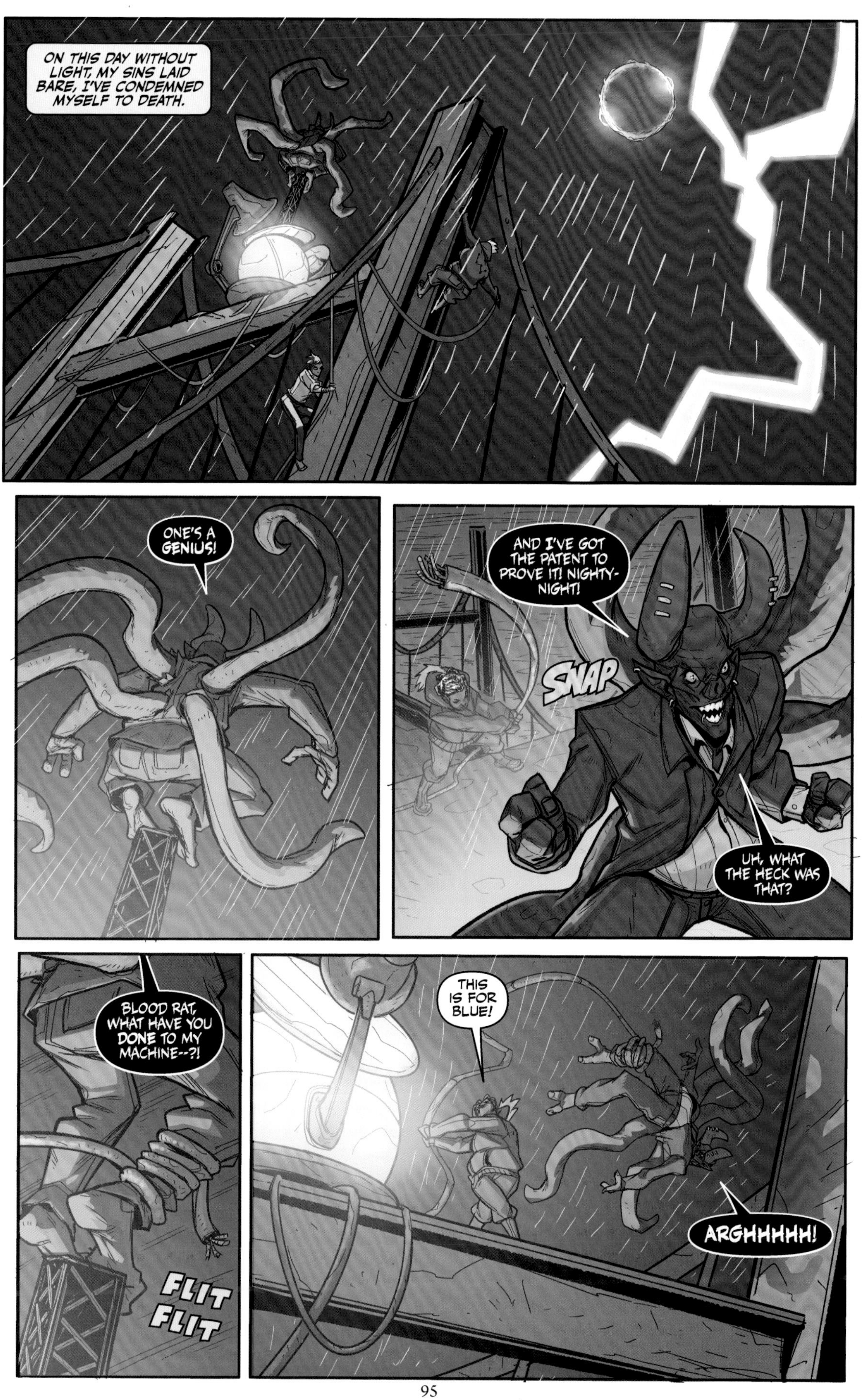
ON THIS DAY WITHOUT LIGHT, MY SINS LAID BARE, I'VE CONDEMNED MYSELF TO DEATH.
ONE'S A GENIUS!
AND I'VE GOT THE PATENT TO PROVE IT! NIGHTY-NIGHT!
SNAP
UH, WHAT THE HECK WAS THAT?
BLOOD RAT, WHAT HAVE YOU DONE TO MY MACHINE--?!
FLIT FLIT
THIS IS FOR BLUE!
ARGHHHHH!

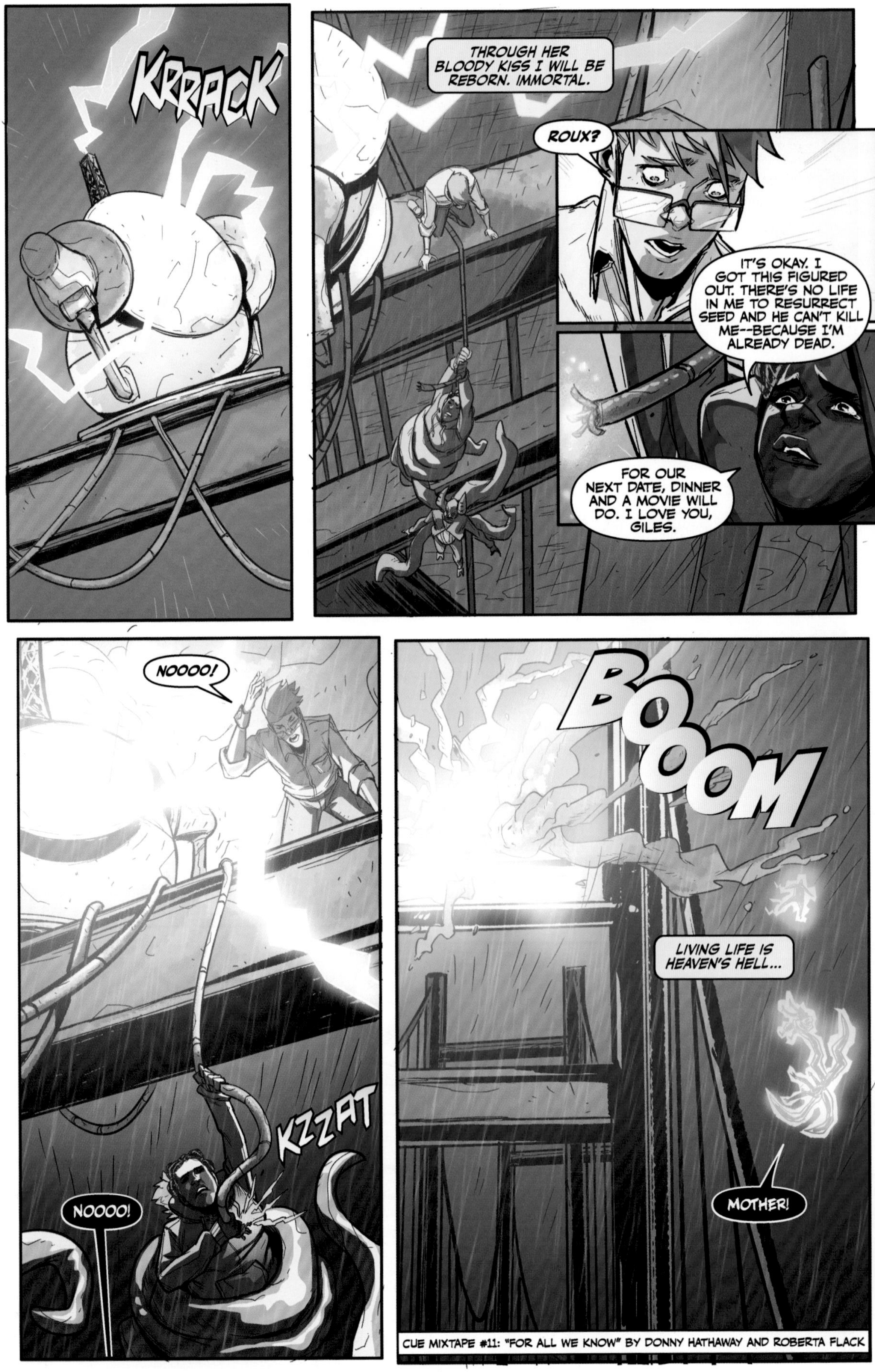
KRRACK
THROUGH HER BLOODY KISS I WILL BE REBORN. IMMORTAL.
ROUX?
IT'S OKAY. I GOT THIS FIGURED OUT. THERE'S NO LIFE IN ME TO RESURRECT SEED AND HE CAN'T KILL ME--BECAUSE I'M ALREADY DEAD.
FOR OUR NEXT DATE, DINNER AND A MOVIE WILL DO. I LOVE YOU, GILES.
NOOOO!
KZZAT
NOOOO!
BOOOOM
LIVING LIFE IS HEAVEN'S HELL...
MOTHER!
CUE MIXTAPE #11: "FOR ALL WE KNOW" BY DONNY HATHAWAY AND ROBERTA FLACK

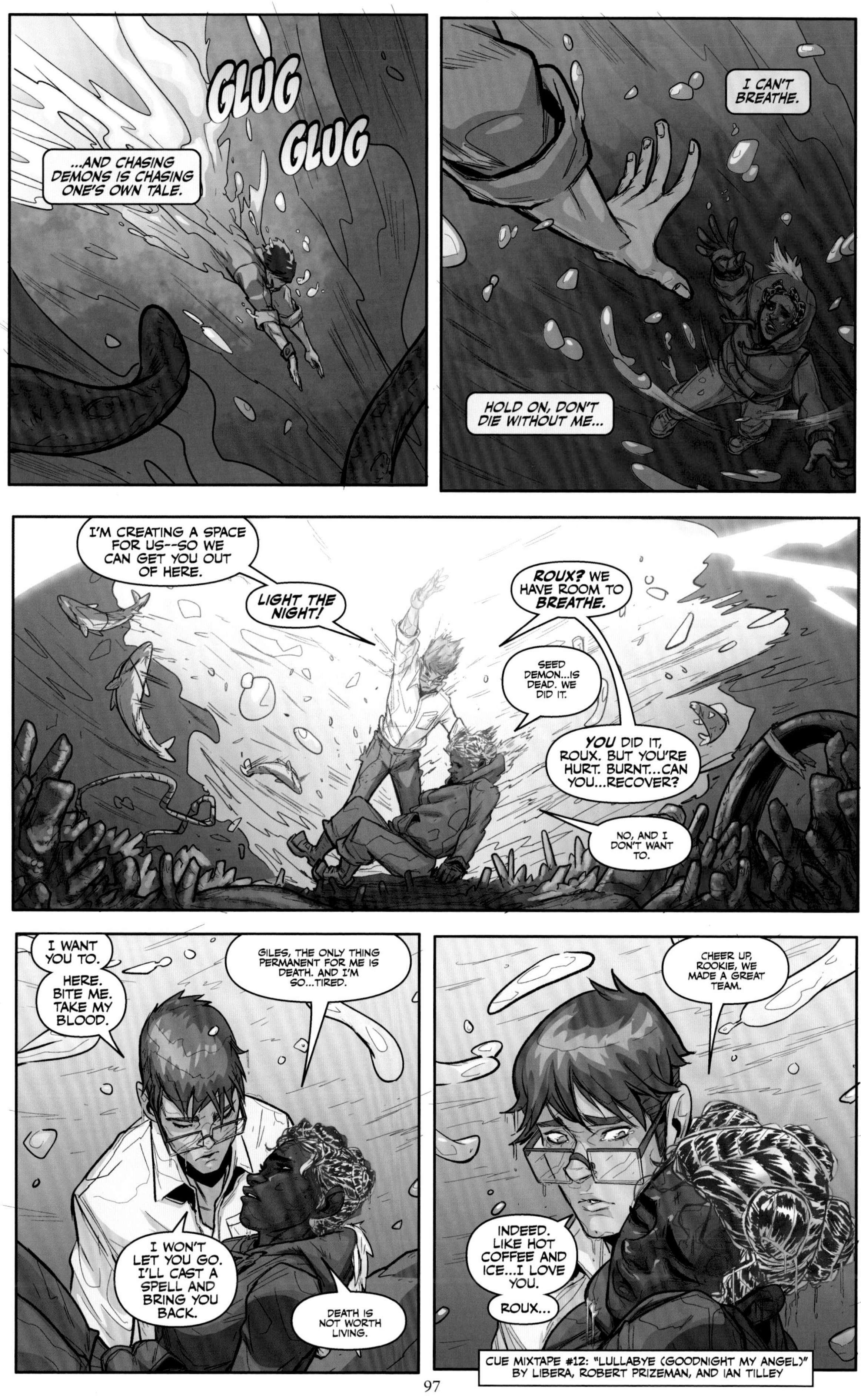
GLUG
GLUG
...AND CHASING DEMONS IS CHASING ONE'S OWN TALE.
I CAN'T BREATHE.
HOLD ON, DON'T DIE WITHOUT ME...
I'M CREATING A SPACE FOR US--SO WE CAN GET YOU OUT OF HERE.
LIGHT THE NIGHT!
ROUX? WE HAVE ROOM TO BREATHE.
SEED DEMON...IS DEAD. WE DID IT.
YOU DID IT, ROUX. BUT YOU'RE HURT. BURNT...CAN YOU...RECOVER?
NO, AND I DON'T WANT TO.
I WANT YOU TO.
HERE. BITE ME. TAKE MY BLOOD.
GILES, THE ONLY THING PERMANENT FOR ME IS DEATH. AND I'M SO...TIRED.
I WON'T LET YOU GO. I'LL CAST A SPELL AND BRING YOU BACK.
DEATH IS NOT WORTH LIVING.
CHEER UP, ROOKIE, WE MADE A GREAT TEAM.
INDEED. LIKE HOT COFFEE AND ICE...I LOVE YOU.
ROUX...
CUE MIXTAPE #12: "LULLABYE (GOODNIGHT MY ANGEL)" BY LIBERA, ROBERT PRIZEMAN, AND IAN TILLEY

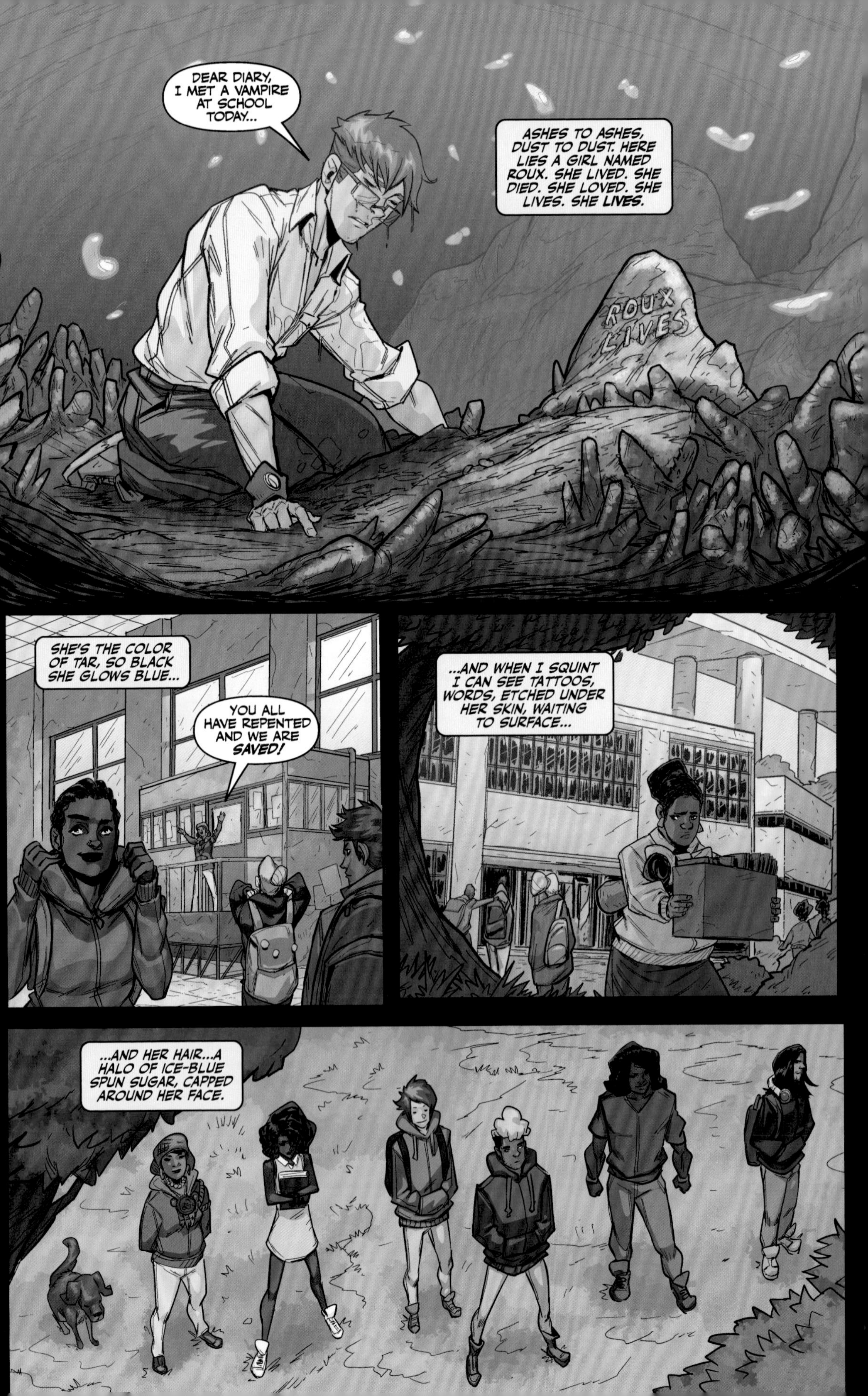
DEAR DIARY, I MET A VAMPIRE AT SCHOOL TODAY...
ASHES TO ASHES, DUST TO DUST. HERE LIES A GIRL NAMED ROUX. SHE LIVED. SHE DIED. SHE LOVED. SHE LIVES. SHE LIVES.
ROUX LIVES
SHE'S THE COLOR OF TAR, SO BLACK SHE GLOWS BLUE...
YOU ALL HAVE REPENTED AND WE ARE SAVED!
...AND WHEN I SQUINT I CAN SEE TATTOOS, WORDS, ETCHED UNDER HER SKIN, WAITING TO SURFACE...
...AND HER HAIR...A HALO OF ICE-BLUE SPUN SUGAR, CAPPED AROUND HER FACE.

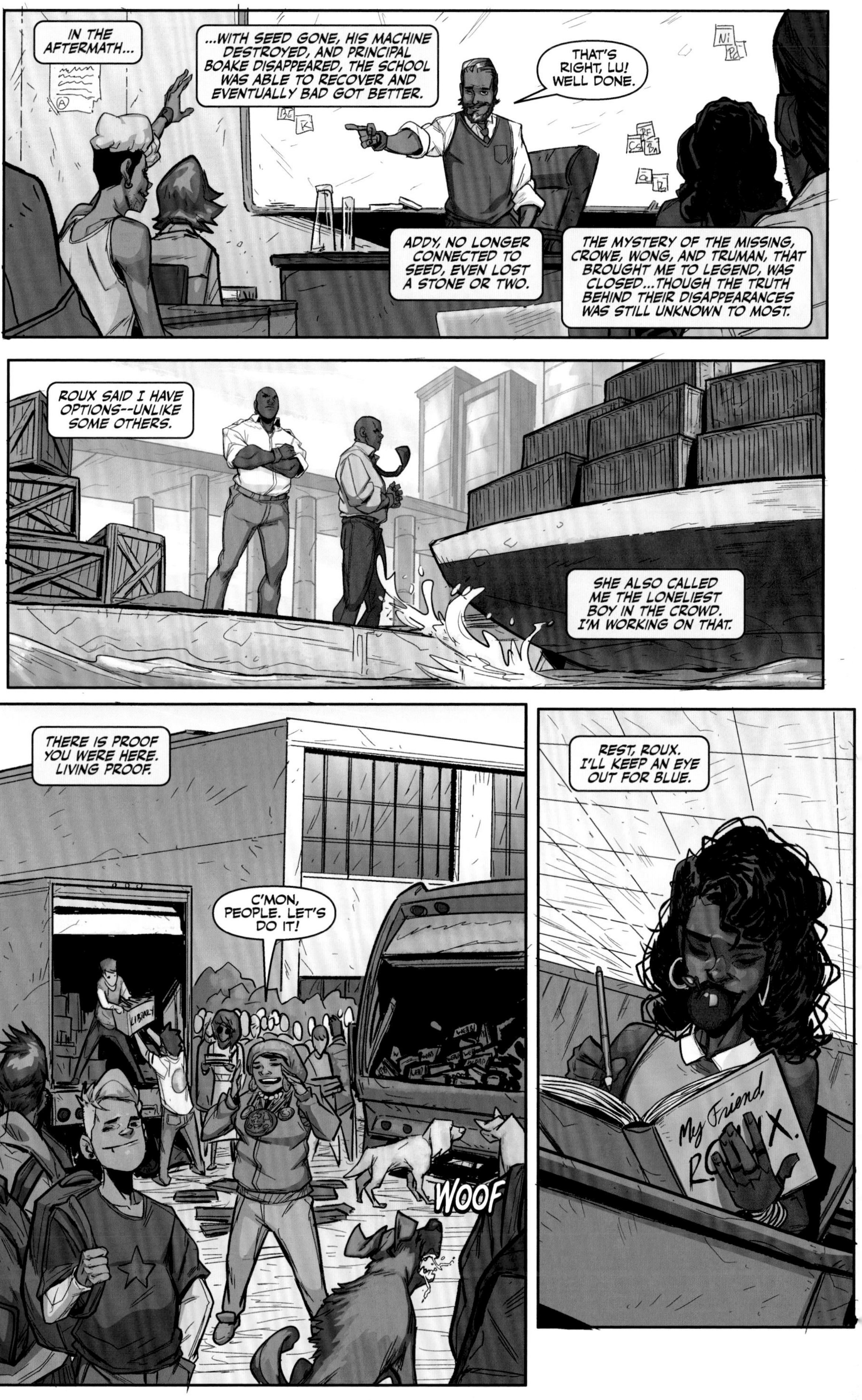
IN THE AFTERMATH...
...WITH SEED GONE, HIS MACHINE DESTROYED, AND PRINCIPAL BOAKE DISAPPEARED, THE SCHOOL WAS ABLE TO RECOVER AND EVENTUALLY BAD GOT BETTER.
THAT'S RIGHT, LU! WELL DONE.
ADDY, NO LONGER CONNECTED TO SEED, EVEN LOST A STONE OR TWO.
THE MYSTERY OF THE MISSING, CROWE, WONG, AND TRUMAN, THAT BROUGHT ME TO LEGEND, WAS CLOSED...THOUGH THE TRUTH BEHIND THEIR DISAPPEARANCES WAS STILL UNKNOWN TO MOST.
ROUX SAID I HAVE OPTIONS--UNLIKE SOME OTHERS.
SHE ALSO CALLED ME THE LONELIEST BOY IN THE CROWD. I'M WORKING ON THAT.
THERE IS PROOF YOU WERE HERE. LIVING PROOF.
C'MON, PEOPLE. LET'S DO IT!
LIBRARY
WOOF
REST, ROUX. I'LL KEEP AN EYE OUT FOR BLUE.
My Friend,

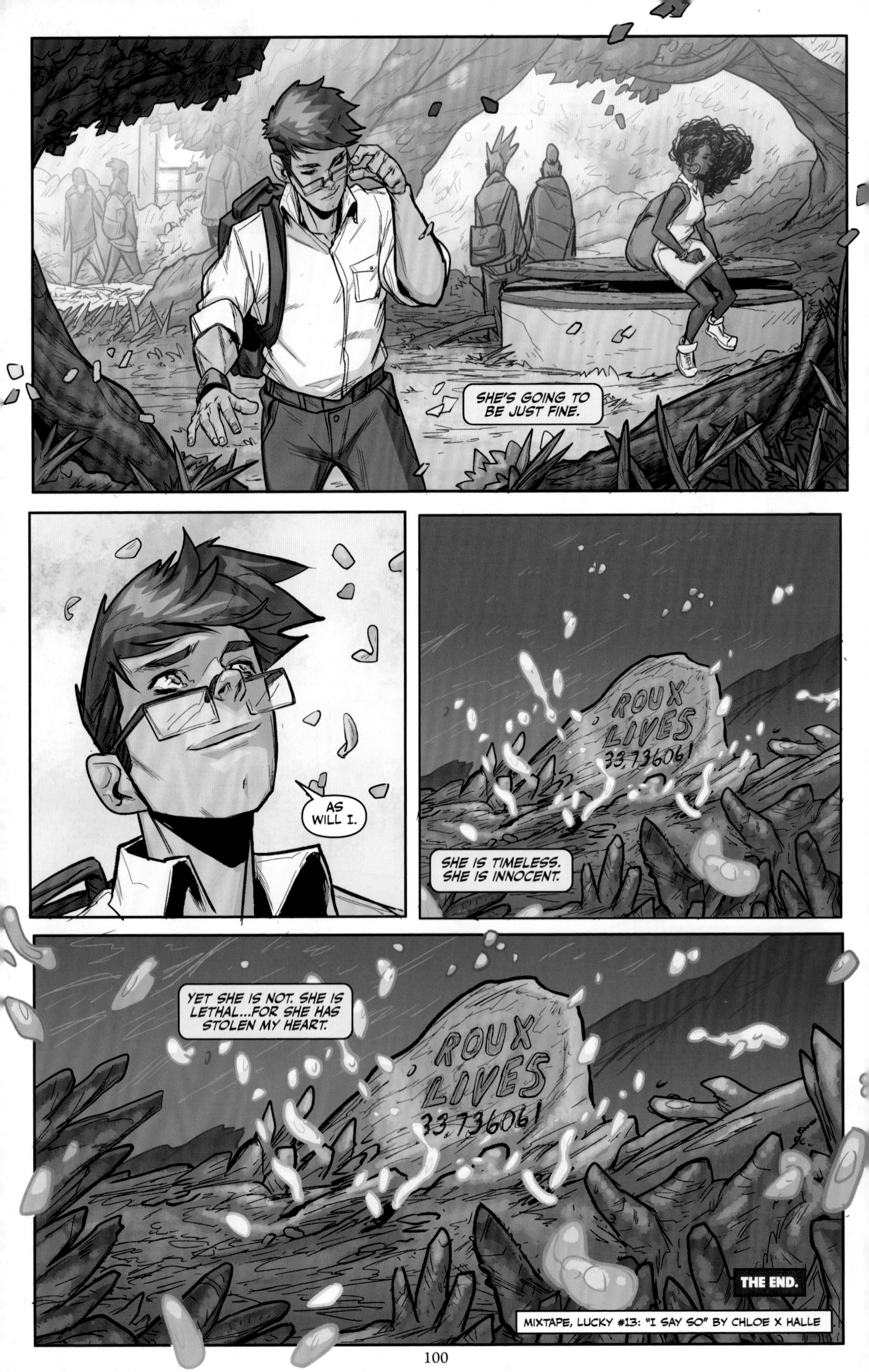
SHE'S GOING TO BE JUST FINE.
AS WILL I.
ROUX LIVES 33.736061
SHE IS TIMELESS. SHE IS INNOCENT.
YET SHE IS NOT. SHE IS LETHAL...FOR SHE HAS STOLEN MY HEART.
ROUX LIVES 33.736061
THE END.
MIXTAPE, LUCKY #13: "I SAY SO" BY CHLOE X HALLE

MIXTAPE: GIRL BLUE

PART 1

#1 - *"We The People"*
by A TRIBE
CALLED QUEST

#2 - *"Untitled 04/8.04.2014."*
by KENDRICK LAMAR

#3 - *"Shutter Island"*
by JESSIE REYEZ

#4 - *"Lost Queen"*
by PHARRELL
WILLIAMS

#5 - *"Figure Eight"*
by BLOSSOM DEARIE

#6 - *"Requiem in D Minor
K. 626"*
by WOLFGANG
AMADEUS MOZART

#7 - *"Cucurrucucu Paloma"
(Live 1995)*
by CAETANO VELOSO

#8 - *"Blackbird"*
by SARA GAZAREK

#9 - *"Liebesträume
S541/R211: No. 3"*
by FRANZ LISZT

#10 - *"Girl Blue"*
by STEVIE WONDER

PART 2

#1 - *"March of the Poozers"*
by DEVIN TOWNSEND

#2 - *"Black Coffee"*
by SARAH VAUGHAN

#3 - *"Me Voy"*
by IBEYI, *featuring*
MALA RODRIGUEZ

#4 - *"Midnight Cowboy"*
by JOHN BARRY

#5 - *"Can't Forget About You"*
by NAS *featuring*
CHRISETTE MICHELE

#6 - *"Zing! Went the Strings
of My Heart"*
by JUDY GARLAND

#7 - *"Stardust"*
by BING CROSBY

#8 - *"Black Dog"*
by LED ZEPPELIN

#9 - *"Be For Real"*
by HAROLD MELVIN
& THE BLUE NOTES

#10 - *"Mood Indigo"*
by DUKE ELLINGTON
& LOUIS ARMSTRONG

PART 3

#1 - *"At the Purchaser's Option"*
by RHIANNON
GIDDENS

#2 - *"St. James
Infirmary Blues"*
by SILK ROAD
ENSEMBLE

#3 - *"POWER"*
by KANYE WEST

#4 - *"Gett Off"*
by PRINCE

#5 - *"Pushin' Against a Stone"*
by VALERIE JUNE

#6 - *"She Bad Bad"*
by EVE

#7 - *"Lost Inside of You"*
by BARBRA
STREISAND

#8 - *"Wreckless Love"*
by ALICIA KEYS

or

"22nd Century"
by NINA SIMONE

PART 4

#1 - *"Glasgow Love Theme"*
by CLAIRE JONES

#2 - *"Bang Bang"*
by JESSIE J, ARIANA
GRANDE, *and*
NICKI MINAJ

#3 - *"We Must Love Each Other"*
by DR. MARTIN
LUTHER KING, JR

#4 - *"Dreams"*
by GIRL BLUE

#5 - *"The End of the World"*
by JULIE LONDON

#6 - *"Awaken"*
by DARIO
MARIANELLI,
JACK LIEBECK,
and
BENJAMIN
WALLFISCH

#7 - *"WTF (Where They From)"*
by MISSY ELLIOT
and PHARRELL
WILLIAMS

#8 - *"Looking In"*
by MARIAH CAREY

#9 - *"Painted on Canvas"*
by GREGORY PORTER

#10 - *"Finesse"*
by BRUNO MARS
and CARDI B

#11 - *"For All We Know"*
by DONNY
HATHAWAY
and ROBERTA FLACK

#12 - *"Lullabye (Goodnight
My Angel)"*
by LIBERA, ROBERT
PRIZEMAN, *and*
IAN TILLEY

LUCKY #13 - *"I Say So"*
by CHLOE x HALLE

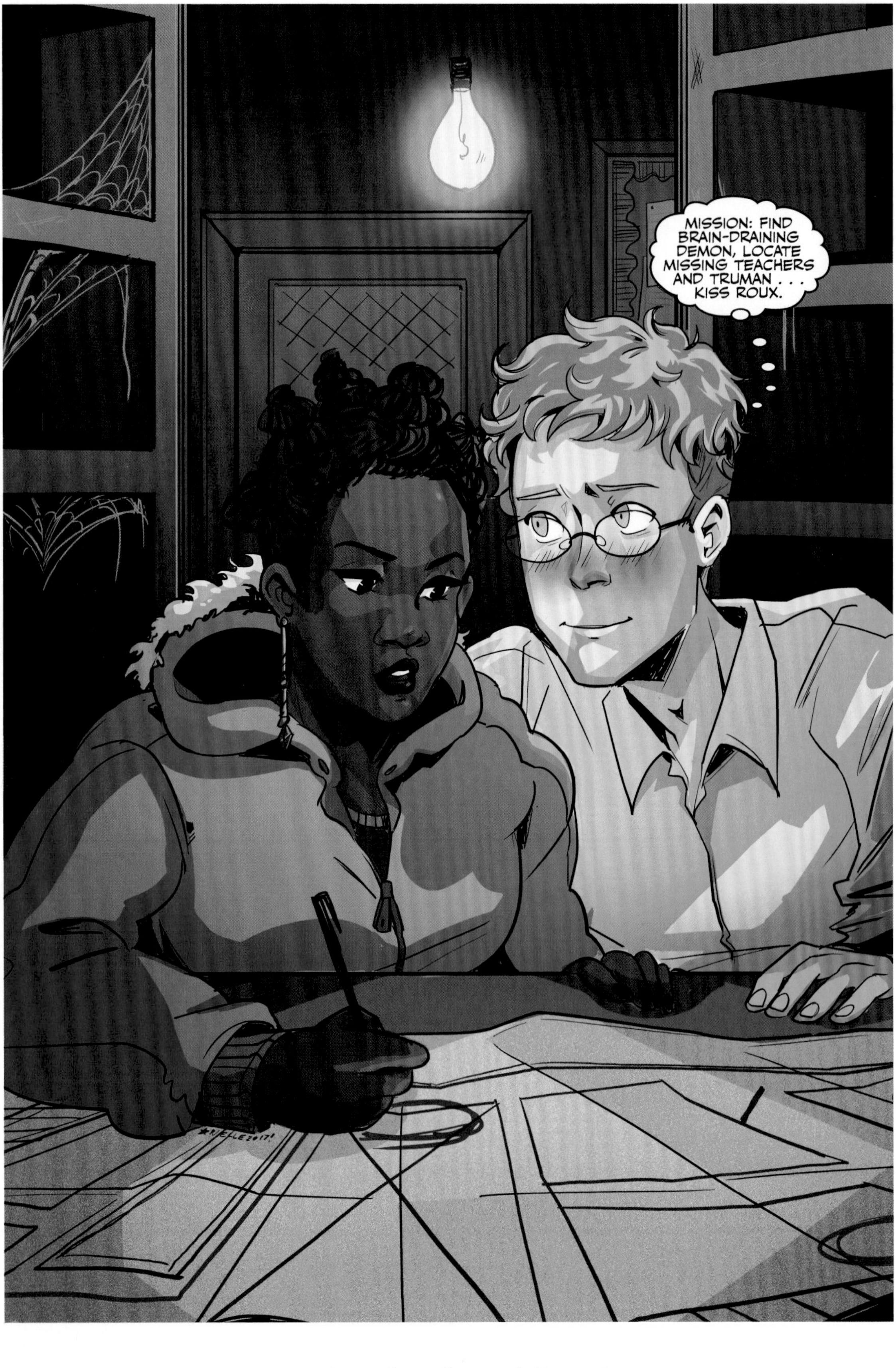
MISSION: FIND BRAIN-DRAINING DEMON, LOCATE MISSING TEACHERS AND TRUMAN . . . KISS ROUX.

Art by Arielle Jovellanos with Comicraft

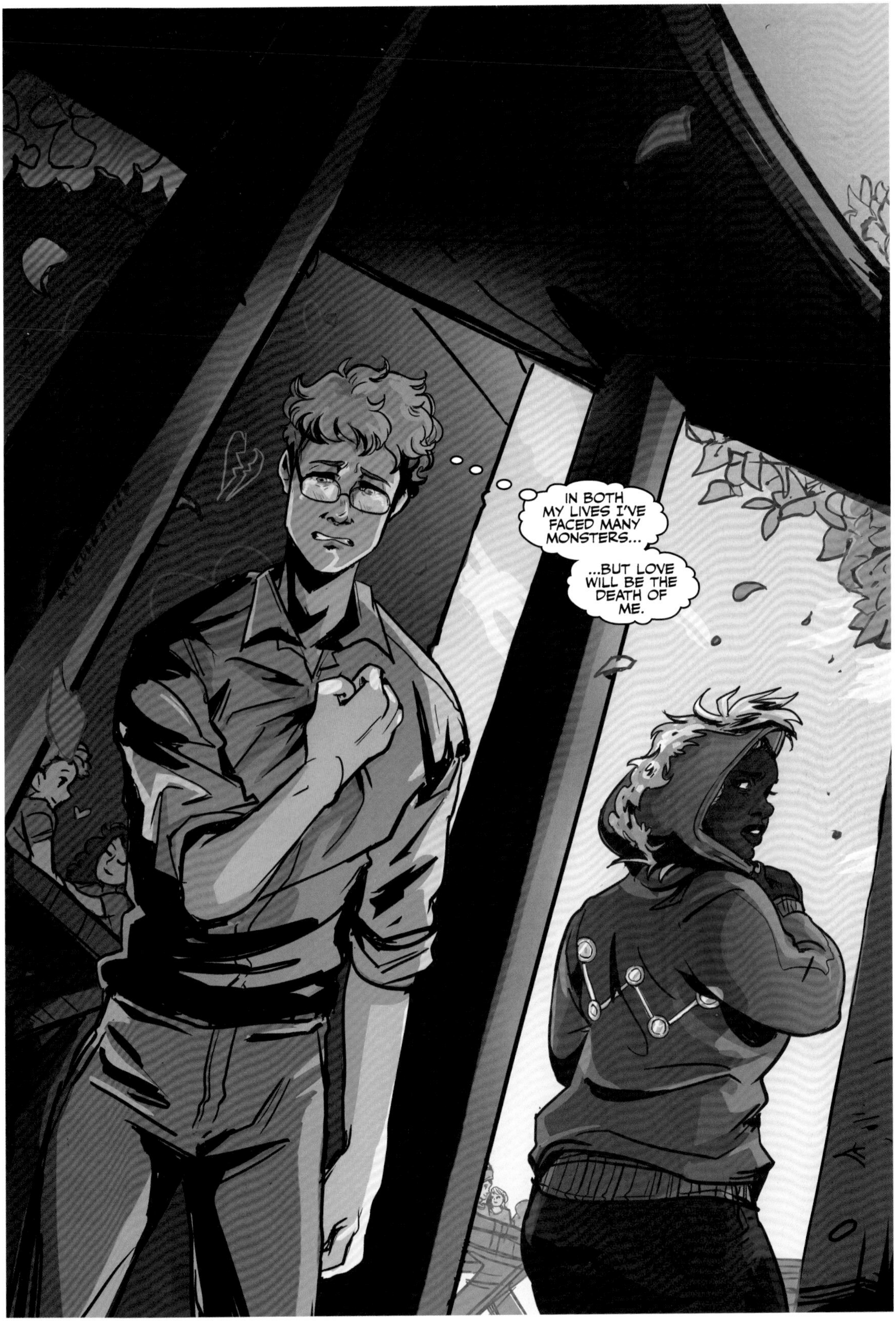
IN BOTH MY LIVES I'VE FACED MANY MONSTERS...
...BUT LOVE WILL BE THE DEATH OF ME.

Art by Arielle Jovellanos with Comicraft

Buffy the Vampire Slayer™

BUFFY THE VAMPIRE SLAYER SEASON 8

VOLUME 1: THE LONG WAY HOME
Joss Whedon and Georges Jeanty
ISBN 978-1-59307-822-5 | $15.99

VOLUME 2: NO FUTURE FOR YOU
Brian K. Vaughan, Georges Jeanty, and Joss Whedon
ISBN 978-1-59307-963-5 | $15.99

VOLUME 3: WOLVES AT THE GATE
Drew Goddard, Georges Jeanty, and Joss Whedon
ISBN 978-1-59582-165-2 | $15.99

VOLUME 4: TIME OF YOUR LIFE
Joss Whedon, Jeph Loeb, Georges Jeanty, and others
ISBN 978-1-59582-310-6 | $15.99

VOLUME 5: PREDATORS AND PREY
Joss Whedon, Jane Espenson, Georges Jeanty, Cliff Richards, and others
ISBN 978-1-59582-342-7 | $15.99

VOLUME 6: RETREAT
Joss Whedon, Jane Espenson, Georges Jeanty, Karl Moline, and others
ISBN 978-1-59582-415-8 | $15.99

VOLUME 7: TWILIGHT
Joss Whedon, Brad Meltzer, and Georges Jeanty
ISBN 978-1-59582-558-2 | $16.99

VOLUME 8: LAST GLEAMING
Joss Whedon, Scott Allie, and Georges Jeanty
ISBN 978-1-59582-610-7 | $16.99

BUFFY THE VAMPIRE SLAYER SEASON 8 LIBRARY EDITION

VOLUME 1
ISBN 978-1-59582-888-0 | $29.99

VOLUME 2
ISBN 978-1-59582-935-1 | $29.99

VOLUME 3
ISBN 978-1-59582-978-8 | $29.99

VOLUME 4
ISBN 978-1-61655-127-8 | $29.99

BUFFY THE VAMPIRE SLAYER OMNIBUS: SEASON 8

VOLUME 1
ISBN 978-1-63008-941-2 | $24.99

VOLUME 2
ISBN 978-1-63008-942-9 | $24.99

BUFFY THE VAMPIRE SLAYER SEASON 9

VOLUME 1: FREEFALL
Joss Whedon, Andrew Chambliss, Georges Jeanty, and others
ISBN 978-1-59582-922-1 | $17.99

VOLUME 2: ON YOUR OWN
Andrew Chambliss, Scott Allie, Georges Jeanty, and others
ISBN 978-1-59582-990-0 | $17.99

VOLUME 3: GUARDED
Joss Whedon, Jane Espenson, Drew Z. Greenberg, Georges Jeanty, and others
ISBN 978-1-61655-099-8 | $17.99

VOLUME 4: WELCOME TO THE TEAM
Andrew Chambliss, Georges Jeanty, Karl Moline, and others
ISBN 978-1-61655-166-7 | $17.99

VOLUME 5: THE CORE
Andrew Chambliss, Georges Jeanty, and others
ISBN 978-1-61655-254-1 | $17.99

BUFFY THE VAMPIRE SLAYER SEASON 9 LIBRARY EDITION

VOLUME 1
ISBN 978-1-61655-715-7 | $29.99

VOLUME 2
ISBN 978-1-61655-716-4 | $29.99

VOLUME 3
ISBN 978-1-61655-717-1 | $29.99

BUFFY THE VAMPIRE SLAYER SEASON 10

VOLUME 1: NEW RULES
Christos Gage, Rebekah Isaacs, Nicholas Brendon, and others
ISBN 978-1-61655-490-3 | $18.99

VOLUME 2: I WISH
Christos Gage, Rebekah Isaacs, Nicholas Brendon, and others
ISBN 978-1-61655-600-6 | $18.99

VOLUME 3: LOVE DARES YOU
Christos Gage, Rebekah Isaacs, Nicholas Brendon, and Megan Levens
ISBN 978-1-61655-758-4 | $18.99

VOLUME 4: OLD DEMONS
Christos Gage and Rebekah Isaacs
ISBN 978-1-61655-802-4 | $18.99

VOLUME 5: IN PIECES ON THE GROUND
Christos Gage, Megan Levens, and Rebekah Isaacs
ISBN 978-1-61655-944-1 | $18.99

VOLUME 6: OWN IT
Christos Gage and Rebekah Isaacs
ISBN 978-1-50670-034-2 | $18.99

BUFFY THE VAMPIRE SLAYER SEASON 10 LIBRARY EDITION

VOLUME 1
ISBN 978-1-50670-645-0 | $29.99

VOLUME 2
ISBN 978-1-50670-657-3 | $29.99

BUFFY THE VAMPIRE SLAYER SEASON 11

VOLUME 1: THE SPREAD OF THEIR EVIL
Christos Gage and Rebekah Isaacs
ISBN 978-1-50670-274-2 | $19.99

VOLUME 2: ONE GIRL IN ALL THE WORLD
Christos Gage, Georges Jeanty, Rebekah Isaacs, and Megan Levens
ISBN 978-1-50670-292-6 | $19.99

ANGEL & FAITH SEASON 9

VOLUME 1: LIVE THROUGH THIS
Christos Gage, Rebekah Isaacs, and Phil Noto
ISBN 978-1-59582-887-3 | $17.99

VOLUME 2: DADDY ISSUES
Christos Gage, Rebekah Isaacs, and Chris Samnee
ISBN 978-1-59582-960-3 | $17.99

VOLUME 3: FAMILY REUNION
Christos Gage, Rebekah Isaacs, Lee Garbett, and David Lapham
ISBN 978-1-61655-079-0 | $17.99

VOLUME 4: DEATH AND CONSEQUENCES
Christos Gage and Rebekah Isaacs
ISBN 978-1-61655-165-0 | $17.99

VOLUME 5: WHAT YOU WANT, NOT WHAT YOU NEED
Christos Gage and Rebekah Isaacs
ISBN 978-1-61655-253-4 | $17.99

ANGEL & FAITH SEASON 9 LIBRARY EDITION

VOLUME 1
ISBN 978-1-61655-712-6 | $29.99

VOLUME 2
ISBN 978-1-61655-713-3 | $29.99

VOLUME 3
ISBN 978-1-61655-714-0 | $29.99

ANGEL & FAITH SEASON 10

VOLUME 1: WHERE THE RIVER MEETS THE SEA
Victor Gischler, Will Conrad, Derlis Santacruz, and others
ISBN 978-1-61655-503-0 | $18.99

VOLUME 2: LOST AND FOUND
Victor Gischler and Will Conrad
ISBN 978-1-61655-601-3 | $18.99

VOLUME 3: UNITED
Victor Gischler and Will Conrad
ISBN 978-1-61655-766-9 | $18.99

VOLUME 4: A LITTLE MORE THAN KIN
Victor Gischler, Cliff Richards, and Will Conrad
ISBN 978-1-61655-890-1 | $18.99

ANGEL SEASON 11

VOLUME 1: OUT OF THE PAST
Corinna Bechko and Geraldo Borges
ISBN 978-1-50670-346-6 | $17.99

VOLUME 2: TIME AND TIDE
Corinna Bechko and Zé Carlos
ISBN 978-1-50670-347-3 | $17.99

VOLUME 3: DARK REFLECTIONS
Corinna Bechko and Geraldo Borges
ISBN 978-1-50670-387-9 | $17.99

SPIKE

A DARK PLACE
Victor Gischler and Paul Lee
ISBN 978-1-61655-109-4 | $17.99

INTO THE LIGHT
James Marsters and Derlis Santacruz
ISBN 978-1-61655-421-7 | $14.99

WILLOW

WONDERLAND
Jeff Parker, Christos Gage, and Brian Ching
ISBN 978-1-61655-145-2 | $17.99

GILES

GIRL BLUE
Joss Whedon, Erika Alexander, and Jon Lam
ISBN 978-1-50670-743-3 | $17.99

BUFFY: THE HIGH SCHOOL YEARS

FREAKS AND GEEKS
Faith Erin Hicks and Yishan Li
ISBN 978-1-61655-667-9 | $10.99

GLUTTON FOR PUNISHMENT
Kel McDonald and Yishan Li
ISBN 978-1-50670-115-8 | $10.99

PARENTAL PARASITE
Kel McDonald and Yishan Li
ISBN 978-1-50670-304-6 | $10.99

ADULT COLORING BOOKS

BUFFY THE VAMPIRE SLAYER ADULT COLORING BOOK
Karl Moline, Georges Jeanty, Rebekah Isaacs, Steve Morris, and others
ISBN 978-1-50670-253-7 | $14.99

BUFFY THE VAMPIRE SLAYER BIG BADS & MONSTERS ADULT COLORING BOOK
Karl Moline, Georges Jeanty, Yishan Li, Pablo Churin, and others
ISBN 978-1-50670- 458-6 | $14.99

AVAILABLE AT YOUR LOCAL COMICS SHOP OR BOOKSTORE!

To find a comics shop in your area, visit comicshoplocator.com. For more information or to order direct:
On the web: DarkHorse.com • Email: mailorder@darkhorse.com • Phone: 1-800-862-0052 Mon.–Fri. 9 AM to 5 PM Pacific Time